POPULAR SCIENCE

DO-IT-YOURSELF

ENCYCLOPEDIA

POPULAR SCIENCE

DO-IT-YOURSELF

ENCYCLOPEDIA

. . . *Complete* How-To *Series for the Entire Family* . . .

•

written in simple language

•

with full step-by-step instructions

•

and profusely illustrated

ILLUSTRATED EDITION

Volume 4

Dri - Flo

ACKNOWLEDGMENTS

The editors of this series would like to express their thanks and appreciation to the following companies for their assistance in preparing special sections within this volume, for their technical advice and their permission to use special material, photographs, art and educational charts.

ALLIED RADIO CORPORATION   ARMSTRONG CORK CO.   · B. F. GOODRICH CO.   BIDDLE MANUFACTURING CO.   BLACK & DECKER BRYANT ELECTRIC CO.   CHICAGO TOOL AND ENGINEERING CO. CORNELL EXTENSION DIVISION   CUMMINS OF JOHN OSTER MANU- FACTURING CO.   DELTA POWER TOOL DIVISION, ROCKWELL MANU- FACTURING CO.   DELTAWOOD INC.   DEWALT, INC.   DU-FAST DURA METAL PRODUCTS CO.   DOUGLAS FIR PLYWOOD ASSOCIATION EDISON ELECTRIC INSTITUTE   E. L. BRUCE CO.   FAN KIT CO. MALL TOOL CO.   MARSH WALL PRODUCTS, INCORPORATED   MA- SONITE CORPORATION   MASTIC TILE CORPORATION   MILLERS FALLS TOOLS   MONSANTO CHEMICAL CO.   MOSAIC TILE CO. NICHOLSON FILE CO.   O M SCOTT & SONS   ORCHARD PARK VE- NEER & CONTAINER CORPORATION   PRICE & RUTZBECK CO.   PRO- PELLER FAN MANUFACTURER'S ASSOCIATION   RICHMOND-ELECTRON CORPORATION   ROBBINS AND MYERS, INC.   RUBBER MANUFAC- TURERS ASSOCIATION   SAKRETE, INC.   SCOTT-MITCHELL HOUSE, INC.   STANLEY TOOLS, DIVISION OF THE STANLEY WORKS   SU- PERIOR FIREPLACE CO.   THE DRILO CORPORATION   THE HOME INSURANCE CO.   UNI-BILT DIVISION, VEGA INDUSTRIES, INC. UNITED STATES RUBBER CO.

Drill, Electric— Attachments

The quarter-inch electric drill can serve as the "workhorse" of a compact workshop. Here are but a few of the many, many attachments which can be used with an electric drill (clockwise starting with the upper right hand corner) :

1. wire brush for metal polishing and rust removal
2. grinding wheel for sharpening tools, knives, garden tools
3. rubber base with sandpaper disc for rotary sanding of wood or metal
4. buffing wheel for polishing metal and household silverware
5. buffing bonnet made of lamb's wool for polishing metal and furniture
6. rotary saw with tilting arbor attachment cuts through 2x4's
7. hedge trimmer
8. circular saw base with blades to cut different sized holes in metal.
9. masonry bits for drilling into concrete, brick and stone
10. drill bits for making holes in wood and metal
11. large diameter high-speed wood bits with ¼″ shank to fit drill
12. spade bit for fast drilling of holes from ½″ to 1″ in diameter
13. drum sander is helpful for sanding edges of curved surfaces
14. planer attachment for smoothing edges of boards to 2″ wide
15. saber saw attachment for cutting curves and interior patterns.

No matter how you buy your quarter-inch drill, whether as a separate unit or as a kit with two to fifty extra attachments there are countless numbers of new devices being designed every day to do more and more of the hard tedious work.

Sanding Attachments

To help with your sanding chores, rough or furniture finish, there is a variety of sanding attachments on the market. You can have your choice of drum style, belt style, disc or oscillating. Disc sanding requires a flexible rubber backing pad with a recessed center for the locking screw. Discs are available in all grades depending upon the work to be done. They are fastened to the rubber backing pad and held in the proper position with the locking screw. You will have to practice with the disc sander for a while to develop the proper skill and technique. The disc must be kept as flat as possible while tilting the machine so that about half of the abrasive surface is in contact with the work. A sweep-motion is necessary with this type of tool. Don't keep the tool in one spot too long or bumps, ridges and swirls will be cut into the surface you are working on.

The oscillating sander is extremely useful for the final sanding or finishing operations for fine cabinet work and rubbing down a var-

A belt sander attachment to really speed up the finishing on any wood working project. Little or no pressure on the tool is required to get a good clean working surface.

Photograph courtesy Mall Tool Co.

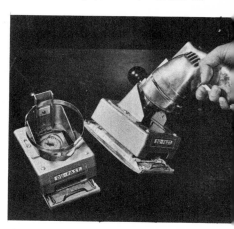

An orbital sanding attachment for fine cabinet sanding and polishing. The photo shows how easy it is to attach the unit to the quarter-inch drill, and be ready to work in seconds.

Photograph courtesy Du-Fast

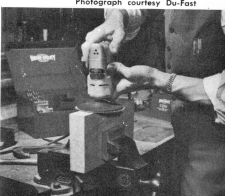

A flexible rubber backing disc attached to an arbor is used with sanding discs to finish this wood surface. The countersunk lock screw in the center of the backing pad permits the disc to be used flat.

Photograph courtesy Black & Decker

Here the sanding attachment is shown mounted in the drill and the drill attached to a bench stand which has a table and a miter gage for sanding frames and corners.

Photograph courtesy Black & Decker

nish finish. The movement of the sand pad is governed by a cam arrangement which guides it in a backward and forward motion as the machine is moved over the surface of the work.

The belt sander is the fastest method you can use to prepare surfaces for painting, staining or varnishing. With the proper grades of abrasives it is ideal for removing old paint and varnish. The sander must be equipped with the proper belt to prevent overloading of the tool and it is necessary to start the motor before permitting the abrasive surface to touch the work. Very little pressure is required, but the sander must be kept moving to prevent the grooving and gouging of the work surface.

The quarter-inch drill can be converted into a drum sander through the use of an arbor and a sanding drum. This tool will be particularly useful for concave and convex shapes on furniture and various other projects.

The same flexible rubber backing pad can be covered by a lamb's wool bonnet to do any polishing chore. Fine furniture, cars, tools and equipment can be polished quickly and easily with this tool. There is also a handle attachment available on the market to permit the unit to be used as a floor polisher. The attachment resembles a broom or mop handle with a strap arrangement to grip the unit and

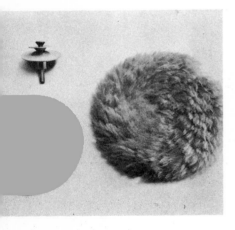

Lamb's wool bonnet fits over flexible rubber disc and is attached by means of an arbor (center of photograph) into chuck of drill.

A quarter-inch electric power drill equipped with a buffing wheel to clean up metals. Tripoli, rouge or emery can be used to buff and polish metals.

Photograph courtesy Black & Decker

hold it while you move it over the floor area to be polished. Do not overheat the surface of the work and be careful at edges and in corners, or you will damage the finish.

Buffing Wheel

A cloth buffing wheel mounted in an arbor and properly charged with an abrasive will give a high polish to metals. Use tripoli, rouge or emery for this process. Another handy attachment to have for this buffing process is a bench stand. There are a great many styles and sizes available for you to choose from.

During your buffing, if your cloth cloth wheel should become overloaded clean it by using a file or file card held against the wheel while it is revolving.

Remember in buffing or in any work where there is a danger of flying metal particles, always use safety glasses or a suitable faceplate.

Grinding Wheel

The quarter-inch drill fitted with an arbor and a grinding wheel mounted in a bench stand will make it possible for you to do much of the work usually done on a bench or pedestal grinder. A tool rest will be valuable for accurate work on chisels and plane blades. The portability of this type of grinder also makes it possible for the grinding tool to be taken right to the job.

A quarter-inch drill has been teamed up with the hack saw attachment to cut through BX cable. These saw attachments can also cut sheet metal, wood and plastics.

Photograph courtesy Mall Tool Co.

The drill and bench stand have been converted to a bench grinder by the attachment of an arbor and a grindstone. This is a handy way to sharpen tools, knives and grind metal parts.

Photograph courtesy Black & Decker

A wire brush attachment cleans off tools, old paint, scale and rust. This quarter-inch drill is mounted on a special bench stand to leave both hands free to control and feed the work.

Photograph courtesy Black & Decker

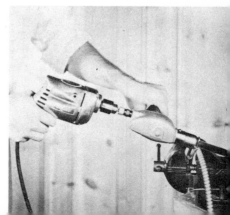

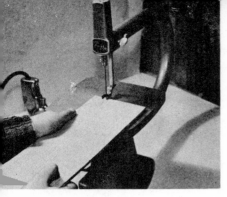

A jig saw table, a complete unit, utilizes the power provided by the quarter-inch drill. Other complete units resembling miniature combination power tools have been developed.

Photograph courtesy Cummins of John Oster Mfg. Co.

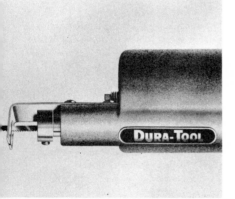

This is a jig saw and filing attachment for drill presses. The unit holds a high speed hack saw blade or a Swiss file.

Photograph courtesy Dura Tool

Wire Brush

The same arbor can usually be used to mount a wire brush for cleaning, buffing, burnishing and removing old paint, scale and rust. The wire brushes are available in a variety of grades for the particular finish you desire.

Wire brushes are good tools for finishing aluminum and copper projects. In addition to the various wire brushes and grinding wheels, end brushes, cup brushes, cup or cone grinding stones, rotary files and routing tools can be bought to fit this tool.

Circular Saw Attachment

A number of portable circular saw attachments have been designed to fit the quarter-inch drill. The circular saws will take the backaches out of cutting wood as thick as dressed 2x4's. The more elaborate saw attachments permit the operator to cut a compound mitre with one pass of the saw. The latest development for the portable saw is the designing of a table or bench to which the saw and drill are attached. Although a far cry from a regular bench saw, the unit performs a good many of the more complicated and intricate cuts needed for cabinet work.

Jig Saw Attachment

A jig saw attachment is also available to use as a portable tool or with a special table as a coping or

The power hammer attachment to this drill makes it particularly useful when hammering steel cut nails into concrete. The unit is easily attached to any quarter-inch electric drill.

scroll saw. In the jig saw family is also included the hack saw attachment which saws easily through metal, wood, or plastic.

There is a number of various types of reciprocating saw attachments which also may be used for cutting wood, metal, plastic, pipe, electrical conduit and light sheet metal. This tool utilizes a short length of hack saw blade to do the cutting. Since the attachment cuts on the pulling stroke the teeth of the blade should point toward handle.

Power Hammer

The star drill and hammer for cutting holes in stone, tile, cement or brick have been replaced with an attachment which features a power hammer added to the quarter-inch drill which does all hole cutting in a very short time. The principle is similar to that employed in the air hammer used by a riveter. Additional accessories for this tool include chisels, masonry drill bits, a calking tool, riveting tool, punch and hammer.

Clutch To Control Speed

An adjustable clutch device permits the operator to fix the desired pressure of the nut or screw he drives with a new screw driving attachment for the electric drill.

Nibblers To Cut Metal

Metal shears or nibblers have been developed to cut sheet metal quickly in straight or curved lines and leave a smooth edge. Most of the types developed can be used on metal up to No. 18 gage in thickness.

This drill is being used with a speed reducer so that more power is developed when working with a masonry bit. Most reducers cut the speed in half.

This attachment nibbles at the metal in order to cut it. It can be used with all thin gage metals and is useful in cutting straight edges, curves and interior cutouts.

Photograph courtesy Mall Tool Co.

A drill level designed to permit the craftsman to drill at any angle without guides, clamps and braces. This is a circular bubble level mounted on a bracket and attached to the drill housing.

The right angle drive attachment makes it easy to use a quarter-inch drill in corners, between studs and in many other inaccessible spots.

Photograph courtesy Millers Falls Tools

Complete Drill Workshops

Bench tools with their own stands and tables such as drill presses, jig saws, grinders, honers, and lathes which depend for their power supply on the quarter-inch drill have been developed. There are a number of separate units as well as combination units, resembling a miniature all-in-one workshop which are available to the model maker and home craftsman.

Angle Drives

Various attachments which convert the quarter-inch drill into right angle buffers, sanders, drills and grinders have been designed to permit the use of the tool in awkward and cramped positions.

Guide for Drilling

A drill level designed to permit the operator to drill at any angle without the use of clamps and vises has been developed as an attachment for the portable tool. There are a number of types on the market. They usually consist of a circular bubble level mounted on a graduated bracket which is calibrated from 0° to 90°. A special fastener permits the level to be attached to the housing of any portable drill.

Angle Saw

Right after the development of the angle converter attachment, has come the development of the angle saw attachment. It is a versatile power tool attachment, less than 7″ long, which will cut its own starting hole. It has been used in industry to cut iron pipe, corrugated sheet

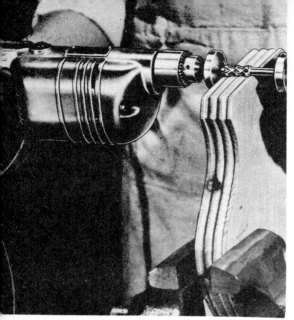

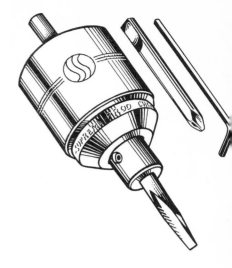

This is the portable shaper unit which can be chucked into the quarter-inch drill. The tool comes with a variety of heads and can be used on furniture that is assembled as well as on separate parts for furniture.

Photograph courtesy Biddle Mfg. Co.

Another screw driver attachment features a built-in clutch. The spinning drill chuck drives the screw only when you press the drill. This model includes blades for slotted head and Phillips head screws.

Photograph courtesy
Scott-Mitchell House, Inc.

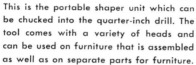

This is the hedge trimmer attachment which is easy to use and light in weight. While the handyman is working, his wife can cut the hedges quickly and easily with this handy attachment.

Photograph courtesy Mall Tool Co.

metal, wood and other materials. An assortment of special blades is also available to work with this tool.

Other Attachments

Attachments for the quarter-inch drill have also been developed to help the handyman in other chores around the house. Aside from the accessories developed for the shop, an attachment which clips the hedge, shrubbery and vines has also been designed to fit the portable tool.

Furniture, toy and model makers will find the new shaper attachment for the quarter-inch drill a great help. This tool reduces complicated adjusting and in many cases can be used on furniture and projects that have already been constructed. The tool can be used with a variety of cutting heads including the flute cutter, single bead cutter, and V-cutter.

Among the host of other attachments are a paint stirrer; a gadget to grip a paintbrush while it is spun clean; a mortiser and even a special attachment to clean white-wall tires.

Planing, always a problem, has also been made easier and quicker for the craftsman through the design of a wood planer attachment which will fit the quarter-inch drill. The drill plane combination is perfect for all kinds of light edge type planing jobs on cabinet work and particularly to free sticky doors, windows, screens and storm windows. The majority of them can take off $\frac{1}{16}''$ on each pass and plane a $2''$ width.

More and more attachments are being developed for this versatile tool each day. A good quarter-inch drill properly taken care of and provided with the best attachments will last a long time and help make your work easier and more accurate.

Photograph courtesy The Drilo Corp.

This attachment drives wood, machine, cap, sheetmetal screws, nuts and bolts. The operator has control of the speed range from zero to full speed of drill.

Photograph courtesy Price & Rutzebeck Co.

This is the handy angle saw which will cut intricate patterns in sheet metal and can be used on iron pipe, wood, plastics and other metals.

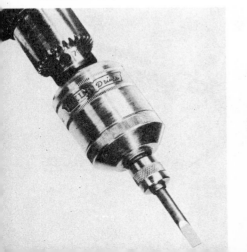

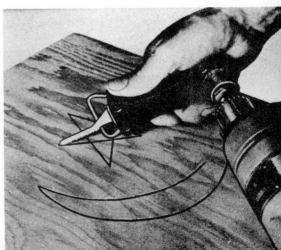

Drill—Hand

The hand drill is used for rapid drilling of small holes. Hand drills come in various sizes and shapes but all of them operate on the same principle—a gear attached to a crank and handle is turned clockwise. This in turn revolves a pinion gear which turns the chuck. Since the drill bit is in the chuck, it drills into the work.

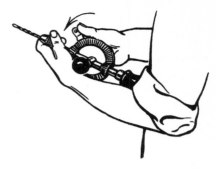

To insert a drill bit, set it into the chuck and push forward or away from you on the handle.

Using the Chuck

To place a drill bit into the chuck, open the chuck by revolving it by hand so that the jaws open and form a hole slightly larger than the diameter of the drill bit. Insert the bit and tighten the chuck by pushing the crank away from you. While holding the chuck shell tight, continue pushing forward to lock the bit securely.

To remove the drill bit, the re-

To remove the drill bit, follow the opposite technique—pull the handle towards you.

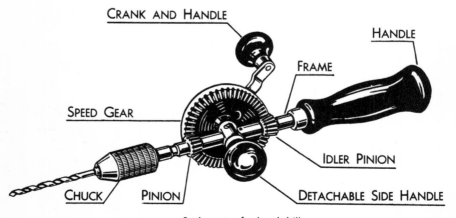

CRANK AND HANDLE

HANDLE

FRAME

SPEED GEAR

IDLER PINION

CHUCK   PINION

DETACHABLE SIDE HANDLE

Basic parts of a hand drill.

verse procedure is followed. Hold
the chuck tightly with your left hand
and turn the crank backward or
towards you with the right hand.
Once the jaws of the chuck have
loosened their grip on the bit, with-
draw it with your left hand.

Working the Hand Drill

Here are several basic operating
rules to follow when using a hand
drill. Many apply to the operation
of any type of drill.

1. Before drilling the hole, use
an awl or center punch to mark the
exact location of the center of the
hole to be drilled. This is essential
when drilling hardwood and metal
but useful when drilling into soft-
wood.

2. When drilling through metal,
relieve the pressure on the drill
slightly before breaking through the
other side. This will help you avoid
breaking the drill bit.

3. Hold the drill straight and do
not wobble when turning the crank
and handle. If you do, you will make
the hole over-size and may possibly
break the drill bit.

4. Hold the drill steady in the
direction desired and exert an even
pressure when operating. Turn the
crank at a constant speed and avoid
going too fast.

5. It is sometimes desirable to
hold the drill by the side handle and
press the body against the frame
handle like a breast drill—one with
a specially-shaped frame handle to
fit against the body.

Sketches from "Tool Guide"
courtesy of Stanley Tools

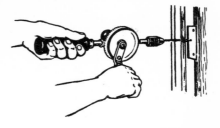

When drilling, hold the hand drill straight
and avoid wobbling as you drill the hole.

Exert an even pressure on the handle when
drilling and turn at a constant speed.

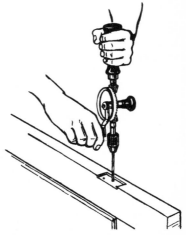

It is sometimes necessary to press your
body against the handle and hold the side
handle with your left hand in order to
have the drill bit penetrate the work being
drilled.

Drill Press

The drill press is arranged to hold and rotate the drill bit at the proper angle with the work. Drill press sizes range from the small bench type to huge multiple-spindle jobs weighing many tons. You will probably have occasion to use the smaller drill presses only. These usually have a separate motor which drives the drill spindle and chuck by means of a V-belt.

A drill press can be used for many different jobs. The introduction in recent years of additional at-

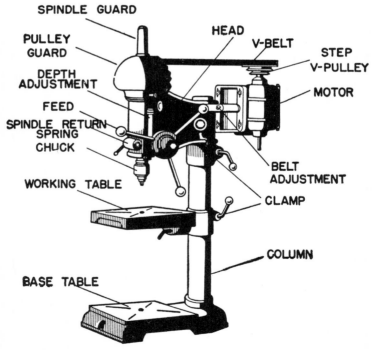

SPINDLE GUARD
PULLEY GUARD
DEPTH ADJUSTMENT
FEED
SPINDLE RETURN SPRING
CHUCK
WORKING TABLE
BASE TABLE
HEAD
V-BELT
STEP V-PULLEY
MOTOR
BELT ADJUSTMENT
CLAMP
COLUMN

Basic parts of a drill press.   Sketch courtesy of Delta Power Tool Division, Rockwell Mfg. Co.

tachments has transformed the drill press into a multi-purpose tool. While it can do fairly well jobs other than boring holes, for which it was designed, it does not do them as well as the power tool designed specifically for the job.

In addition to drilling a hole, a drill press can be used for:

1. cutting a mortise by inserting a hollow-chisel mortising attachment which drills square holes.

2. cutting a groove with router bits.

3. cutting a tenon.

4. planing a board with a special planer attachment.

5. internal cutting with a router bit.

6. shaping an edge by a shaper attachment that fits on the spindle.

7. sanding an edge with a drum sander.

8. sanding a surface if the board is narrower than the face plate to which the sandpaper is adhered.

9. cutting plugs to fill holes above countersunk screws, by means of a plug cutter.

10. shaping moldings with special cutter blades.

What size drill press should the handyman buy? The size of a drill press is determined by the maximum diameter that can be center drilled in a circular piece of work—the distance from the center of the chuck to the forward edge of the column.

For average work, the handyman should use a 13″ to 15″ drill press. If you intend to use the drill press extensively, it is better to buy an 18″ model. On the other hand, if the drill press is for infrequent op-eration, you can use a drill press stand with your electric hand drill or buy an 11″ to 13″ drill press.

One advantage of the drill press over the portable electric drill is that you have speed control. Four grooves are usually found on the cone step pulley of the motor and four on the spindle pulley. High speed—3,000 to 3,600 R.P.M.—is suitable for small drills but is about 10 times too fast for a ½″ drill. When you're in doubt, use the slowest speed. That means changing the belt to the smallest-diameter groove of the motor pulley.

An electric drill can be converted into a light-duty drill press by attaching it in a special stand. This model can be used as a vertical drill press as well as a horizontal press.

Photograph courtesy of Cummins of John Oster Mfg. Co.

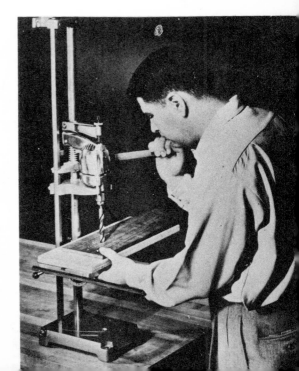

The feed pressure is easily controlled on the drill press by means of a feed wheel with long handles. A depth stop is provided to stop the progress of a drill at a predetermined depth. That's important when you're drilling blind holes—those that don't go all the way through.

Securing the Stock

If you try to hold stock on the drill press table with your hands while drilling it may prove dangerous. The drill may catch or jam and start the stock spinning like a buzz saw. If this happens the stock may fly loose and become a high-speed projectile, endangering all within range. Hold the stock down with something besides your hands. The best way is to use a drill vise or a C-clamp. You may even have to design special holding jigs for some jobs.

Use the drill vise for small jobs. Clamp larger pieces of stock to the drill table. Before you turn on the power, revolve the drill a few turns by hand to make sure it is properly centered.

Drill Vise

An adjustable vise which can be secured to the table of the drill press offers the fastest and best method of securing work for a drill press job. Using this vise, the handyman has both hands free to operate the machine and there is no danger of the work breaking away from his grip.

Drill press vises come with V grooves to hold round work—rods and tubes—either in the vertical or horizontal position. Some vises remain perfectly level with the table of the drill press. The better models are adjustable so that they can be set at an angle to the spindle for angle drilling and other jobs which require tilting of the work. Unless you have a tilting table on your drill press, it is best to purchase a tilting drill press vise and make it do the job instead.

Adjustable drill press vise can be rotated in any plane for angle drilling or angle cutting or mortising with attachments.

A drill press vise—this model remains parallel with the table of the press.

Photographs courtesy of
Chicago Tool & Engineering Co.

Drive Nail

Drive nails are used for fastening in masonry. A hole is drilled on the concrete for the shield, which is then slipped into place. The driving action of the nail into the shield secures the anchorage.

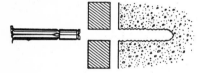

Star Dryvin and drilled hole should be the same diameter.

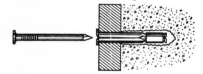

Install Star:Dryvin Shield thru fixture into hole.

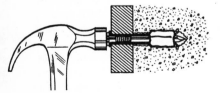

Hammer nail home! *You now have permanent, secure anchorage.*

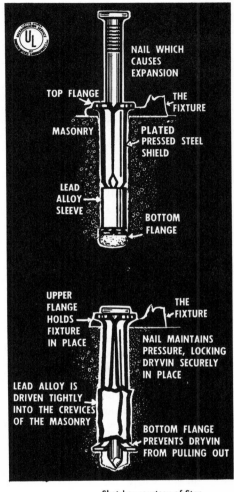

Sketches courtesy of Star
Expansion Bolt Co.

Drive Screw

This is sometimes called a screw nail, but it has a slotted head. This type of screw is intended to be set by blows of a hammer, yet it can be removed with a screwdriver. It is faster to set the screw in place with a hammer than by using a screwdriver.

A drive screw.

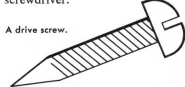

Driveways and Sidewalks

Driveways and sidewalks should be placed for the convenience of the homeowners and their guests, and should give easy access to the entrances of the house, to the garage, and for service deliveries, such as groceries and fuel. The following suggestions are intended particularly for small village and city properties, but may be modified and adapted to many situations.

Location of Driveway

Place the driveway on the service side of the house, for convenience to the side entrance or kitchen doorway and for the delivery of household supplies. All services to the house and grounds should be on the same side.

Place the driveway about 8′ or more from the side of the house, if possible, to allow room for a pass court and for any base planting of flowers or shrubs. Make the driveway direct, straight, or slightly curved except for corners to give access to the garage and to make a turning space. The dimensions for a turning space are ample for most cars, but it is advisable to try turning your car in the area to be sure the space is large enough.

Make the pass court long enough for one or more cars, and place the court near the front or main entrance to the house, so guests may easily use the main en-

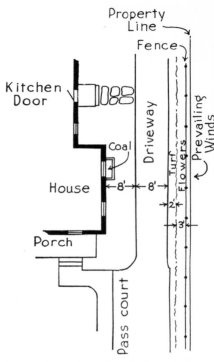

trance instead of the kitchen door. The pass court should be in a level or nearly level part of the driveway. A wall may be needed if the slope is up or down from the driveway.

Unless service is needed to both sides of the house, do not have a driveway around the house. If it is necessary to put fuel, vegetables, or other things in the basement on the side opposite the logical place for the driveway, drive over the lawn; the truck will not seriously damage the lawn if the soil is dry or frozen.

Construction

Make the driveway of "all-weather" construction, with a coarse-stone foundation surface with finer stone, concrete, or any

black-top surface that will not become soft and sticky in hot weather. Make the finished surface level with the lawn or, on sloping ground, level with the shoulder on each side.

Details of construction follow: Grade the road bed to easy slopes, excavate to a depth of 10″ for a stone road, 12″ for a black-top road, and 9½″ for a concrete road.

Sketch from Cornell Extension Bulletin 693, "Driveways and Sidewalks" by Donald J. Bushey

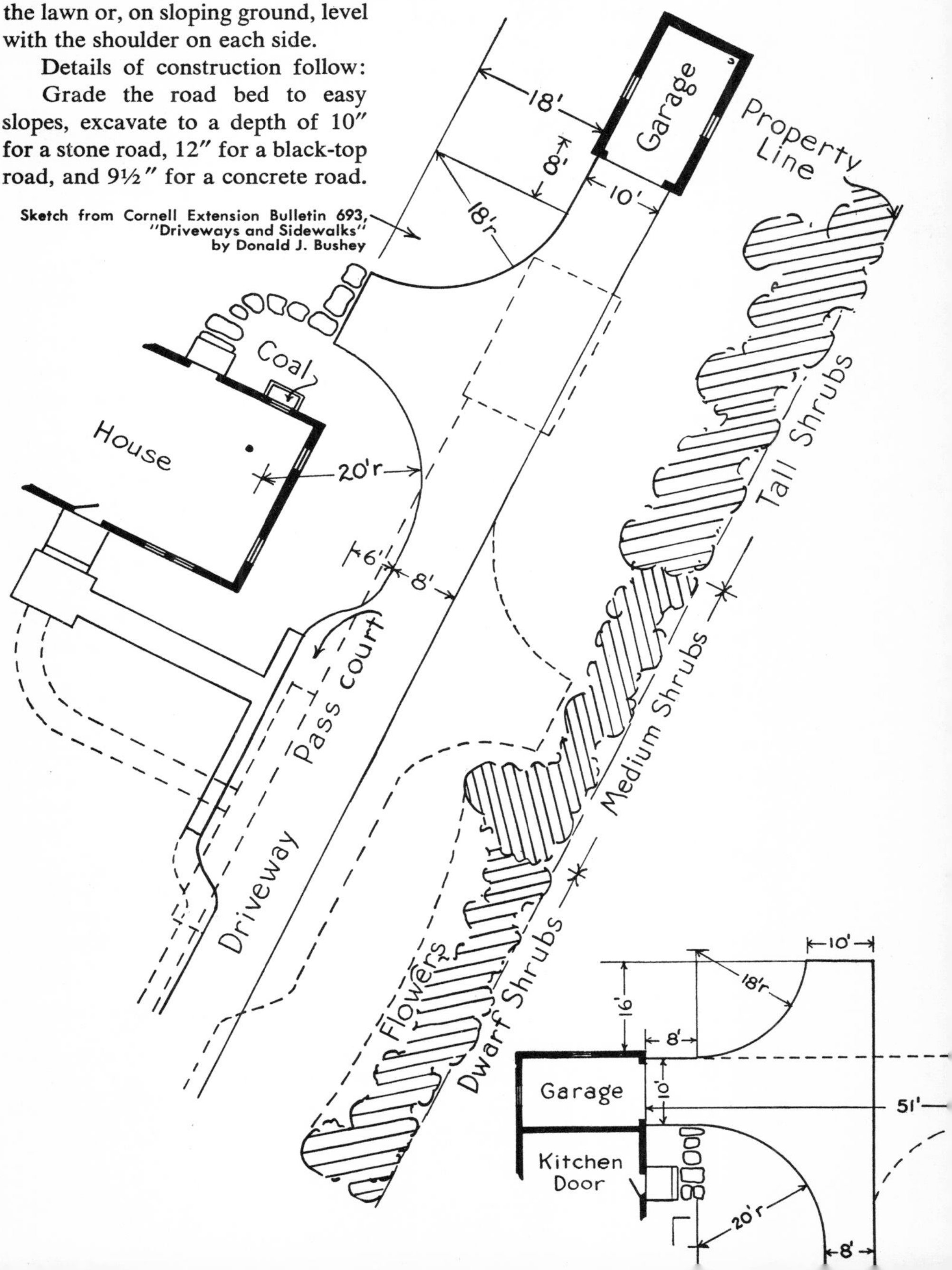

Garage

Property Line

Coal

House

20'r

18'

8'

10'

18'r

Tall Shrubs

Medium Shrubs

Dwarf Shrubs

Flowers

Driveway

Pass court

6'

8'

Garage

Kitchen Door

10'

18'r

16'

8'

10'

51'

20'r

8'

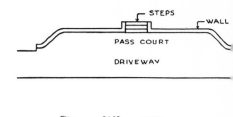

Put a layer of coarse stone or quarry shuck in the bottom of the excavation and roll or otherwise compact the layer. This layer should be 8″ deep for stone and black-top roads and 4″ deep for a concrete road.

For a stone road, put a 2″ layer of fine crushed stone (from ¼″ to 1″ in size) on the surface and roll it. To maintain this road, fill the surface holes and hollows with fine crushed stone and roll the road firmly. Keep the crown in the center.

For a black-top road, put a 2″ layer of fine crushed stone on the base, keep a 2″ crown, and roll the road. Put a 2″ layer of an asphalt mix on the surface and roll the road. Asphalt mix is sold under a variety of trade names.

Make side forms 5½″ high and place between them No. 3, 6″x6″ highway wire. Pour concrete (1-2-3½ mix) between these forms, embedding the wire. Crown the surface

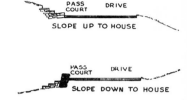

at the center and smooth with a wood-float finish. Make the expansion joints 50′ apart.

Select the appropriate type of grading with drainage for your situation, regardless of the type of road construction used.

If the natural slope of the ground permits, keep a gentle slope downward from the road on both sides. The road should be higher

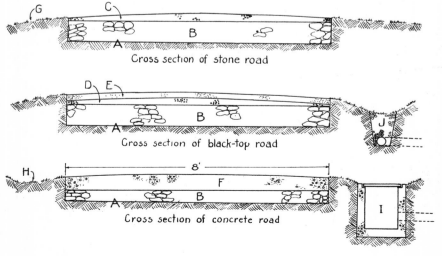

Cross section of stone road

Cross section of black-top road

Cross section of concrete road

than the adjacent grades so no water will stand on the surface of the road. If the natural grade is slightly sloping, make shallow, smoothly rounded grass gutters to carry the surface water to a suitable outlet. In low, wet places, install concrete catch basins with a tile leading to a suitable outlet. Sometimes a ditch with a tile at its base and covered with gravel will carry excess water away satisfactorily.

See *Concrete*.

Landscape Treatment

The space between the driveway and the edge of the maintained lawn or property line may be only a few feet in width. If any planting is desired in this area, consider: (1) the direction of the prevailing winds and (2) the width of the area. If the winds are from this edge of the lawn toward the driveway, a hardy shrub planting or a fence of fairly close construction would cause snowdrifts to form in the drive. Here you might use a fence of open construction such as a three-rail fence. You could use vines, such as clematis or China fleece-vine (silver lace-vine) on the fence as either may be cut to the ground in the fall, so snow will not drift in the driveway. They make a full growth and flower in one season. Annual vines, such as morning glory or sweet peas, also are suitable. An annual or perennial flower border may be planted between the fence and the drive.

If you want a border planting and no fence, shrubs such as hills-of-snow, hydrangea, Anthony Waterer spirea, or peonies may be used in a space from 5′ to 6′ wide. They

also may be cut to the ground each fall.

If the prevailing winds are in a direction from the house toward the driveway, use a three-board fence, a picket-fence, or a woody shrub planting at the edge of the lawn. Use only dwarf shrubs at the front near the road. These low-growing plants will not obstruct the view, and will be no hazard at the intersection. You may plant medium-sized shrubs that grow from 4′ to 6′ high opposite the house and plant taller growing shrubs toward the back.

A fence treatment is best for a space as narrow as 2′, but may still be used if the lawn is wider. A shrub border should not be planted in a space less than from 8′ to 10′ wide.

Sidewalks

The first thing to consider in laying a sidewalk is the main walk.

MAIN ENTRANCE—Extend the main walk from the front or main entrance of the house to the driveway or pass court, either paral-

Three-rail fence

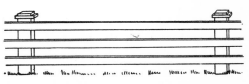

Three-board fence

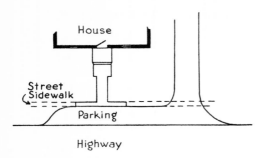

Highway

more in width. It may be made of concrete, concrete base with flagstone, large flagstone with grass growing in the joints, or any blacktop construction that will not become soft and sticky in hot weather. Make the surface of the walk flush with the lawn.

Sidewalk construction is similar to road construction but need not be so heavy. The base for the concrete or asphalt sidewalk need be only 4″ deep and may be of gravel,

lel to the front of the house and not nearer than 6′ from the foundation, or curve it slightly to the driveway or pass court. Or you may want to lay the walk from the main entrance of the house straight to the street sidewalk or roadside. This is usually best if the house is close to the road. Or perhaps you want to lay the walk on a slight curve, in a gradual reverse curve, or in an arc bearing in the direction most frequently traveled to or from this entrance of the house.

In either of the plans you may make parking space by widening the shoulder of the highway.

Make the main walk 3½′ or

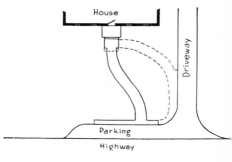

Highway

cinders, or sand. Put 4″ of concrete (1-2-3½ mix) on top of this and smooth it with a woodfloat finish. Put the expansion joints 50′ apart and make creases 5′ apart with a joining tool.

Stepping Stone Walk

Crannied Stone Walk

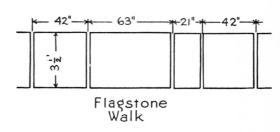

Flagstone Walk

Sketches from Cornell Extension Bulletin 693, "Driveways and Sidewalks" by Donald J. Bushey

For an asphalt sidewalk, put 2″ of asphalt mix on top of the 4″ base and thoroughly roll it. Use a material that will not get soft and sticky in hot weather.

Flagstone walks may be laid on 2″ or 3″ of sand or cinders. The excavation for this type of walk need be only deep enough to permit the surface of the stone to be flush with the surface of the lawn. No part of a walk should be lower than the adjacent grade as this would allow water to stand on the surface. Sometimes on sloping ground one edge of a walk is made from ¼″ to ½″ lower than the opposite edge which permits surface drainage.

SERVICE WALKS—Extend the service walks from the side or rear entrance of the house to the driveway, garage, barns, vegetable garden, or other frequented parts of the property.

Make these walks from 2′ to 2½′ wide. They may be of solid construction, as suggested for the main walk, but usually stepping stones set in the ground with their top surface level with the lawn are satisfactory.

Landscape Treatment

Usually an unbroken lawn extending from both sides of the walk is best. If, however, you do plant an annual or perennial flower border parallel to the walk, leave a narrow lawn strip between the walk and the flower border. Also, leave a path through the flower border for access from one side of the lawn across the walk to the opposite side, so you will not have to lift the lawnmower over the flowers.

Drop Siding

This term is usually used to refer to wood pieces forming the outside covering of a home. Generally ¾″ thick and about 6″ wide, these pieces are machined into various patterns. Drop siding has tongue-and-groove or shiplap joints so that the pieces interlock vertically or horizontally, depending upon how the siding is installed. Drop siding with these joints have more structural strength than bevel siding, which is often made of thinner wood.

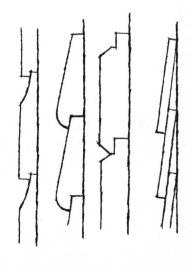

DROP   BEVEL

Drugs, Poisonous

In the medicine cabinet you may have containers of drugs, medicines, or cosmetics which are poisonous if swallowed internally. For the sake of safety, especially if there are small children in the household who cannot read labels, such "external use only" articles should be kept on a separate shelf, preferably the highest shelf in the cabinet.

The labels should be clearly explanatory, and an identification mark should be placed on them, which all the members of the family know and recognize. For instance, paint a band of red nail polish on the bottles, boxes, or tubes of these poisonous drugs. Or stick a piece of adhesive tape on each container, or use some other method of identification which is most convenient.

Drum Sander

A drum sander is a sanding machine for smoothing large flat surfaces, of which the drum-type floor sander is one example. The term is now commonly used, however, to designate a small variety of drum sander or spindle sander which is particularly useful for sanding curved surfaces such as the edges of jigsawed or shaped work. Drum-sander attachments are most frequently used with the drill press and portable electric drill.

One type consists of a rubber "rod" with a stem which fits into the drill chuck. A sleeve or tube of abrasive paper fits over the rubber "rod" or drum.

These circular sanders come in many different sizes as well as shapes. In addition to the drum shape, you will find the cone shape useful when finishing household projects.

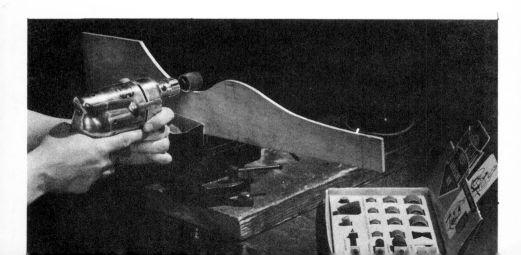

Dry Rot

While this is a commonly used term, actually there is no such thing as "dry rot." Decayed wood is often dry after it has rotted, but not while the decay is taking place. See *Decay, House Structure*.

Drying Oils

The oils used by the paint industry have the property of becoming solid when exposed to air. They are therefore called "drying oils." The important vegetable oils in this class are linseed, tung and perilla. The only animal oil which can be used is fish oil. Soybean oil is also used by the paint industry but possesses the drying property to a lesser extent.

Drywell

Drywells are used primarily for rain run-off. They are dug into the ground and water is channeled into the drywell by soil pipes connected to the downspout.

For a full discussion of drywells and how to build them, see *Gutters*.

Dual Control Lights

When two switches are used to control a single light, it is necessary to use three-way switches. Lighting arrangements of this type are commonly found in homes. For example, there are switches at the top and at the base of a stairwell controlling the single light illuminating the stairs. Or there may be a switch in the kitchen and another in the garage to control the light over the driveway.

Dual control lights are a convenience of modern living. The light can be turned on or off from either point. Each switch works independently from the other. You can turn the light on with one, then turn it off with the other. The next time you wish to turn on the light, either switch will do the job.

Wiring a dual control light is not difficult. It is generally necessary to use a three-wire cable between the two switches in place of the conventional two-wire cable used in most home wiring. This cable is readily available in any hardware or electrical supply store.

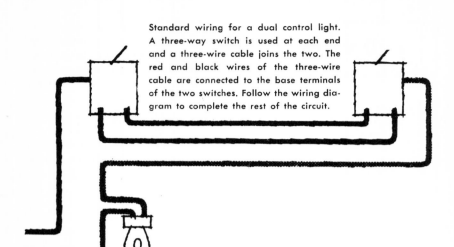

Standard wiring for a dual control light. A three-way switch is used at each end and a three-wire cable joins the two. The red and black wires of the three-wire cable are connected to the base terminals of the two switches. Follow the wiring diagram to complete the rest of the circuit.

There are times when you cannot see the light from one of the switches. Under the circumstances, it is difficult to tell whether or not the light is on. Unlike the conventional double-pole switch which has imprinted "on" and "off" on the handle, the three-way switch has no such markings. If you have this type of a wiring plan in your home—say the light inside the garage is controlled from the garage and from inside the house, you can add a pilot light to the system as part of the kitchen switch. Standard three-way switches do not come with pilot light attachments, but you can use Despard fixtures in this instance to full advantage. Merely combine a three-way Despard switch with a Despard pilot light.

See *Electrical Wiring.*

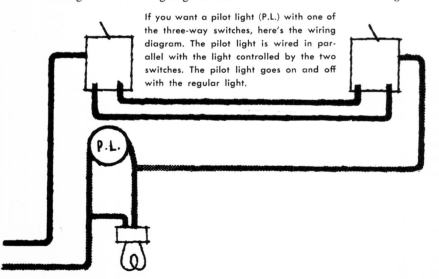

If you want a pilot light (P.L.) with one of the three-way switches, here's the wiring diagram. The pilot light is wired in parallel with the light controlled by the two switches. The pilot light goes on and off with the regular light.

Dull Rubbing

When a surface has on it a completely dry layer of finishing material such as paint or varnish, and you wish to dull the finish, you may rub it with abrasive paper, pumice, or steel wool and oil or water. This process is referred to as "dull rubbing."

Dutch Bond

This is a style of laying brick which is sometimes called English cross bond. It is a bond in which the courses or rows of brick are alternately made up of headers and stretchers.

Sample of Dutch Bond.

Dutch Door

While few people remember that the original purpose of a Dutch door was to keep the barnyard fowl out of the kitchen, everyone appreciates the beauty and usefulness of a Dutch door. You can use one to advantage in many parts of your home. It is particularly handy in the kitchen so that mother can keep a watchful eye on the toddler having fun in the backyard. It is also decorative as a front entrance door.

You can make an unusual Dutch door out of a modern material such as Texture One-Eleven fir plywood. All you need are two 8′ panels of this plywood plus one panel of utility grade ¼″ exterior plywood.

Here are the cutting plans depending upon the height of your door. Only the height of these parts is given; cut the width as required for your individual door.

Door Height	A & C	B & D	E	F
6′6″	45″	33″	46″	32″
6′8″	46″	34″	47″	33″
7′0″	48″	36″	49″	35″

Pieces A and B are used for the outside face of the door.

Pieces C and D are cut out of ¼″ utility grade exterior plywood.

Pieces E and F are used for the inside face of the door.

1. Cut the pieces to the required size as noted in the table.

2. Join pieces A and C together and pieces B and D together with glue and #9 flathead screws ½″ long, spaced 3″ to 4″ apart along the perimeter. However, along the upper edge of pieces B and D, set the screws so that they are 1½″ below that edge.

3. Cut a groove in pieces D and B as shown in the sketch; this should be deep enough to permit the metal weatherstripping to fit into it.

4. Attach piece E to the combination A and C with glue and 1″ coated finishing nails spaced about 2″ to 3″ apart. Countersink the head slightly. Do the same with piece F by attaching it to pieces B and D.

5. Fasten a piece of metal weatherstripping—the T type—as shown.

6. You are now ready to hang the Dutch door. You need a pair of hinges for the top and another for the bottom. Note that the top of this door can be opened and the bottom

half can remain locked if you use a bolt latch on the lower half.

7. Finish the door by sanding the surfaces smooth and painting all exposed edges and surfaces.

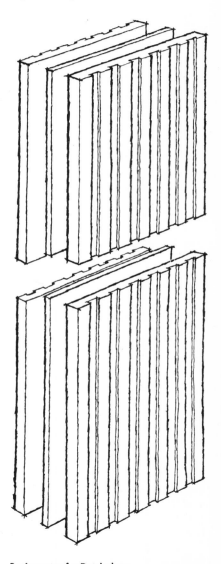

Detailed view of center closing.

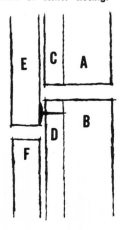

Basic parts of a Dutch door.

Eaves

The eaves are the projecting edges of a roof. It is an architectural term to designate that portion of the roof which overhangs the walls of the house.

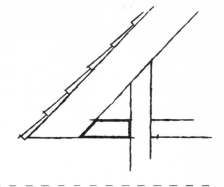

Eaves of a home.

Edger

This garden tool is used to trim the edge of the grass where it joins the pavement. The most frequently used type consists of a wheel with a rotating cutter and disc. The disc runs along the edge of the ground flat against the side of the concrete walk or driveway while the cutter removes any overhanging grass.

Within recent years, power edgers have become available for the homeowner. There are several different types. Some are electrically driven and consist of a small cutter disc. Others are gasoline-powered and are made in the form of three wire whips attached to a rotating wheel.

Edgers are used to give your lawn a tailored look.

An electrically-operated trimmer and edger.

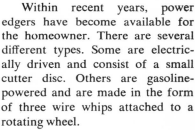

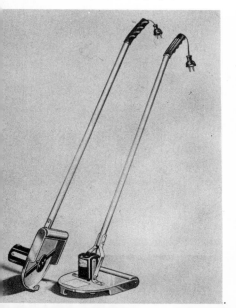

Efflorescence

This is a condition sometimes found in brick or concrete. It is the formation of whitish powder (white crystallization) on the surface of brick caused by excessive mineral salts in new brick. It also occurs in concrete and is caused by moisture seepage from green or uncured concrete.

See *Bricks*.

Elbow

This is a plumbing fitting used to change the direction of a pipe. Elbows are made for cast iron pipe, soil pipe and copper tubing.

There are a number of different types of elbows available for plumbing work. Some elbows or L's are used for a 90° turn; others are made for a 45° turn.

Most cast iron elbows are threaded on the inside or have a female thread. However, an elbow which is threaded on the inside on one side and threaded on the outside on the other is called a 'street elbow.'

See *Plumbing*.

A cast iron elbow—a 90° L.

A 90° L used with rigid copper tubing.

A 'street elbow'—this 90° elbow has one end threaded on the outside and the other threaded on the inside.

Electrical Hazards

Besides the information contained in the section on *Accident Prevention,* the following discussion gives the various causes of hazards due to improper safeguarding in the handling of electrical products.

Shock

Electrical shock results when a perceptible electric current passes through a part of the body. If the current is very small, it may produce only a slight tingling sensation. If somewhat larger, the current may produce involuntary muscular contractions which may become decidedly painful. If a dangerous current passes through the body, in addition to causing violent muscular contractions, it may prove fatal.

The amount of current which may flow through the body from electrical circuits of 110 to 220 volts and the consequent severity of the shock depends upon several conditions, the most important of which is the electrical resistance of the skin at the points of contact with the circuit. Dry, thick skin offers a high resistance to electric current, whereas the resistance is low if the skin is thin and moist. It is the current and not the voltage which causes electric shock. The voltage is important only to the extent that together with the resistance it determines the amount of current which will flow through the body under a given set of conditions.

Most electrical circuits installed in residences have one of the conductors grounded, and consequently a shock may be received by touching a single conductor when a person is in electrical contact with the ground. This contact with the ground may be direct (as when standing upon soil, wet concrete, etc.) or it may be made by touching pipes, radiators, water faucets, and other metal objects which have a direct connection to ground. It may also result from standing upon a wet floor. Many of the worst electrical accidents, especially the fatalities at low voltage, occur to persons who make contact with an electrical circuit under wet conditions.

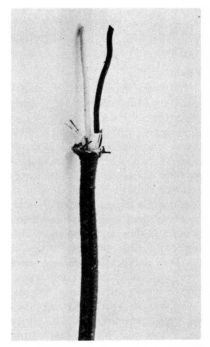

Be wary of loose wires—don't touch with your hands until you're sure the current is off.

Burns

If the current passing through the body is large enough, it may actually sear the tissue, especially at the point of contact with the skin. This seldom happens except on circuits of high voltage. It is most likely to happen when the voltage is high enough for the electricity to spark or arc to the skin before actual contact is made with the electrical conductor.

Burns are also caused at times from immediate proximity to an electric arc which has formed between two conductors so that the current does not flow through the person's body. Such arcs may result from a short-circuit or an electrical circuit, through which current is flowing, that is broken at the switch.

Fires

The fire hazards of electricity usually consist of the overheating of conductors which are carrying too large a current, or of an electric arc in the presence of combustile material. An overheated conductor may set fire to its insulating covering. An electric arc, in addition to producing a large quantity of localized heat, may spatter molten metal about and thus set fire to surrounding combustible material.

The overheating of electrical conductors may be brought about by trying to operate lamps, motors, or appliances which take too much current for the circuit to which they are connected. This can result from connecting too many appliances to one circuit, or it may arise from some fault in the insulation.

It is important from a fire-prevention standpoint that all joints and connections in electrical circuits be tight and permanent. To prevent trouble when they are not, it is best that joints be made inside a metallic enclosure such as an outlet box or switch box. When an electrical installation includes loose or improperly made joint in wires or connections to devices, such as switches and sockets, dangerous heating or sparking may occur at these joints or connections even when the currents are not excessive.

Prevention of Hazards

The design of electrical circuits should be, and usually is, such as to make it improbable that these hazards will exist in residential buildings All wiring should be installed in accordance with the regulations set forth in the National Electrical Code and the National Electrical Safety Code. To avoid contact with live parts, electrical conductors are covered with insulating material and are not exposed to contact. Excessive voltages may occur from contact of outdoor high voltage wires with the wires supplying the premises. To prevent this hazard, the wires of the house circuit are usually grounded. To prevent the exposed metal covers of electrical equipment and the metal coverings of wires from presenting a hazard in case of insulation failure resulting in contact with the electrical conductors, these metal parts are usually grounded when the electrical equipment is installed.

The use of electrical appliances should be avoided when the hands

Use a string to control the pull light over the lavatory—metal, water and electricity don't mix.

are wet or when standing upon a wet floor or ground, for an electric shock under these conditions may be fatal. If the use of a portable appliance under such conditions seems unavoidable, then all exposed metal parts on the appliance should be connected to ground. Insulation is especially subject to breakdown when exposed to moisture, and the current may consequently leak from the electrical conductors or the motor winding to the frame of an appliance such as a washing machine. Grounding the frame of the machine will prevent such leakage from giving a shock to the operator. This may be done by use of a separate wire connecting the exposed metal directly to a cold water pipe or by use of a three-conductor cord where one conductor is used for grounding the exposed metal parts of the appliance. A polarized plug and receptacle are needed to insure that improper connection of the grounding conductor will not occur.

Overloading circuit

To avoid overloading the electrical wiring, automatic overcurrent protective devices are provided in branch circuits. These protective devices consist of a fuse or circuit-breaker designed to open the circuit, if for any reason the current becomes too high. The rating of the fuse or circuit-breaker is selected to correspond to that of the wire. If a fuse or circuit-breaker of too high rating is used, the wiring may become overheated to the extent of causing a short circuit and starting a fire.

Fuse

The blowing of a fuse is a warning that some fault has occurred or that a circuit is overloaded. Before a blown fuse is replaced, the fault should be ascertained and remedied. A fuse of the proper rating may

Use only UL approved fuses to control the electrical circuits in your home.

then be inserted in place of the blown fuse. To replace a blown fuse by one of larger rating or to replace the fuse by other metal which will not give the intended protection is to remove a very necessary safeguard. In order that fuses may give the intended protection, it is necessary that their integrity be rigidly maintained. The fuse is to the electrical installation what the safety valve is to a steam boiler. To render a fuse inoperative is taking a chance with life and property which is similar to tying down the safety valve of a steam boiler.

Fuse plugs of 15 amperes, the rating suitable for ordinary branch circuits, may be easily distinguished from those of higher rating by their hexagonal shape. This may be a hexagonal opening in the cap through which the window of mica or other material shows, a hexagonal-shaped recess in the cap, or hexagonal impression raised or depressed on the (metal) cap. Fuses of ratings larger than 15 amperes do not carry such a hexagonal design.

Disconnecting Current

The entire supply of electric current may be cut off where it enters the house system by pulling or disconnecting the main switch, which is usually located in metal box near the meter in the basement.

Each adult member of the household should be familiar with the means for disconnecting the current. The method of operation will vary according to the type of design. In most equipment, a handle protrudes from the box or enclosure,

Don't touch the main fuse box if you're wet
or if there's water on the floor.

and the circuit is disconnected by pulling the operating lever down; on circuit breakers or pulling out type switches, the method of opening is indicated on the outside of the enclosure. In case of fire or other emergency, or when a house is to be left unoccupied for long periods, the main switch should be opened.

Portable Appliance Cords

Cords to portable electrical appliances such as lamps, pressing irons, and fans, cannot, of course, be either out of reach or guarded by exterior metal covers. For this reason the insulation of such cords is more subject to deterioration by mechanical injury and moisture than fixed wires. These cords in general present a greater shock hazard than other parts of the electrical installation. The use of such cords is one of the principal reasons for the grounding of circuits.

Cords are adversely affected by moisture, oil, heat, and handling. Where any abrasion of the protective covering is noted, the condition should be promptly corrected. If the cord is kinked or sharply bent in handling, some of the cord strands may break and later pierce the insulating covering. Persons contacting these exposed strands may receive a shock. Cords should be made as short as convenient and, where practicable, located and used away from radiators or set tubs, kitchen ranges or sinks, bathroom fittings, cement basement floors, or other objects well connected with the ground, whereby a person touching the cord may become a part of an electric circuit and receive a shock.

Where the surfaces are very damp and especially where the air may be moist with steam, as in bathrooms, kitchens, and laundries, the conditions are especially bad for the cord and permit more severe shock if the cord is abraded or otherwise injured. For this reason, cords used in laundries, bathrooms, and similar places should have special waterproof coverings. A special type of cord is supplied for heating appliances. In general, in such places, the floor on which users stand should be covered with dry wood, rubber, or other insulating material, and caution should be observed in handling the cord. The National Electric Code gives types and uses of flexible cord.

Lamps and Appliances

The same general considerations that apply to the use of cords in various locations apply to the use of portable appliances in the same locations.

Frayed electrical cords are a hazard; repair them at once.

Members of the household using portable appliances should keep away from grounded objects. The use of such appliances by persons while in bathtubs or when likely to touch faucets, laundry tubs, kitchen ranges, or other grounded objects is particularly dangerous. The danger is greater for persons in bathtubs because the skin is wet and a large surface of the body may be in contact with the conducting water. Accidents involving electric shock under these circumstances may be expected to be fatal.

In nearly all cases where an electrical accident has occurred in the bathroom, the victim's body was wet. In most cases the person was in a bathtub. Under this condition he may have attempted to turn the switch of an electric light or appliance. In these instances the part of the switch, appliance, or socket that he touched was uninsulated and in contact with the ungrounded part of the electric circut.

Electric fixtures in the bathroom preferably should be controlled by a wall switch near the entrance door. Key and chain sockets should be avoided; ceiling fixtures are best. No electrical appliances which require handling should be used in the bathroom unless specially designed for such use, as electric shavers. To permit accessibility for aid in case of accident, bathroom doors should remain unlocked if practicable, or have a lock that can be opened from the outside in an emergency.

Brass-shell sockets should not be installed in the basement or places liable to have damp floors if key sockets are used. Only porcelain or

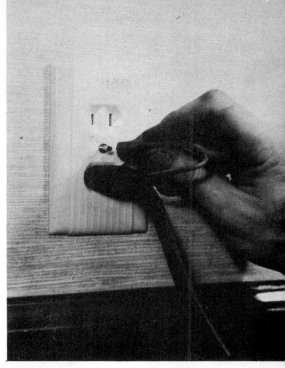

When working about the house, use a screw-in ground connection when using portable power tools, like an electric drill.

composition sockets should be employed under such circumstances.

Portable extension lamps are often put together by inexperienced persons, and records show them to be frequently involved in severe accidents or fires. Extension lamps should not be made up of twisted lamp cord and brass-shell sockets. They should be equipped with a socket of non-absorptive insulating material, and the insulated conductors should be inclosed within an outer protective covering.

Electric-lamp bulbs become very hot when free ventilation is interrupted. Where these lamps come in contact with curtains, carpets, woodwork, or bedding, the use of suitable inclosing wire basket guards

Always ground your portable power tools when working in the basement.

is essential. Such guards also protect the bulbs against breakage. Paper or cloth articles should never be placed in contact with lamp bulbs, and such materials should be used for lamp shades only if very liberal ventilating space is left between the shade and lamp bulb.

Where it is necessary to make use of portable lamps or appliances in such places as a garage having a cement or earth floor, use a special type of portable cord containing an additional wire for grounding the frame or case of the appliance. Special types of plug and receptacle are necessary for the use of this cord to prevent insertion of the plug in the ordinary type of receptacle. The ap-

pliance or lamp may, therefore, be used only where the special receptacles are installed. Such receptacles are not usually installed in residences, but are becoming common for use in factories. In some states they are now required for cetain industrial installations.

A rather common hazard is the overloading of lighting fixtures by the attachment of portable appliances. Large numbers of electrical appliances are coming into use because of their convenience and intrinsic safety as compared with heating and power appliances depending on other forms of energy. Lighting fixtures are generally designed for supplying current to lamps, but not for supplying some of the larger appliances or several of the smaller ones. A single lamp socket rated 660 watts cannot be used with safety to supply a flatiron or toaster rated 1,000 wats. Use of a multiple outlet plug or similar device in a lamp socket provides an even greater opportunity for overloading.

Water Heaters

There have been offered for sale portable immersion water heaters in which the current-carrying parts come into direct contact with the water to be heated. Ordinarily part of the current will flow through the water to the containing vessel and is a shock hazard to anyone placing his hands in the water or touching the container. The use of such types of water heater is not recommended.

To get quick results in heating water, a larger current is usually needed than can be supplied by the

When using a portable drop light, make sure it has a wire cage around the bulb and keep it away from anything that's inflammable.

ordinary branch circuit. Water heaters intended to be plugged in on such circuits should consequently be viewed with suspicion and should not be employed if rated at more than 15 amperes. Any appliance which does not have the rated current or wattage and voltage plainly marked should not be used.

Satisfactory water heaters of both the storage and instantaneous types are available for permanent installation, but these usually require a separate circuit to supply the needed high current.

Radio and Television

In erecting an antenna, care should be taken to avoid contact with or crossing over or under electric power, light, telephone, or telegraph conductors. Contact between antenna wires and power conductors has often caused fatal shock.

During a lightning storm it is a good plan to disconnect outdoor antennas from the radio or television set and connect them to an effective ground. Information on grounding is contained in the National Electrical Safety Code. It is always necessary to have a lightning arrester connected to the lead-in wire from an outside antenna.

Before attempting to replace the tubes or pilot light in a radio set, make sure the set is disconnected from the supply circuit by pulling out the plug supplying the set. Because of the high voltage circuits present in television equipment, be careful when making repairs.

Radio Transmitting Stations

Installations of amateur transmitting stations should be made only by competent persons familiar with local regulations and the rules of the National Electrical Safety Code. As therein required, radio transmitting equipment should be kept disconnected from the antenna system when not in use and the antenna effectively grounded. This can be done by use of a double-throw, single-pole switch outside the building. The antenna should not be attached to the radio apparatus inside the house during severe lightning storms.

Antennas used for transmitting should be carefully erected with poles or towers guyed in such a manner that they cannot fall even if the antenna wire should be accidentally broken. The following situations should be avoided in erecting antennas and guy wires: (a) attachments to electric power, light, telephone or telegraph poles; (b) crossing over railroad tracks or public roads; and (c) crossing over or under electric power, light, telephone or telegraph wires.

As some of the circuits in radio transmitting equipment present a serious shock hazard, construction or arrangement should be such as to prevent contact with these circuits during operation of the equipment.

Laundry Appliances

Electrical appliances and machinery used in laundry work, such as washing machines, involve a special hazard, since they are frequently used in a basement or other damp place. Even when the laundry room is not permanently damp, water is likely to be spilled on the floor. A person standing upon a damp floor is especially liable to a severe electrical shock from contact with a live wire or machine frame, because a good conducting path to ground is thereby provided.

It is obvious that in laundries and places equally subject to dampness, exposed metal parts of motors or machines should not be permitted- to become alive through any failure of insulation. There is an easy way to prevent this, and it is by making a positive connection to ground. Motors permanently installed are regularly grounded, but with portable machines this is not customary. If the portable laundry appliance is not provided with a

grounding conductor in the cord (it will be marked with a green color), grounding should be provided by using a separate wire not smaller than No. 10 AWG, connecting one end to the frame of the washing machine and the other end to the nearest cold water pipe. A ground clamp is used for this purpose. If a grounding conductor is provided in the flexible cord, the receptacle used for its connection should be of the type to receive the attachment properly, and should provide a reliable ground connection for the grounding conductor.

A motor-operated wringer should be equipped with a guard or with a device which will stop the motor or release the wringer in case one's hand gets caught.

Switches

Next to portable appliances, switches are the most handled portion of electrical equipment equipment, and the live parts should consequently not be exposed to contact. In modern installations this is accomplished by the inclosure of switches under the flush plates of metal wall boxes with only handles or push butttons projecting, or by the use of snap switches with fiber-lined metal enclosures. Where snap switches are used in damp locations, and particularly in bathrooms, the covers should be of porcelain or other material not so likely to fail under damp conditions as is a fiber lining.

Switches should be placed in convenient locations. This is especially true of the main or service switch which is installed for the pur-

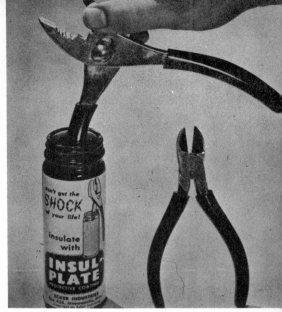

pose of cutting off the building wiring from the source of electrical supply This switch should be accessible at all times and stored material should not be placed so as to block access to it. When a house is to be left unoccupied for long periods, it is well to open this switch.

Outdoor Hazards

Electrical wiring outside of buildings is either placed underground or is mounted upon overhead structures, such as wood poles or steel towers with suitable clearance from buildings, trees, and other objects and suitable separations of the several conductors.

Every householder can help eliminate a serious hazard by reporting to the electric-light company, or other proper authority, any wires which have fallen in the street or which have broken or sagged down so as to be within reach of pedestrians or vehicles. Contacts of conductors with trees are not so serious, but even this should not be permitted to continue. Broken or sagging wires are most likely to be observed after heavy storms.

The reduction in the safe clearances of overhead wires constitutes the only danger to the public from such wires. They are responsible for a considerable number of fatalities annually. These occur from contact with fallen or broken wires, from unauthorized climbing of poles, rom contact of other wires with the electric-power wires, and occasionally from some tall object such as a derrick being moved in the street where there is insufficient clearance.

You can buy tools with insulated handles or else there's a plastic liquid into which you can dip the handles to produce an insulated covering.

The covering of high-voltage wires cannot be depended upon to supply sufficient insulation for safety, and no one should touch a high-voltage wire even though it is covered with such insulation.

The flying of kites near overhead wires has been responsible for a number of accidents, particularly where wire has been used as a kite string or where cotton string has become wet. Children should be instructed not to fly kites near overhead wires or to throw strings or pieces of wire over the power wires. They should also be warned against climbing of poles or trees near which electric wires pass.

Another frequent cause of injury has been the attempt to erect radio-antenna conductors in locations where it was necessary to carry them over electric light or power wires. Contact with the power wire by an antenna wire held in the hand subjects the victim to a severe and probably fatal electrical shock. Antenna wires should never be erected in the immediate vicinity of electric light or power wires.

Electric light companies usually trim trees near which their wires pass so as to avoid contact. With later growth of the trees such contacts frequently develop, and trees should be kept trimmed so as to avoid this. Such a contact may rub the insulating covering of a wire until it is bare, and the wet surface of a tree during a rainstorm may be sufficiently conducting so that it becomes hazardous to touch the tree at any point.

Persons should also avoid touching wet poles that carry electric light or power wires. Such wires are usually mounted upon insulators, but during a storm the wire may come in contact with the pole or cross arm and if the pole is wet the current may be conducted to a person touching it near the ground. Contact with the guy wires which support poles should also be avoided, since live wires may also sag against them during a storm.

Electric Heaters

In most localities, heating the entire house by electricity is too expensive to be generally used. Portable electric heaters, however, are a convenient source of heat for bathrooms or other areas where occasional heat is needed.

Electric heaters require little maintenance except for the replacement of burned-out heating elements or defective switches. In some cases, switches may be repaired by polishing the contacts that have become pitted or corroded by repeated arcing. Portable electric heaters should be supplied with extension cords of ample capacity, having adequate protection for the wire. Portable electric steam radiators should be checked occasionally to determine whether they contain sufficient water to cover the electric heating element. Radiant electric heaters should not be located too near furniture or draperies as the radiation may overheat and ignite combustible materials. Laundry should not be dried over radiant heaters because of the fire hazard involved.

Electrical Wiring

The average handyman can do many electrical jobs around the house. BUT it is essential that he know exactly what he's doing and that he follow accepted electrical and safety rules. Before going any further, here is one rule to follow at all times: Do not touch any wire or fixture unless the current to that wire or fixture is OFF!

In this section on electrical wiring, you will find a basic explanation of wiring circuits, some terms commonly used, working hints when handling electrical wires and specific wiring problems and their solution. It is strongly recommended that you read through all the sections to obtain all the rules, working techniques and a basic un-

derstanding of what you are doing before you tackle an electrical job about the house.

Working with electricity is simple and a lot easier than doing masonry work. It is, however, more dangerous unless you know the rules. In some communities, only professional electricians are authorized to do any wiring in your home. In other areas, it is possible for the handyman to do the electrical work and have it inspected by local authorities.

When any wiring is to be done, whether it has to be inspected or not, the work must conform to standard wiring rules and regulations. Many of these rules are noted in the following sections. However, you should ask your local building authority for a copy of the local code, and also obtain the national wiring code from the Board of Fire Underwriters.

The Tools You Need for Wiring

The tools you need for an electrical job depend upon the exact job you have in mind. Here, however, is a collection of tools which is useful for interior and exterior wiring of all types:

1. Hammer—for driving nails, staples and fastening hangers.

2. Drill bit—one that will make a hole large enough for the electrical cable, BX or Romex, to pass through.

3. Masonry bit—needed if you have to makes holes in concrete or brick walls.

4. Extension bit—a shaft extension to enable you to drill deep holes or to reach difficult-to-get-at places.

5. Drill—you can use a hand or electric drill or even a brace for boring holes.

6. Keyhole saw—for cutting holes and irregular shapes.

7. Hacksaw—for cutting BX cable, wire lath or wood lath and plaster.

8. Test light—this inexpensive unit is used to trace and test circuits, to check if the current is on or off in the cable as you work.

9. Wire stripper—this adjustable plier-like tool will quickly and easily strip the insulation off the wires you need for joining to switches, outlets, pilot lights or fixtures.

10. Blow torch—this liquefied petroleum torch is compact and convenient for an average handyman to use. It is needed to heat the wires when they are to be soldered.

11. Folding rule—for measuring distances, wire and openings.

12. Chisel—for notching studs, rafters, joists and lath to make an opening for the cable or conduit to pass through.

13. Lever-jaw wrench—can be used as a pliers, lock wrench and a pipe wrench while working.

14. Linesmen's pliers—this tool is used for cutting wires, gripping locknuts, etc. Note that the model shown in photograph has heavy rubber handles that form an insulation over the pliers as an added safety measure when working with wires.

15. Pocket knife—for cutting insulation and cleaning wires.

16. Fish tape—used to pull wire through a wall, floor or conduit.

17. Conduit bender — this 'hickey' will help you bend conduit in the approved manner. It is possible to bend the conduit without collapsing the walls of the tube or pipe.

18. Screwdriver — to tighten screws on connectors, switches and outlets and elsewhere when a screw has to be driven.

19. Offset screwdriver — to reach hard-to-get-at screws, especially inside of switch, outlet and junction boxes.

20. Long-nose pliers—helpful in bending ends of wire to fit under screw terminals.

The Materials You Need

WIRE is your first requirement. Which type you use depends upon where the wire will be used and upon your local electrical code. You can use armored cable, commonly

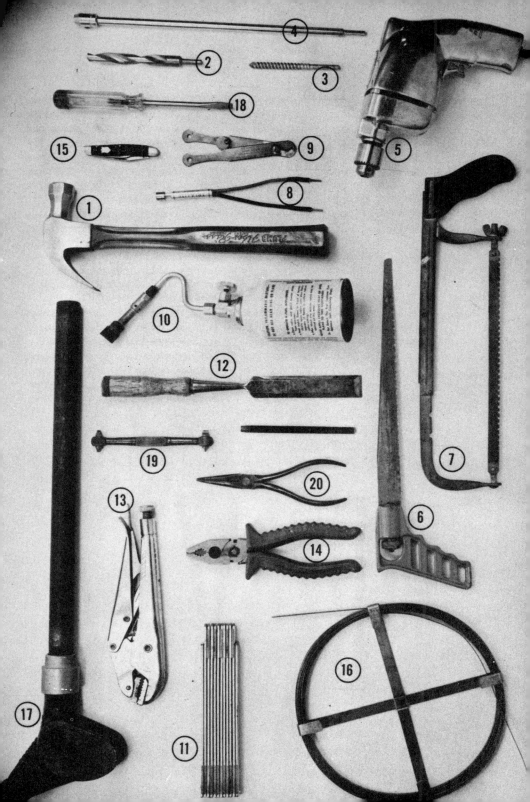

called BX cable, non-metallic sheathed cable, called Romex, rubber-covered cable or insulated wires through a conduit or pipe. It is best to use the same type of cable as is now used in your home, although this is not essential. However, adding BX cable to a home wired in Romex requires special grounding for the BX, and adding Romex to a home wired with BX requires the use of a grounding wire in the Romex so that all boxes are properly grounded.

The size of the wire is determined by the load it will carry. If the wire is to be used outdoors, it is necessary to use rubber-covered cable or insulated wires through pipe or conduit. Inside the home, you can use either Romex or BX, depending upon the local code requirements.

SWITCHES are used to make or break a line; that is, to close the circuit or open it. When the circuit is closed, the switch is in the 'on' position. When the circuit is open, the switch is in the 'off' position. Several different types of switches are used in the home:

1. The standard switch normally used is a SPST—single-pole, single-throw switch. That is, the switch is used only on one line—it is connected in series with the black or 'hot' wire. It can be opened or closed.

2. Another type of switch that can be used in special applications for the same purpose is a DPST—double-pole, single-throw switch. It is connected to both the white and black wires; it opens or closes both lines when the switch handle is moved.

Three types of cable a handyman can use: BX or armored cable, Romex or non-metallic sheathed cable, or rubber-covered cable.

These switches NOT used on electrical lines are presented to show the details of single-pole double-pole, single-throw and double-throw operation. The one on the left is a DPDT—double-pole, double-throw switch. Note that the handle can be moved into the top or bottom position or left in the center. There are two wire terminals for each position, making it a double-pole, and there are two closed positions for the handle, making it a double-throw. The switch on the right is a DPST—double-pole, single-throw. The two wire terminals make it a double-pole, but there is only one closed position. Therefore, it is called a single throw.

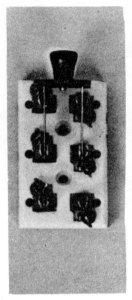 

3. When two switches are used to control a single light, a three-way switch is used. It is necessary to run a three-wire cable between the switches in this type of wiring. See *Dual-Control Light*.

4. When three switches are used to control a single light, a four-way switch is necessary. This is a switch which has four terminal screws and is wired to two three-way switches as shown in a wiring diagram later in this section.

Standard electric switches used in the home. These include a SPST, a three-way switch and an outlet.

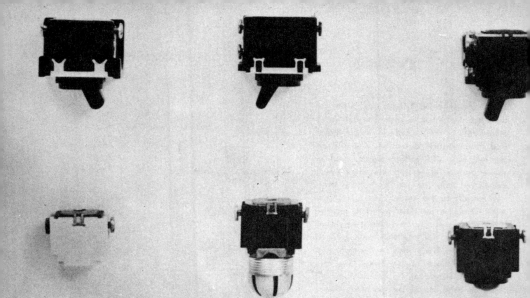

These are Despard electric fixtures; several can be mounted within a special plate in a single box. From upper left across: SPST, 3-way switch, 4-way switch; bottom row across: outlet, pilot light, neon pilot light.

These are some of the accessory items you need for electrical wiring jobs. They include switch, junction and outlet boxes, cable connectors, staples, solderless connectors, solder and tapes.

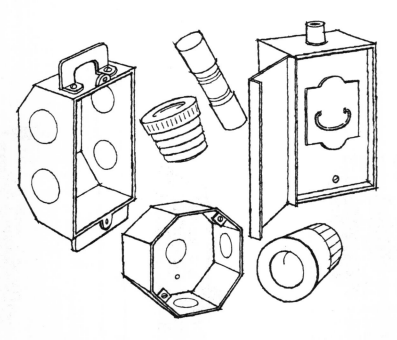

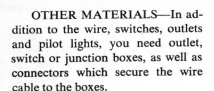

OTHER MATERIALS—In addition to the wire, switches, outlets and pilot lights, you need outlet, switch or junction boxes, as well as connectors which secure the wire cable to the boxes.

1. A switch box, usually rectangular in shape, can be used to house a switch or even an outlet.

2. A junction box, usually octagonal in shape, is used for the joining of wires or for attaching a light fixture.

3. An outlet box, usually a shallow rectangular shaped unit, is used to house an outlet.

You also need solderless connectors or solder and tape for joining the wires, and straps or staples to anchor the cable to the wall and joists as it is installed.

Wiring Symbols

The following electrical symbols are used in house plans and blueprints. They will help you read the plans more intelligently and also enable the handyman to figure out special wiring circuits.

GENERAL OUTLETS

Lighting Outlet

Ceiling Lighting Outlet for recessed fixture (outline shows shape of fixture)

Continuous Wireway for Fluorescent Lighting on ceiling, in coves, cornices, etc. (Extend rectangle to show length of installation)

Lighting Outlet with Lamp Holder

Lighting Outlet with Lamp Holder and Pull Switch

Fan Outlet

Junction Box

Drop-Cord Equipped Outlet

Clock Outlet

CONVENIENCE OUTLETS

Duplex Convenience Outlet

Triplex Convenience Outlet (Substitute other numbers for other variations in number of plug positions.)

Duplex Convenience Outlet— Split Wired

Duplex Convenience Outlet for Grounding-Type Plugs

Weatherproof Convenience Outlet

Multi-Outlet Assembly (Extend arrows to limits of installation. Use appropriate symbol to indicate type of outlet. Also indicate spacing of outlets as X inches.)

Combination Switch and Convenience Outlet

Floor Outlet

Range Outlet

Special-Purpose Outlet. Use subscript letters to indicate function. DW-Dishwasher, CD-Clothes Dryer, etc.

SWITCH OUTLETS

S Single-Pole Switch
S_3 Three-Way Switch
S_4 Four-Way Switch
S_D Automatic Door Switch
S_P Switch and Pilot Light
S_{WP} Weatherproof Switch
S_2 Double Pole Switch

LOW-VOLTAGE SWITCHING SYSTEMS

$\underline{S}$ Switch for Low-Voltage Relay Systems

$\underline{MS}$ Master Switch for Low-Voltage Relay Systems

Relay-Equipped Lighting Outlet

Low-Voltage Relay System Wiring

AUXILIARY SYSTEMS

Push Button

Buzzer

Bell

Combination Bell-Buzzer

Chime

Annunciator

AUXILIARY SYSTEMS

Electric Door Opener

Maid's Signal Plug

Interconnection Box Bell-Ringing Transformer

Outside Telephone

Interconnecting Telephone

Television Outlet

MISCELLANEOUS

Service Panel

Distribution Panel

Switch Leg Indication. Connects outlets with control points.

While electrical engineering is a complex subject reserved for the professionals, it is essential that the handyman be familiar with certain basic terms before he starts any electrical project. As you read through this list, you'll be amazed at all the terms with which you are already familiar even though you might have done only a few simple wiring jobs. However, for the sake of clarity and safety in following the detailed instructions given later in this section, here are several of the more important terms together with their meaning:

AC—Alternating current: the type of power used in most home wiring systems; usually 60 cycles, but 25- and 50-cycle systems are used in a few localities.

AMPERE—This is a unit of measure of the rate of flow of electricity, something like the gallons per minute in a water system.

BUSHING—An insulator which fits around the wires at the end of a BX cable to prevent the cut metal from fraying the insulation covering the wires.

CIRCUIT—The complete flow of electricity is traced through what is technically called a circuit; it is the flow of current through a wire from the source of supply to one or more outlets and then back to the source of supply through another wire.

CIRCUIT-BREAKER — It performs the same function as a fuse in opening or breaking the circuit when there is an overload of current, but needs only to be reset.

CONDUCTORS—The trade name for electric wires.

CONDUIT—This is metal tubing resembling pipe through which wires are run; it is used frequently when running wires underground or in areas where exposed wires are in danger of being frayed, broken or cut.

BX—Common trade term used for armored cable.

CONNECTOR—Also called a BX connector, this fitting is used to secure the conductors to an outlet, junction or switch box.

DC—Direct current: the type of power still used in some areas for home wiring; also the current flow from batteries where one wire is always 'positive' or hot and the other always 'negative' or ground.

FUSE—A safety device which breaks the flow of current or electricity whenever a circuit is overloaded.

GROUNDING—The connection of the electrical system to the earth, a precaution necessary to prevent damage from lightning and to minimize the danger from shocks.

H.P.—Horsepower: a unit of measure of work; one H.P. equals 746 watts.

HOT WIRES—The power-carrying wires, usually black or red, as distinguished from the neutral wires, usually white.

INSULATION — A protective sheathing used over wires to prevent the escape of electricity.

JUNCTION BOX—A metal box, either square or octagonal, in

which wires from different circuits are joined.

OUTLET—A device or fixture that permits tapping off electricity at convenient locations for lights or appliances.

OUTLET BOX—A unit in which an outlet or to which a fixture such as a ceiling light is secured and joined to the wiring system.

OVERLOAD—Term used to describe an electrical condition in which too much current is flowing through the line for the fuse controlling that particular line.

POLARIZING—Identification of wires by color throughout the entire system to help assure that hot wires will be connected only to hot wires and that neutral wires run in a continuous uninterrupted connection back to the ground terminal.

RECEPTACLE—Similar to outlet: a unit to which electric cords can be plugged in conveniently.

ROMEX—Term used for non-metallic sheathed cable.

SERVICE ENTRANCE SWITCH —Technical name for a fuse box; it is the main panel through which electricity is brought into the building and then distributed to various branch circuits. It contains the main disconnect switch for the entire wiring system as well as fuses or circuit-breakers for the individual lines.

SHORT CIRCUIT — Popularly called a 'short,' it is an improper connection between hot wires or between a hot wire and a neutral wire.

SWITCH—A device for breaking the flow of current.

SWITCH BOX—A metal unit, usually a rectangle but can be square, in which a switch or switches are connected to the circuit.

THREE-WAY SWITCH—A type of switch which is used in pairs to control the same light from two different points.

UNDERWRITERS' LABORATORIES—A nationally accepted organization which tests all types of wiring materials and devices to make certain that they meet minimum standards for safety and quality. If the item meets their approval, it usually carries a UL seal or tag. Don't take chances with inferior materials—look for the UL seal or tag when you buy.

VOLT—This is a unit used in measuring electrical pressure, like pounds in a water system.

VOLTAGE DROP—This term is used to indicate the loss of voltage which occurs when wires are overloaded or when the current has to travel a great distance through a wire.

WATT—This unit shows the current drain taking into account both voltage and amperage. For example, 1 watt is equal to 1 ampere at 1 volt, or 75 watts on a bulb indicates that the bulb consumes about .64 (slightly more than %10ths) of an ampere at 115 volts.

WATT HOUR—One watt used for one hour equals 1 watt hour; 1,000 watt hours equals 1 kilowatt hour (Kwh), which is the unit by which electricity is metered.

Adequate Wiring For Your Home

Adequate wiring in your home depends upon (a) the load which the service entrance lines will carry to your home, and (b) the number of branch circuits to carry full power to the appliances and lighting fixtures. Today's home has many more appliances than homes of 10 or 20 years ago. Now there are washing machines, clothes dryers, freezers, air conditioners, TV sets—appliances commonly found in the home today which were not present years back.

The addition of more appliances puts a greater strain on the electrical wires. You just cannot keep adding appliances in a home without providing for more current to enter a home. Just as an analogy—if you were to add four or five bathtubs to your home today without changing the main water pipe, you would not expect the tubs to be filled at the same rate as the single tub is today. The same is true of electricity. As you add appliances, it is necessary to increase the load-carrying capacity of the service wires.

Check with your local public utilities to determine what size wires are used in your service connection box and what load they are meant to carry. A #6 wire should be used for the service entrance, or a #4; if there is any doubt, it's better to use a #4, for you will always have additional current capacity available.

Here are some standard arrangements for service entrance hook-ups:

1. For minimum service you should have 3-wire #6 service conductors — usually 115-230 volts with a 60-ampere switch or fuse. This will provide for a range circuit, three 15-ampere branch circuits and one 20-ampere branch circuit.

2. For maximum service, you should have 3-wire #4 service conductors—115-230 volts with a 100-ampere switch or fuse. This is the size required for a seven-circuit installation in a home.

BRANCH CIRCUITS

The service conductors are divided into branches so that if an overload or short occurs in one circuit, only the fuse of that circuit will be affected. The current in the rest of the lines will continue while the current in only the one line will stop.

You must have at least one 20-ampere appliance circuit for your kitchen and laundry area. This circuit should be independent of the lights in those rooms. It is best to have one separate circuit for the kitchen and another for the laundry.

A separate 15-ampere lighting circuit is recommended for every 500 square feet of floor space in your home. These circuits can be used to power the room lights, radios, fans and other smaller appliances.

Heavier appliances require additional circuits. It is best to check the load on each circuit before introducing another item. A room space heater, for example, draws about 10 amperes. You can readily see what would happen if it were connected in a circuit which is already drawing about 15 amperes or even 10 amperes. The fuse would

The Wattage Requirements of Major Appliances in the Home

Fixed Appliances	Average Wattage*
KITCHEN	
1. Refrigerator	205
2. Range	10800
3. Fan	85
4. Dishwasher	1155
5. Food Waste Disposer	330
LAUNDRY	
6. Water Heater	2500
7. Automatic Washer	1000
8. Clothes Dryer	4350
9. Ironer	1500

UTILITY ROOM	
10. Furnace Fan	225
11. Oil Burner	245
12. Stoker	250
13. Heat Pump	3 & 5 HP
14. Electronic Air Cleaner	60
15. Air Conditioner (Central)	(2 to 5 HP)
16. Water Pump	265
17. Dehumidifier	210
18. Home Freezer	255
MISCELLANEOUS	
19. Attic Fan	370
20. Room Air Conditioner	800
21. Bathroom Heater	1095

Source: Edison Electric Institute

blow because too much current is passing through the line. See the accompanying tables showing the average wattage of appliances in the home.

Source: Edison Electric Institute

The Wattage Requirements of Portable Appliances

Appliances	Number	Average Wattages*
1. Bed Covering	1 to 2	185
2. Bottle Warmer	1	400
3. Broiler	1	1325
4. Clock	3 to 5	2
5. Coffee Maker (Automatic)	1 to 2	830
6. Cooker (Egg)	1	520
7. Fan (Desk)	1 to 3	70
8. Floor Polisher	1	240
9. Fruit Extractor	1	80
10. Germicidal Lamp	1 to 3	20
11. Grill	1	770
12. Hair Dryer	1	235
13. Heater (Radiant)	1 to 2	1095
14. Heating Pad	1 to 2	55
15. Heat Lamp (Infra-red)	1 to 3	250
16. Hot Plate	1	1140
17. Iron (Hand)	1 to 2	1000
18. Mixer (Food)	2 to 6	120
19. Percolator	1 to 2	490
20. Radio	2 to 6	90
21. Radio Phonograph	1 to 2	100
22. Razor (Electric)	1 to 2	15
23. Roaster	1	1300
24. Sewing Machine	1	75
25. Sun Lamp	1 to 3	390
26. Television	1 to 2	280
27. Toaster	1 to 2	990
28. Vacuum Cleaner	1 to 2	315
29. Vibrator	1	45
30. Waffle Baker	1	855

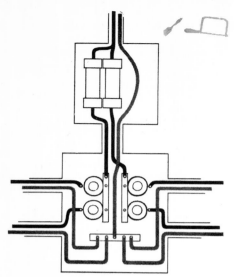

Cartridge fuses are normally used in the service entrance box to control the main electrical lines. The screw-in glass fuses are used as safety devices to control the branch circuits.

When the Fuse Blows

When a fuse blows or burns out, it is a sign that you may have an overload or a short circuit. It's easy to see if a plug-type fuse is burned out, but cartridge fuses do not change in appearance.

It is a good idea to have a list of the switches, outlets and lights that each fuse controls pasted on the inside of the cover of the fuse box. In this way, you will know instantly which fuse controls what line when you are doing any electrical wiring repairs or installations.

When a fuse blows, you should:

1. Turn off the master switch controlling the service conductors bring current into the house.

2. Remove the blown fuse and replace it with a 25-watt bulb to test the line.

3. Put the current on again. If the bulb burns dimly, the line is overloaded. This means that some appliances should be disconnected. It is a sign that you should have a new line added to carry the extra load normally required.

4. If the bulb burns brightly, there is a short circuit somewhere in the line. If you have a helper to watch the bulb, you can go the line and unscrew or turn off the lights on that circuit and disconnect any appliance. Do one at a time; when the test bulb goes out, you have found your trouble.

5. Leave the appliance disconnected or the switch off and put in a new fuse. Turn the main switch on again.

6. If the fuse blows again immediately after you have screwed it in place, your difficulty may be more serious. There may be another short in the line caused by an appliance, switch or light, or there may be a short in the line itself. Here is where you can use professional help.

7. If nothing happens to the fuse, it is necessary to correct the short in the appliance, switch or lamp socket at a convenient time. Remember to shut off the current if it's necessary to replace a switch or fixture socket.

One note of caution: do not change fuses in the dark! Keep a flashlight handy near the fuse box for just such emergencies.

WIRES IN THE BRANCH CIRCUITS

When wiring branch circuits, it is best not to put all the lights and outlets in any one room on the same

circuit. If that fuse were to blow you'd have no source of current in the room. Frequently, local wiring regulations require that ceiling lights and wall outlets be installed on separate circuits.

Here are the recommended sizes of wire to use in different parts of the home:

1. For room lighting circuits— for ceiling or wall fixtures, portable lamps, radio, TV and movable appliances, such as a vacuum cleaner, use 2-wire #14 or #12.

2. For an electric range, use 3-wire #6 cable and protect each of the 'hot' or black wires with a 30 ampere fuse.

3. For the kitchen appliances— refrigerator, mixer, toaster, grill, etc., use 2-wire #10 cable protected by a 20-ampere fuse.

4. If you have a water heater operating on the electrical circuit, you should have a 2-wire #12 cable protected by a 20-ampere fuse.

5. If you have an electrically operated clothes dryer, use 3-wire #6 or #8 cable and protect the two black wires when the unit is operated on 220 volts with two fuses.

6. If you have a substantial number of power tools, it is best to use a separate circuit to the workshop; use 2-wire #10 cable protected by a 20-ampere fuse.

What Size Wire to Use

The size or diameter of the wire determines the electrical load it will carry just as the diameter of a pipe determines the amount of water it will permit to flow through. A thin wire carrying a heavy load will overheat; this will waste current in

Keep a list pasted to the inside of the fuse box showing the switches, light fixtures and outlets each fuse controls.

addition to being dangerous. The amount of current the wire will deliver will not be sufficient for the motor to run or the bulbs to light at top efficiency.

Every wire has a maximum allowable current-carrying capacity

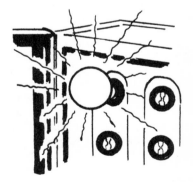

Use a 25-watt bulb to test the line when a fuse blows.

Sketch from "How To Do It Safely," Courtesy of The Home Insurance Co.

as shown in the accompanying table. In addition, the longer the wire, the greater the current loss or voltage drop. Therefore, it is necessary to plan your wiring so that you do not have an execessively long run for any one line. If, however, such a long run is necessary, it is essential to use a heavier or thicker wire, checking carefully the voltage drop of that wire.

The different types of wire given in the table "Maximum Current Carrying Capacity of Flexible Wires" are classes used by Underwriters' Laboratories to specify the type of insulation and covering over the wires. Generally, you will find this classification listed on the reel when you purchase wire, or it may be listed on a tag when the wire comes in a roll.

MAXIMUM CURRENT CARRYING CAPACITY OF FLEXIBLE WIRES

Size of Wire (Number)	Rubber Type*	Heavy Rubber or Thermoplastic** (amperes)	Asbestos****	Heavy Asbestos***
18	5	7	10	17
16	7	10	15	22
14	15	15	20	28
12	20	20		36
10	25	25		47
8	35			
6	45			
4	60			
2	80			

* Types PO, C, PD, PWP, K, E and ED
** Types S, SO, SJ, SJO, SV, POSJ, ST, STT, STV, and POT
*** Types HC, HPD and HSJ
**** Types AVPO and AVPD

The diameter of the wire increases as the number designation gets smaller. A #18 wire is lighter or smaller than a #10. In the accompanying sketch you will find the actual diameters of copper wire without the insulation.

Voltage drop is a vital consideration if you are running any power tools in your house. If the wire fails to deliver the proper voltage to your motor, not only will the power tool fail to work at top performance but your motor will burn out quickly. In the accompanying table is a guide showing the distance in feet which different types of wire will carry a 110-volt current of different amperage with less than a 2% voltage drop.

AMPERES	DISTANCE (IN FEET)					
	#14	#12	#10	#8	#6	#4
1	450	700	1100	1800	2800	4500
2	222	350	550	900	1400	2200
3	150	240	350	600	900	1500
4	110	175	275	450	700	1100
5	90	140	220	360	560	880
10	45	70	110	180	280	450
15	30	45	70	120	180	300
20		35	55	90	140	225
30			35	60	90	150
40				45	70	110
60					45	75

Working with Wires

The first step in good electrical wiring is to know the right and the wrong way to make wire connections. In joining two or more wires, two essential requirements must be met. First, the wires must be bright and clean before they are joined. Secondly, the connection must be tight—either well fastened with solder and covered with tape or joined with solderless connectors.

Here is a guide for the handyman for cutting, splicing and connecting wires. Remember, joining the ends of two separate wires is known as a splice. Joining a wire at right angles to a continuous wire is called a tap.

When removing the insulation from a wire, it is best to cut at a slant as in sharpening a pencil. Expose about ½″ to ¾″ of the copper conductor. When removing the insulation, be careful not to scrape off the tin coating usually found on the wire; this tin coating makes soldering easier.

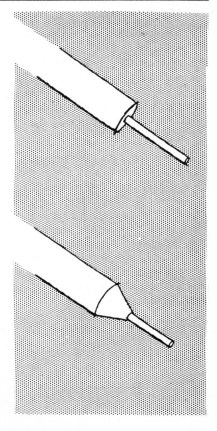

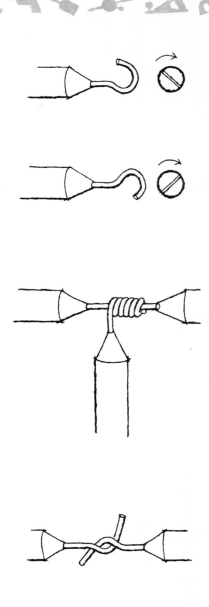

When connecting wire to a screw terminal, bend the end of the wire into a loop to fit around the screw. Attach the loop in the direction in which the screw turns when it is tightened. This will hold the wire under the head of the screw. If inserted in the opposite direction, there is always a chance of the wire working loose as the screw is tightened.

A tap splice is the joining of one wire at right angles to a continuous wire. For connecting the end of one wire at a point on a continuous wire, remove the insulation from the end of that single wire. Also bare a section of the continuous wire. Wrap the continuous wire around the exposed length as tightly as possible, making certain that both wires are clean. Then solder and tape.

A splice is the joining of two separate wires. It is necessary to remove about 3″ of insulation from each of the two wires. After making certain that the wires are clean, cross the wires about 1″ from the insulation. Then make 6 to 8 turns, using your fingers, with each wire and tighten the twisted sections with pliers to produce a splice similar to that shown in the sketch.

All splices have to be soldered and then taped. Always heat the wires with a soldering iron or gun or a blowtorch, making certain not to melt the insulation. After the two wires have been properly soldered, wrap rubber tape around the splice. It is best to extend the tape about 1″ to 2″ on either side of the joining of the wires. The rubber tape is then covered with friction tape. The friction tape should be wound from the opposite direction. It is possible to cover the splice with plastic tape. This new tape need not be covered with friction tape, although it is required in some communities by the local electrical code.

Solderless connectors eliminate the need for soldering the joining of wires. The connectors are made of an insulating material and once they are set over the wires, there is no possibility of shorting. Simply screw the connector over the two wires.

If both wires to be joined are solid, they are merely pressed closed together and the solderless connector is screwed over the two. On the other hand, if one is stranded and the other is a solid wire, it is better to twist the stranded wire around the solid wire in a clockwise direction and then screw the solderless connector over both. If you should wind the stranded wire around the solid one in the wrong direction, they will work loose as the solderless connector is screwed on. Should this happen, rewind the two wires at once and replace the connector.

Electrical Circuits

The electricity after leaving the main fuse box in your home goes through different branch circuits Each of these circuits is capable of carrying electricity to specific outlets and lighting fixtures. Generally, a circuit in a home is designed to carry 15 amperes or to deliver about 2650 watts with normal 110–120 volts.

How effectively the electricity does its job depends upon the individual circuit. Probably the best way to explain electrical circuits is to use Christmas-tree lamps as an example.

Until recently, most Christmas-tree lights were connected by a single wire. There was a plug at one end and a single wire ran from bulb to bulb and finally returned to the plug. If one lamp was burned out or loose in the socket, none would light. These lamps were in *series*. Now, however, many Christmas-tree lamp cords are available where two wires run from socket to socket. These lamps are in *parallel*. The failure of one lamp will not affect the others. See the accompanying sketches for a visual explanation.

Wiring in series presents many problems. If any one item is not functioning, then the entire set of won't work. A switch is wired in series with a light fixture. When the switch is 'off,' then the lamp is off; but if the switch is 'on,' the lamp burns brightly.

To make the individual parts independent, outlets and lamps are wired in parallel. The flow of current remains uninterruped even if one switch is 'off' or a lamp is burned out.

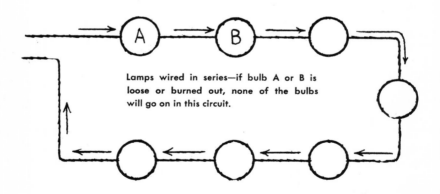

Lamps wired in series—if bulb A or B is loose or burned out, none of the bulbs will go on in this circuit.

Lamps wired in parallel—even if bulb A is burned out, bulb B as well as the others will light because current is available through the entire set of wires.

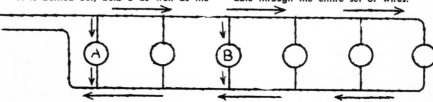

SWITCH

OUTLET

BULB

A switch is always wired in series with the fixture or outlet it controls. Here the switch is wired in series with a lamp. When the switch is 'off,' the lamp is out; but when the switch is 'on,' the lamp lights.

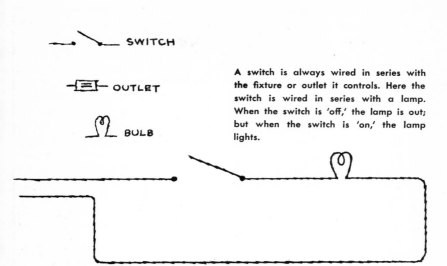

In this wiring diagram, the outlet is wired in parallel, but the switch and lamp are in series. The switch can be 'on' or 'off' and it will control only the lamp; the outlet will always have electricity available for use.

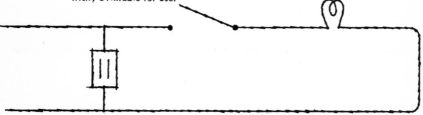

Although the lamp and outlet are wired in parallel in this circuit, the switch is in series with both. Thus if the switch is 'off,' neither the lamp nor the outlet will receive any electricity.

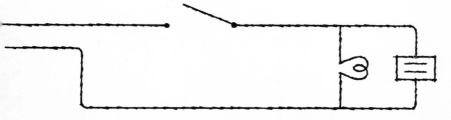

Common Wiring Diagrams

There are many wiring arrangements you can use inside and outside of your home. Here are several of the more common wiring diagrams to meet the need of the homeowner.

1. WALL SWITCH TO CONTROL CEILING LIGHT—If the wires from the fuse box reach the light fixture first, the black wire passes through the fixture box uninterrupted while the fixtures wires are connected in series with the white wire. Both the black and white wires continue along the ceiling and down the wall to the switch. One wire is connected to each terminal. If you are using a mercury-type switch, make certain that it is positioned properly; one section is marked "top."

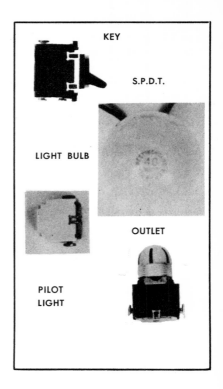

KEY

S.P.D.T.

LIGHT BULB

OUTLET

PILOT
LIGHT

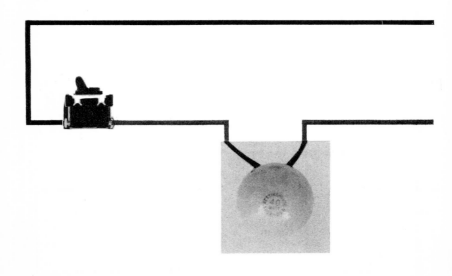

2. WALL SWITCH TO CONTROL CEILING LIGHT— The wires from the fuse box might come to the wall switch first. In this case, the black wire from the fuse box is connected to the switch. The black wire from the ceiling fixture is attached to the other terminal of the switch and the white wire from the ceiling light is joined to the white wire coming from the fuse box.

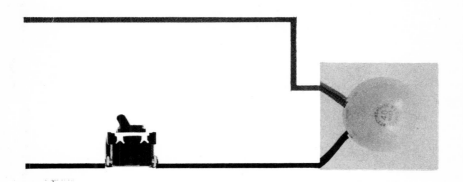

3. ONE SWITCH AND MORE THAN ONE CEILING LIGHT —A single wall switch can be used to control more than one light. All that is necessary is that the second light be wired in parallel. In this case the black wire from the second light is connected to the black wire from the switch and the black wire from the first light. The white wire from the second light joins the white wire of the first light and the white wire from the fuse box.

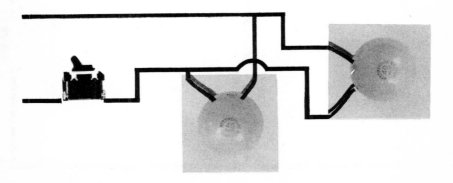

4. WIRING AN OUTLET—An outlet is wired in parallel with the white and black wires coming from the fuse box. If the outlet is wired in a branch circuit, then the white wire is attached to one terminal and the black to the other.

5. WIRING AN EXTRA OUTLET ON A LINE—To add an extra outlet to an existing outlet, it is necessary to wire it in parallel with the existing unit. Just run a black wire from the terminal connected to the black wire from the fuse box and add a white wire to the terminal from the fuse box.

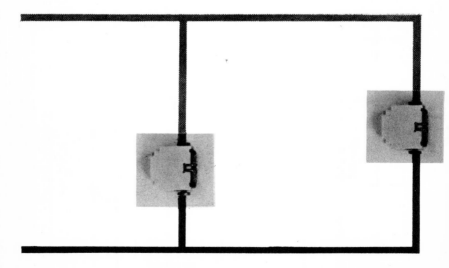

6. ADDING A PILOT LIGHT—
Often you require a pilot light
at the switch to indicate whether or not the light is on. This
type of wiring circuit is sometimes found at the base of an
attic stairway—the pilot light
lets you know whether or not
the attic light is on without
your going up the stairs. The
pilot light is wired in parallel
with the light in the attic or
wherever the light is that the
switch controls.

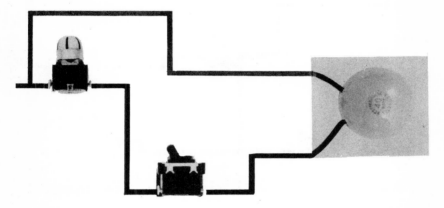

7. AN OUTLET WITH A
SWITCH—Maybe you want an
outlet next to the switch and to
have the outlet work independent of that switch. This can be
done easily if the wires from
the fuse box come to the switch
before the ceiling light. The
outlet is wired in parallel with
the wires from the fuse box before either wire is connected to
the switch or ceiling light.

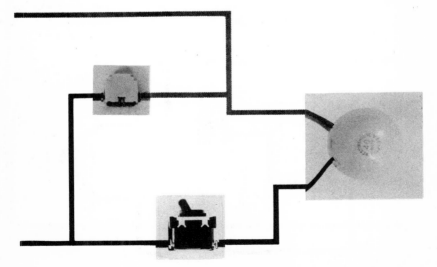

8. AN OUTLET WORKING OFF A SWITCH—Perhaps you'd prefer to have the outlet 'on' only when the switch and light are on. In this case, the outlet is again wired in parallel in the circuit, but it is connected after the switch. The current must flow through the switch before it reaches either outlet or the light. Outlet is controlled by switch.

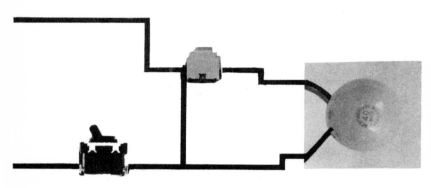

9. SEPARATE NIGHT LIGHT ON A LINE—In a child's room, a night light is a great convenience. It can be wired in to act independently of the regular room light. Two switches are needed—one controls the night light and the other the room light. Although complex looking, this wiring diagram is exceedingly simple. In consists of two series circuits: the switch and night light in one circuit and the other switch and room light in the other circuit. The wiring, however, is combined; the black wire from the fuse box is connected to one switch and then to the other by means of a jumper. The white wires from both the night light and room light are joined to the white wire from the fuse box.

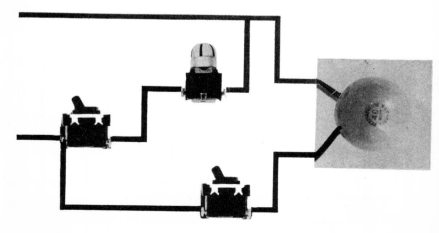

10. THREE-WAY LIGHTS FOR STAIRWAYS—To control a light from two different places, is is necessary to use a three-way switch. A three-wire cable is used between the two switches as each has three terminals. The red and black wires of the three-wire cable connect the two switches; the white wire is connected to the light. It is possible to have more than one light. However, all the lights have to be in parallel along the white wires between the two boxes.

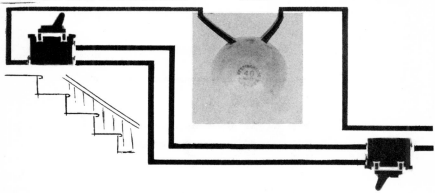

11. TWIN-CONTROL WITH A PILOT LIGHT—Using three-way switches to control a hall light presents no problem—it's easy to tell if the light is on or off. However, if that light is inside a garage and one of the switches is located in your kitchen, you may have to walk out of your home into your garage to tell if the light is on or off. Unlike the standard switch used to control room light, a three-way switch has no 'on' and 'off' position. Merely pushing the lever turns the light on or off. In this wiring diagram, a four-wire cable is needed between the house and the garage with the pilot light and one switch in the house, and the light and the other switch outside the house in the garage.

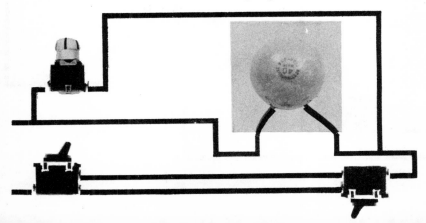

12. THREE SWITCHES FOR ONE LIGHT—A more complex wiring system is needed when you have three switches to control a single light. You'd encounter this wiring set-up if you have a light along your driveway and have a switch in the house, another in the garage and a third at the entrance gate to the driveway to control the light. With this wiring, you need one four-way switch and two three-way switches. Only three-wire cable is run between the connecting switches as shown in the accompanying diagram. Follow wiring carefully.

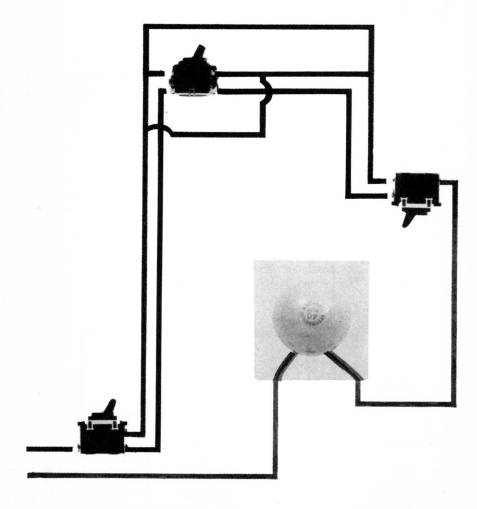

The Main Fuse Box

All electrical wires come to you from the power company through a single service entrance switch. In many main fuse boxes, there is a single 'on-off' switch to control all the current. In homes without such a switch, the main fuse box has two cartridge fuse holders. A fuse is set across the main power line; removing this fuse shuts off the house current. Note that a fuse is wired in series. It is used only on the black line—the white line is the ground and there is no interruption in that line.

An electrical ground is any conductor that connects directly to the earth. It may, however, go through another conductor, such as a water pipe. Grounding the main fuse box is a must! It is required by the National Electrical Code and must be made in the prescribed manner.

Normally, a #4 or a #6 wire is used for grounding. This copper wire is heavy enough to be exposed, provided that the wire is free from danger of mechanical injury. If you should use a #8 wire, on the other hand, it must be of the armored type or else enclosed in a conduit.

The ground wire can be connected to the water pipe and a jumper provided to by-pass the water meter. You can also attach the ground wire to a copper rod, at least ½″ in diameter, or a steel or iron pipe, at least ¾″ in diameter. The rod or pipe must be at least 8′ long, and should be located at a minimum of 2′ from the building. The rod or pipe is driven into the earth so that at least 1′ to 2′ are un-

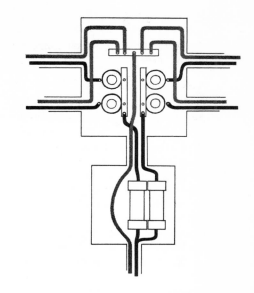

Grounding at the main fuse box.

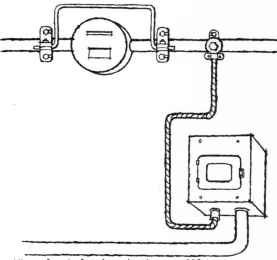

View of main fuse box showing two 110-volt lines plus a neutral line entering from the outside of the home and a fuse box with four branch circuits, each controlled by an individual fuse.

derground. The ground wire is attached to the rod or pipe by means of a ground clamp, which connects the two firmly.

Wiring at the Main Box

In many homes two main conductors are brought to the fuse box although in some homes there are three wires. In the latter, two of the wires carry 110 volts and the third is the neutral or ground wire to complete the circuit. It is possible with this system to obtain 220 volts for operating an electric kitchen range, a motor or any other appliance, such as a dryer, on a 220-volt line.

The main conductors are protected upon entering the home by cartridge fuses. A separate cartridge fuse is used for each 110-volt line. In some communities, a glass 30-ampere fuse is used, while in other areas circuit breakers are permitted on the line. Note that no circuit breaker or fuse is used on the neutral or ground line.

After leaving the main fuse box, the electrical wires enter another box in which the branch lines or circuits are located. Some fuse boxes are large enough so that the main and branch fuse connections are in a single unit.

Generally, the main 'hot' leads are connected to the individual circuits through a receptacle into which a fuse is placed. A 15-ampere fuse is normally used for a branch circuit although a 20-ampere fuse is used for kitchen appliances as well as a washer in the laundry room. The neutral or ground wire is connected to a termi-

nal board and there are taps (screws in a metal plate) which are numbered to correspond to the individual branch circuits.

To Add Additional Branch Circuits

If the main fuse box is capable of delivering the required power, it is possibe to add additional branch circuits. This is often necessary when you add a freezer or a washer and prefer a separate circuit for

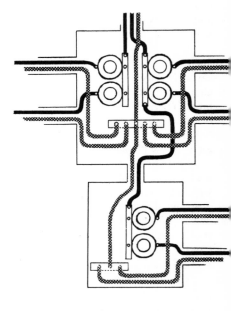

Adding an extra fuse box—note that the 'hot' lead is attached to one of the main or black wires in the main fuse box and another wire (usually white) is attached to the neutral bar in the main box. You muse be extra careful when making a circuit connection of this typel The current in the main line is on unless you have pulled the main switch or removed the controlling fuses. Always do this before you start the wiring.

these appliances. However, you cannot add extra circuits if your main fuse box is already carrying its maximum load.

A new fuse box is anchored near the current main fuse box, although it is possible to place it anywhere inside the home you may wish. It is best to locate it near the present one because then you have all the major electrical controls in one place, in case something goes wrong and you have to test the circuits.

You will find a tap on one of the main current bars inside the main fuse box. If there isn't one in your box (point A in the accompanying sketch), you can connect a wire to the bar where another fuse is anchored. Attach a second wire, which will be the neutral of the new line, to the neutral bar in the main fuse box.

These two wires are then connected to the new fuse box and wired in a manner similar to the main fuse box.

Running Wires Through Walls

When adding new outlets or switches to control overhead lights, it is best to run the wires in the cavity between the inner and outer walls. You can use Romex or BX cable, depending upon the requirements in your local community.

To bring a cable up into the wall from the basement, it is necessary to drill a hole between two joists through the plate on which the wall rests. Make all measurements carefully so that you drill the hole properly; you cannot afford to make a mistake and come up in the middle of a room. A brace with an exten-

sion bit or an electric drill with a bit extension and drill bit can be used to make the hole for the cable. Remember to make this hole large enough for the cable to slip through freely. It is not good policy to yank the cable through a small hole and possibly fray the insulated covering.

In some cases, it may be more convenient to draw the wire down from the attic into the wall cavity. This is particularly true in the second floor of a house or a house without a basement. Here it is necessary to drill through the top plate of the wall and to make the opening between two wall studs. An extension bit with a brace or an electric drill will make the job of drilling easy. Always check before drilling to make certain that the opening is made within the wall and not in the ceiling of a room.

Adding to an Existing Line

There are times when you wish to add only a single outlet in an existing line. Remember: all cable connections must be made within a switch, outlet or junction box. Merely cutting the cable and adding a branch to it cannot be done—there just isn't enough cable available to make proper connections. Here is what you have to do:

1. Shut off the power in the line.

2. Cut through the cable—the exterior insulated covering and both wires.

3. Two junction boxes are added in the line; see accompanying sketches.

4. A piece of cable connects the two boxes.

5. The new branch is connected within one of these boxes.

Complete view of wiring to show branch outlet added to a line.

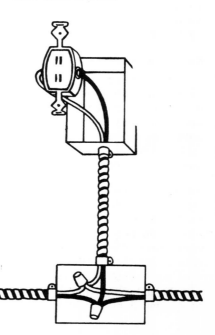

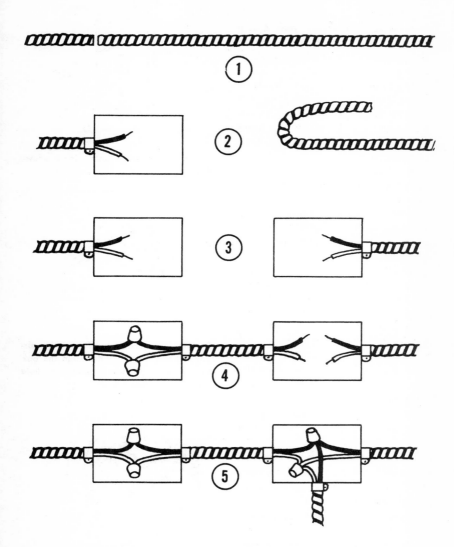

Here is how to add a branch in an existing line: (1) cut through the cable, both the insulation and the wires, (2) attach one end of the cut wire with a connector to a junction box, (3) about a foot or so away, attach the other wire to a junction box, (4) cut a piece of cable to join both boxes and connect it with the wires coming from the power supply, (5) add the branch wire to the outlet to the other junction box and join the wires within the the box as shown.

How To Replace a Switch

Replacing a switch or an outlet is very easy. However, before you start the job, shut off the power to that switch! Here is all you have to do:

1. Shut off the main switch or remove the fuse controlling the branch circuit on which the switch is located. If in doubt, pull the main switch—you can't afford to take chances!

2. Using a screwdriver, take off the cover plate. There are two small screws on either side of the switch handle. If you are changing a double outlet, you will generally find one screw in the center which holds the plate over the outlet.

3. Remove the plate and expose the switch inside the box in the wall. Set the plate and the two screws that hold the plate aside, preferably in a large ash tray or dish so that you won't loose any of the parts.

4. With a screwdriver, remove the screws holding the switch in the box. There are two screws, top and bottom, that go through holes in the switch ends into tapped holes in the box. An outlet is held in a box in the same manner.

5. With the two screws removed and safely put away, pull the switch out of the box as far as the wires will permit. Avoid pulling too hard because you may break the wires if they are old.

6. With a screwdriver, loosen the terminal screws holding the wires to the switch. Be careful when working with solid wire for it may snap.

7. Clean the ends of the two

1. Remove the switch plate using a screwdriver.

2. With the cover plate off and the current off, remove the switch from the box by removing the two screws that hold the switch in place.

3. Pull the switch and the wires out of the box as far as you can, taking care not to break the wires.

wires and set them under the terminal screws of a new switch. The black wire is placed under one of the terminal screws and the white wire under the other terminal screw. Tighten the screws with a screwdriver.

8. Push the wires and switch back into the box so that the holes in the ends of the switch line up with the holes in the switch box. Replace the two screws that hold the switch in the box.

9. Replace the fuse and test the light, being careful not to touch any of the wires or terminals in the box. If the light switch works, remove the fuse again.

10. Now replace the switch plate and tighten the two screws that hold it in place. Be careful not to tighten too much if you have a plastic or glass plate for you are liable to crack it.

11. With the plate in place, replace the fuse and the job is completed.

Electric Appliance Cords

The cords by which electrical appliances are connected to a circuit often cause trouble. In most cases, this is due either to wear or to improper handling, but in some cases may be the result of moisture, oil, or heat.

A cord usually shows the first signs of wear at the point where it is most frequently handled or where bends occur. If the cord is twisted often and bent sharply, the stranded wire beneath the covering may break and perforate the insulation. If it comes into contact with a conductor of the opposite polarity, a

4. Remove the wires by loosening the terminal screws. The new switch is replaced by following the directions in reverse.

short circuit will result, causing a flash or arc which may start a fire. Even if the insulation is not perforated, the failure of the small constituent wire of such a conductor will ultimately result in reduced current to the device, perhaps with a 'hot spot' in the conductor. When all of the small wires in a conductor have failed, the current cannot flow through it, and the appliance will not work. Defective cords should be promptly discarded.

PROPER HANDLING

To avoid twisting a cord, when a screw socket adapter is used, do not screw the plug into the socket with the cord attached to the plug. If possible, separate the screw half of the plug from the cap and screw it into the socket. When this has been done, the prongs of the cap may be inserted into the plug without twisting the cord. For convenience in attaching and to prevent the entrance of foreign objects, if sockets are located close to the floor, the threaded half of the plug should be left in the socket. Most of the modern receptacles are made to accommodate the bayonet-type plug. As the name implies, this plug is equipped with two bayonet-like responding slots in the receptacle. With this type of plug, the cords are not subject to twisting as is the case with a screw plug.

When disconnecting an appliance from a plug, the cap should be grasped to avoid pulling on the cord. This will prevent strain on the wires. Some caps are obtainable with handles attached. If a cord becomes badly damaged, it should be replaced. However, if the cord is sound and has merely been pulled out of the plug, it can readily be reconnected.

REPLACING CORD IN PLUG

To replace the cord in a plug, make certain the cord is not connected! Then loosen the screws inside the plug cap and remove any short pieces of wire which may remain attached to the screws.

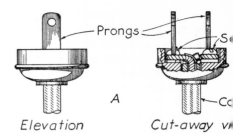

Elevation   Cut-away view

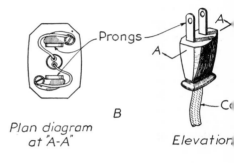

Plan diagram   Elevation
at "A-A"   B

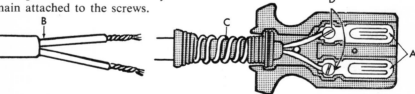

Replacing cord on a heater plug
   a. Terminals
   b. Prepared end of heater cord
   c. Cord passed through bushing and spring
   d. Twisted wires fastened under screw heads

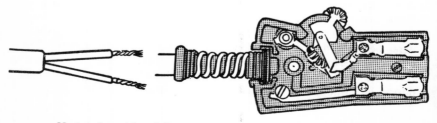

Heater plug with switch

Clip the end of the cord and push it through the hole in the cap from the outer side. Next, split and remove the outside braid of the cord for about 1″ from the end, which will expose the two separately covered wires within. Carefully remove the insulation from these wires for a distance of ½″.

Twist the strands of each wire to keep them together and form each of the conductors into a loop so that the wire runs in a clockwise direction when placed under the terminal screw. Then loop each wire around the blades of the plug, and secure under the terminal screws.

Caution: Make sure there are no bare wires of opposite polarity to come into contact with each other!

Various special types of plugs are now available that require even less work to connect. Some merely clamp on the ends of the wires in such a way as to pierce the insulation and make the connections automatically.

When the cord becomes too worn, it ought to be discarded and replaced with a cord, which is approved by the Underwriters' Laboratories for the specific use for which it is intended.

UNDERWRITERS' KNOT

A special method of securing the wire in a plug is recommended—it is called an Underwriters' knot. It is designed to prevent the pulling out of the wires from the plug if the cord is inadvertently jerked while it is connected to the outlet.

Just follow the accompanying sketches to tie the knot. It is best to pull about 3″ of wire through the

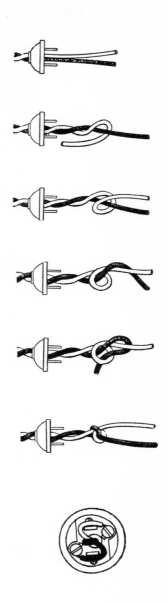

To tie an Underwriters' knot.

plug for the knot and then cut off the excess.

FLAT PLUG

If your appliance cord has an ordinary two-part flat plug, the same procedure for replacing a cord is used as discussed in the foregoing. But you must first remove the wire spring which covers the cord where it enters the plug, then unscrew or unclamp the parts of the plug to open it up flat. When the new cord has been put in, replace the spring at the plug base, then put the two parts of the plug together with the screws or clamps you had removed.

SPLICING CORD

As previously emphasized, when a cord is badly worn, it is best to replace it with a new one. However, for emergency or temporary measure you may want to splice a cord which is broken, or perhaps lengthen a cord you now find too short.

The procedure is to scrape the two wire ends (which are to be connected) clean; use a knife for the purpose. It may be necessary to sandpaper the two wire ends if they aren't very smooth. The scraped, clean areas of the two wires should extend about 3" from the ends. Bring the two wires together, about 2" from the ends, and cross them

over. Then, with the end of each wire, make about 5 or 6 turns until there is a secure fastening. Snip the two ends off with a pair of pliers, and squeeze them tightly to make certain there are no sharp protrusions to penetrate the outer covering. Solder the two ends and cover with rubber and friction tapes, made especially for electrical purposes.

Electric Sockets

A pull chain or key controls a push bar for the switch within the socket. If necessary to make repairs to the socket, it must be taken apart. Turn off current before starting! Use a screwdriver to pry apart the upper part of the socket; you will see where dents are made for the upper part to fit over the lower, and it is by pushing up on the dents that you can separate the two parts.

Inside the socket you will find the terminal screws where the switch mechanism is connected. Loosen these screws, then remove the defective switch, and replace with a new one by connecting it to the wires. The two wires are inserted through the socket cap. Tie the two wire ends with a double knot (called an Underwriter's knot); there are

Connecting a cord to a lamp socket
  a. Bushing with screw
  b. Cap
  c. Porcelain or bakelite socket base
  d. Paper shell
  e. Brass shell

two reasons for this: it relieves strain of the weight on the connection, and it enables the wire ends to fit tightly into the socket cap.

When the two wires are knotted, with a knife scrape off the outer covering on the ends of the two wires. Then attach the two wire ends to the terminal screws; wind the wire around the screws in a clockwise directon. Now tighten the screws, snip off loose wire ends. Replace the fiber insulating shell, and finally put on the outer metal shell, being sure the upper and lower part fit very securely at the dents where they meet.

Trouble-Shooting Fluorescents

Many homes use fluorescent lights since they provide three times as much illumination as a filament lamp consuming the same wattage. Generally, a fluorescent lamp will last from 2500 to 3000 hours and will warn you as it approaches its end by flashing on and off.

There are times when the lamp does not work effectively even before it is due to burn out. Here are some symptoms and cures for faulty fluorescent lamps.

1. The lamp flickers for several seconds before it finally goes on.—There is a voltage drop either in the supply of current to the home or a loss along the individual circuit in the home. Check to see if there is too much of a load on the circuit.

2. The ends of the tube darken while the bulb is still new.—The current has been exceeding 110-115 volts because of faulty power regullation at the generating plant. Some-times reversing the fluorescent tube will correct this difficulty. If, however, the power fluctuation from the power company varies too greatly, it may be necessary to forget about fluorescent bulbs in your home.

3. The bulb burns out rapidly. —You may have been using an incorrect starter with the bulb. Take out the starter and check to see if it is of the type recommended for the fluorescent bulb you are using.

WHEN THE LIGHT WON'T GO ON

If you turn on the switch and the fluorescent bulb won't go on, you should follow this procedure:

1. Check other lights on the same circuit to see that current is flowing in the line.

2. If there is current in the line and the bulb doesn't go on, replace the starter.

3. Should the bulb still fail to go on, remove the fluorescent tube and check the contact points at the end. They may be dirty and should be sanded lightly.

4. Replace the bulb and try again.

5. If the light doesn't go on, shut off the power to that circuit by removing the fuse.

6. Check the contact points in the fixture. They may be bent or corroded. Sand the contact points or straighten them, if bent.

7. Should the lamp not go on after it is replaced in the fixture and the current turned on, then remove the fuse again.

8. With the current off, remove the fixture and check the wiring in-

side to make certain that all connections are properly made.

9. Test the switch by removing it and checking it with a test light in your workshop. The switch may be faulty and, if it is, replace it.

10. If the switch is working, then the ballast inside the fixture is probably at fault and a new one should be substituted.

If you have checked carefully as you worked along, you should be able to replace the entire unit, set the bulb in the sockets and turn on the current. The job will be completed.

How To Read an Electric Meter

Most electric meters have four dials which resemble clocks. They are numbered from 0 through 9 instead of 1 through 12 like a clock. Each clock has only one hand and in two of the clocks, the numbers are read counter-clockwise.

To read your meter, mark down the reading and a month later copy the reading again. Let's assume that the reading shown in the accompanying sketch is that taken at the beginning of the month.

- It is 3456.

The reading at the end of the month as shown in the sketch is:

- 3592, the last reading.

The difference between these two is 136. In other words, you have consumed 136 kilowatt hours of electricity during the month.

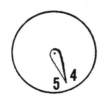

The meter reading (above) is 3456. At the end of the month, the meter reading (below) is 3592. Total electricity used amounted to 136 kilowatt hours.

Electronic Symbols

Here are some of the symbols which are standard in radio, TV and electronic diagrams. The popular component parts are shown accord-

Electronic Schematic Symbols

ANTENNA (BROADCAST)	AIR CORE TRANSFORMER (RF)	CRYSTAL DETECTOR
ANTENNA (TV, FM)	IRON CORE TRANSFORMER (AF)	RECTIFIER
ANTENNA (LOOP)	I.F. TRANSFORMER (DOUBLE TUNED)	PILOT LAMP
GROUND	POWER TRANSFORMER	HEADPHONES
CHASSIS CONNECTION	P — 115 VOLT PRIMARY	LOUDSPEAKER PM DYNAMIC
WIRING Method 1 CONNECTION	S1 — CENTER-TAPPED SECONDARY FOR FILAMENTS OF SIGNAL CIRCUIT TUBES	LOUDSPEAKER ELECTRODYNAMIC
NO CONNECTION	S2 — SECONDARY FOR RECTIFIER TUBE FILAMENT	PHONO PICK-UP
WIRING Method 2 CONNECTION	S3 — CENTER-TAPPED HIGH-VOLTAGE SECONDARY	
	FIXED CONDENSER (MICA OR PAPER)	VACUUM TUBE FILAMENT
NO CONNECTION	FIXED CONDENSER (ELECTROLYTIC)	VACUUM TUBE CATHODE
"A" BATTERY, OR SINGLE CELL	VARIABLE CONDENSER	VACUUM TUBE GRID
"B" BATTERY, OR MULTI-CELL	GANG TUNING CONDENSER	VACUUM TUBE PLATE
RESISTOR	POWER SWITCH S.P.S.T.	3-ELEMENT VACUUM TUBE
POTENTIOMETER (VOLUME CONTROL)	SWITCH S.P.D.T.	TUBE GAS FILLED
RHEOSTAT	SWITCH D.P.D.T.	ALIGNING KEY OCTAL BASE TUBE
AIR CORE COIL (OR CHOKE)	SWITCH D.P.S.T.	METER
IRON CORE COIL (OR CHOKE)	SWITCH ROTARY OR SELECTOR	A — AMMETER MA — MILLIAMMETER μA — MICROAMMETER V — VOLTMETER W — WATTMETER G — GALVANOMETER
IRON CORE COIL PERMEABILITY TUNED	FUSE	MICROPHONE

Chart courtesy of Allied Radio Corporation.

ing to industry-wide agreement in labeling of the parts.

Note that two methods of wire connection and crossover are included in this list of symbols. While both are in common use, the preferred method to show a connection is with the dot in method 1, while the preferred method of showing a crossover or no connection between the wire is the simple crossing of the lines, also shown in method 1.

The symbol for the ground point may indicate an actual connection to the metal chassis of the unit or a connection to a ground lead, usually the B– voltage point. All ground points may usually be assumed to be connected together electrically.

COLOR CODE FOR RESISTORS

All carbon resistors are produced and color-coded to meet the standards set up by the RETMA (Radio, Electronics and Television Manufacturers' Association). Here is your guide to resistors by color bands.

Color-Code Chart							
Band A		**Band B**		**Band C**		**Band D**	
Color	Value	Color	Value	Color	Value	Color	Tolerance
Black	0	Black	0	Black	None	None	±20%
Brown	1	Brown	1	Brown	0	Silver	±10%
Red	2	Red	2	Red	00	Gold	± 5%
Orange	3	Orange	3	Orange	000		
Yellow	4	Yellow	4	Yellow	0000		
Green	5	Green	5	Green	00000		
Blue	6	Blue	6	Blue	000000		
Violet	7	Violet	7	Violet	0000000		
Gray	8	Gray	8	Gold	÷10		
White	9	White	9	Silver	÷100		

Note: The first band (A) shows the first figure of the resistor value, the second band (B) shows the second figure, and the third band (C) indicates the number of zeros to be added. The fourth band (D), which is not included in all resistors, merely indicates the tolerance. If the last band (D) is omitted, the tolerance of the resistor is plus or minus 20%.

Elevation

This term is used to describe a drawing to scale showing the upright parts of a structure or of any work. It is a geometrical projection on a vertical plane.

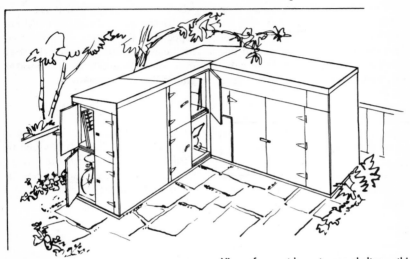

View of an outdoor storage shelter -- this is a perspective drawing of the entire unit.

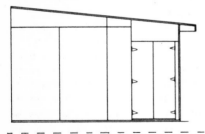

This is the rear elevation -- a view from the back of unit taken from the far right-hand corner in the perspective drawing.

Sketches courtesy of Douglas Fir Plywood Association.

Emergencies

When a sudden occurrence in the home calls for outside help, all the members of the family (including the children) should know whom to summon. It is wise to make up a list of names, addresses, and telephone numbers of:

Fire department
Police department
Family doctor
Druggist
Visiting nurse service
Dentist
Nearest relative
Closest neighbor
Red Cross
Hospital
Ambulance service
Plumber

Electrician
Gas company
and whatever other agencies or individuals you could call upon, should an emergency arise.

The list should be written or printed clearly so that it can be read easily, and it should be kept near the telephone, or pasted inside the door of the medicine cabinet, and everyone in the home should know where it is and be familiar with the list. Thus, a feeling of panic and helplessness will be dispelled should one be alone in the home when an accident happens which needs outside assistance.

In the case of young children, especially, they must be instructed in the use of this list; or told they may signal the telephone operator and tell her to summon aid.

Emery Cloth

Powdered emery is an abrasive made of corundum composed of oxide of alumina, iron, silica and a small portion of lime. It is glued to a thin cloth and is used for removing file marks on metal and for polishing metallic surfaces.

See *Abrasives*.

Enamel

This is applied as a finish to the surface of wood and metal, in the same manner as paint, either with a brush or a spray. The finish produced by coating with enamel is glossy, or sometimes flat, depending on the type used. In interior decoration it is used more in the nature of a 'trim' and for cabinets and furniture, rather than as a finish for large wall areas, except in kitchens and bathrooms where it is used for moisture resistance and washability.

Enamel is available in a heat-proof quality, as a finish for metal radiators, heating grilles, exposed water pipes, and stoves. The variety of colors in which enamel may be purchased gives it a wide range for any interior decorating scheme, either on wood or metal surfaces.

See *Painting*.

End-Grain

The face or edge of a piece of wood exposed when its fibers are cut transversely. End-grain requires

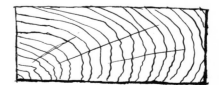

special treatment when finishing.

If the end-grain is to be painted, it should be filled with a wood filler which, when dry, is sanded smooth.

If the end-grain is to be stained, it is often best to apply a very thin

coat of shellac or resin sealer over the surface. In this way, the stain will not penetrate deeply into the fibers and make the edge or end-grain darker than the rest of the surface.

End-Lap Joint

This is a corner joint formed by halving both pieces of wood for a distance equal to their widths.

And end-lap can be cut with hand tools by cutting through half the thickness of each piece with a backsaw and then cutting at right angles so that equal pieces are removed from both pieces of wood to be joined.

The end-lap can also be cut with a power saw. Either you can make a series of parallel cuts through half the thickness of the wood and remove the excess with a chisel, or you can use a dado blade to remove

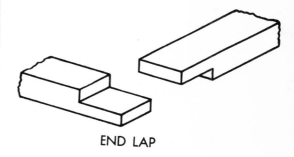

END LAP

Two pieces already cut to form a corner-end lap joint.

the required portion of each piece.

End-lap joints can be fastened with adhesive, nails or screws, or a combination of adhesive and nails or adhesive and screws.

See *Joints*.

End-Matched Lumber

Boards which have been tongued and grooved on both ends and edges are said to be end-matched.

English Bond

A style of laying brick with alternate courses or rows of headers and stretchers.

See *Brick*.

Entrance Switch

Sometimes called a service en-

trance switch, this is the switch that controls the current to all the wires entering a building. It is often part of the main fuse box in the home.

See *Electrical Wiring*.

Entryway

A house which lacks a vestibule, where the door opens directly outdoors, will be greatly improved by the addition of a closed-in or a shielded entryway. Whether the door is flush with the ground level or raised over a small stoop of a few stairs, an enclosure or shield can be added to keep the rain from driving in when the door is opened.

Colorful reinforced plastic panels can be utilized to make such enclosures. These plastic panels are transluscent and shatterproof and can be sawed, nailed and drilled just like wood.

Available in deep and pastel colors as well as white—both flat and corrugated—the panels admit light but maintain privacy. Furthermore, the panels are permanently colored and require no finishing or repainting.

See *Canopy*.

SIDEWALL AND CANOPY

An eggcrate pattern is used for the roof and is covered with plastic Fiberglas. The side wall is made of a wooden frame of 2x2's with flat plastic sheets set inside the wooden framework. A brick or stone planter along the base adds to the decorative appearance. For cutting the framing for the canopy, see **Eggcrate** section under **Furniture**.

Sketches courtesy of Monsanto Chemical Co.

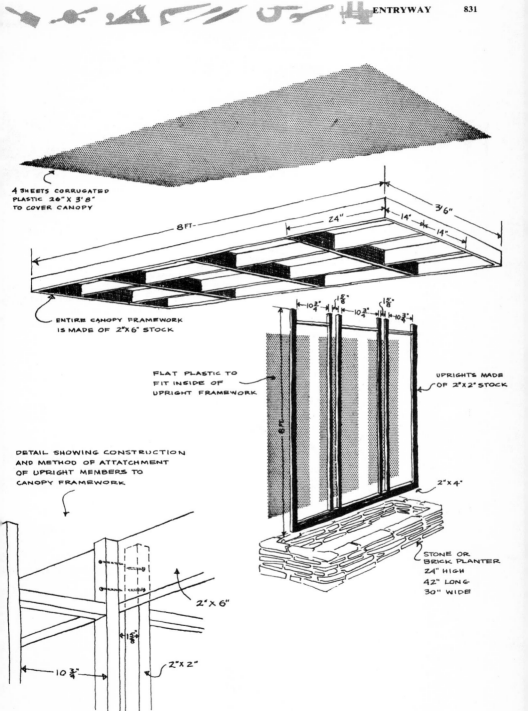

4 SHEETS CORRUGATED
PLASTIC 26" X 3' 8"
TO COVER CANOPY

8 FT.

24"

14"

14"

3' 6"

ENTIRE CANOPY FRAMEWORK
IS MADE OF 2"X 6" STOCK

10¾"

1⅝"

10¾"

1⅝"

10¾"

FLAT PLASTIC TO
FIT INSIDE OF
UPRIGHT FRAMEWORK

UPRIGHTS MADE
OF 2"X 2" STOCK

DETAIL SHOWING CONSTRUCTION
AND METHOD OF ATTACHMENT
OF UPRIGHT MEMBERS TO
CANOPY FRAMEWORK

2"X 4"

STONE OR
BRICK PLANTER
24" HIGH
42" LONG
30" WIDE

2"X 6"

1⅝"

10¾"

2"X 2"

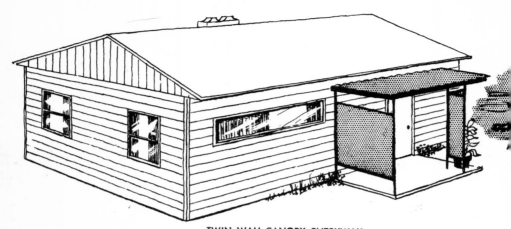

TWIN WALL-CANOPY ENTRYWAY

Here's a way to make the concrete slab in front of your door more interesting. Sun shadow patterns from this entry treatment give a plain house design a 'lift.' Wall framing is made of 4x4's with angle irons used to attach uprights to concrete slab. Eggcrate design of 2x6's is used for the canopy.

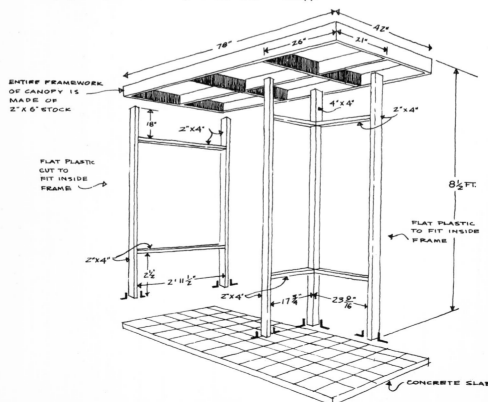

ENTIRE FRAMEWORK OF CANOPY IS MADE OF 2" X 6" STOCK

FLAT PLASTIC CUT TO FIT INSIDE FRAME

4" X 4"

2" X 4"

2" X 4"

8½ FT.

FLAT PLASTIC TO FIT INSIDE FRAME

78"   26"   21"   42"

18"

2" X 4"

2" X 4"

2½"   2' 11½"

2" X 4"   17 ¾"   23 9/16"

CONCRETE SLAB

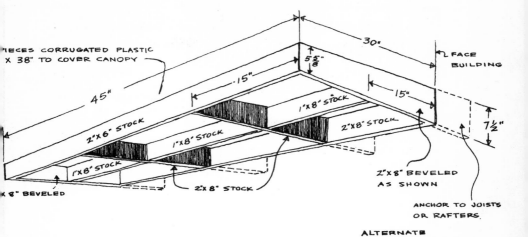

PIECES CORRUGATED PLASTIC
X 38" TO COVER CANOPY

45"

15"

30"

5 5/8"

FACE
BUILDING

15"

7 1/2"

2"X 6" STOCK

1"X 8" STOCK

1"X 8" STOCK

1"X 8" STOCK

2"X 8" STOCK

2"X 8" STOCK

2"X 8" STOCK

8" BEVELED

2"X 8" BEVELED
AS SHOWN

ANCHOR TO JOISTS
OR RAFTERS.

ALTERNATE
BOLT 2"X 8" TO MASONARY
IN BRICK BUILDING

TRANSLUCENT CANOPY

Keep the rain out with modern overhang.
The eggcrate frame is secured to the
house exterior with lag screws in lead
anchors or Rawl plugs, or with screws directly into the studs.

Sketches courtesy of Monsanto Chemical Co.

Equivalents, Weights and Measures

While in this country we use the U. S. weights and measures, it is well to know how they are translated into the metric system which is used in many parts of the world, and then to understand the relationship of the two system as equivalents.

Weight Tables

a. U. S. Avoirdupois Weight

$27\frac{11}{32}$ grains (gr) = 1 dram (dr).
16 drams   = 1 ounce (oz).
16 ounces = 1 pound (lb).
           = 7,000 grains.
2,000 pounds = 1 short ton.

b. Metric Weight

1,000 micrograms
          = 1 milligram (mg).
1,000 milligrams
          = 1 gram (gm).
1,000 grams = 1 kilogram (kg).
1,000 kilograms
          = 1 metric ton.

c. Equivalent of Weight

1 ounce   = 28.3495 grams.
1 pound = 453.59 grams.
0.03527 ounce = 1   gram.
2,2046 pounds
         = 1   kilogram

Capacity Tables (Liquid)

a. U.S. Liquid Measure
8 fluid drams (fl dr)
        = 1 fluid ounce (fl oz).
4 fluid ounces
        = 1 gill.
4 gills   = 1 pint (pt).
2 pints   = 1 quart (qt).
4 quarts = 1 gallon (gal).
        = 231 cubic inches.

At maximum density, 39.164° F., a gallon of pure water weighs 8.345 pounds; at 59° F., the weight is 8.338 pounds.

b. Metric Capacity Measure
1,000 milliliters (ml) = 1 liter (l).
1,000 liters   = 1 kiloliter (kl).
The term "cubic centimeter" has been commonly used instead of "milliliter." Technically, this is not correct, since the cubic centimeter is a measure of volume, not of capacity. For practical purposes, however, they may be regarded as equal.

c. Equivalents of Capacity
1 fluid ounce = 29.5729 milliliters.
1 pint   = 473.167 milliliters.
1 gallon   = 3.7853 liters.
0.2705 fluid dram = 1 milliliter.
33.8147 fluid ounces = 1 liter.
1.0567 quarts = 1 liter.

d. Equivalents for Teaspoonful, Tablespoonful, and Cup
3 teaspoonfuls = 1 tablespoonful.
2 tablespoonfuls = 1 fluid ounce.
16 tablespoonfuls = 1 cup.
8 fluid ounces = 1 cup.
15 milliliters   = 1 tablespoonful.
1 pint   = 2 cups.

Linear-Measure Tables

a. U.S. System

12	inches (in)	=	1 foot (ft).
3	feet	=	1 yard (yd).
16½	feet	=	1 rod (rd).
5,280	feet	=	1 mile.

b. Metric System

1,000 microns	=	1 millimeter (mm).
10 millimeters	=	1 centimeter (cm).
1,000 centimeters	=	1 meter (m).
1,000 meters	=	1 kilometer (km).

c. Equivalents of Length

1 inch	=	2.54 centimeters.
1 foot	=	30.48 centimeters.
1 mile	=	1.60935 kilometers.
0.3937 inch	=	1 centimeter.
39.37 inches	=	1 meter.
0.62137 mile	=	1 kilometer.

Volume (Cubic Measure) Tables

a. U.S. System

1,728 cubic inches (cu in)	=	1 cubic foot (cu ft).
27 cubic feet	=	1 cubic yard (cu yd).

b. Metric System

1,000 cubic millimeters	=	1 cubic decimeter.
1,000 cubic centemeters	=	1 cubic meter.
1,000 cubic decimeters	=	1 cubic centimeter.

c. Equivalents of Volume

1 cubic inch	=	16.39 cubic centimeters.
1 cubic foot	=	28.317 cubic decimeters.
1 cubic yard	=	0.7646 cubic meter.
0.061 cubic inch	=	1 cubic centimeter.
1.308 cubic yards	=	1 cubic meter.

Area-Measurement Tables

a. U.S. System

144	square inches (sq in)	= 1 square foot (sq ft).
9	square feet	= 1 square yard (sq yd).
30¼	square yards	= 1 square rod (sq rd).
43,560	square feet	= 1 acre.

b. Metric System

100 square millimeters	=	1 square centimeter.
100 square centimeters	=	1 square decimeter
100 square decimeters	=	1 square meter.
100 square meters	=	1 are.
100 ares	=	1 hectare.

c. Equivalents of Area

1 square inch	=	6.452 square centimeter.
1 square foot	=	9.2903 square decimeter.
1 square yard	=	0.8361 square meter.
1 acre	=	0.4047 hectare.
0.155 square inch	=	1 square centimeter.
1.1960 square yards	=	1 square meter.
2.471 acres	=	1 hectare.

Expansion Bit

Also called an expansive bit, this is a boring tool which can be set to make varying diameter large holes in wood. The cutter, regulated by an adjusting screw, can be moved closer or farther away from the screw-tip point for boring the proper diameter hole.

Moving the cutter adjusting screw in some types of expansion bits automatically moves the cutter an exact amount. One complete turn of the screw of a Russell Jennings bit enlarges or reduces the hole ⅛"—a half turn, 1/16".

It is best to test the size of the hole on a scrap piece of wood before doing the actual boring. Use a brace with the bit. It is always best to clamp a piece of waste wood on the back of the work to prevent splitting.

The expansion bit.

Sketch from "Tool Guide" courtesy of Stanley Tools.

Expansion bit used in wood.

Expansion bit is used to make large diameter holes with a brace. It is adjustable to within 1/64". Note that a piece of waste wood is used to back up the thin aluminum—this facilitates the drilling. Woodworking tools may be used with this special type of aluminum.

Photograph courtesy of Reynold's Do-It-Yourself Aluminum.

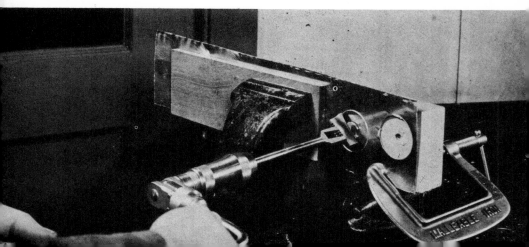

Expansion Bolt

A bolt equipped with a split or hinged casing which acts as a wedge. As the bolt is screwed into the casing, the ends of the casing expand to form a wedge. This type of bolt is used as an anchor in brick or concrete.

See *Anchors for Concrete* and *Bolts.*

An expansion bolt.

Expansion Joint

When two masses are set next to each other and each is subject to expansion and contraction, a special joint is used between them. This joint is flexible, providing space for the mass to move into when it expands. It is flexible enough so that when the mass contracts, the joint expands to fill the gap.

Expansion joints are generally used when laying concrete. A space is left between two large sections of concrete (using a board treated with oil or grease, or a metal divider for easy removal after the concrete has set). This space is filled with asphalt which, while it hardens on the surface, remains pliable inside. Another method of adding an expansion joint is by using specially-treated felt and setting it between the masses of concrete as each section is formed.

If an expansion joint is not used with large masses of concrete, there is a good chance it will buckle and crack. Should this happen, it is necessary to chop openings for expansion joints and to repair the cracked concrete.

It is always best to use an expansion joint when laying a concrete patio abutting the house. This joint can be made by using a 1x4 set between the house and patio. While the wood can remain and act as a cushion, it will eventually rot. Therefore, remove it after the concrete is cured and pour asphalt into the opening.

Extension Bit

Often when using an electric drill, the bit is not long enough to penetrate through a wide piece of wood, or it is not possible to get the drill close enough to the work, for example, when drilling through a

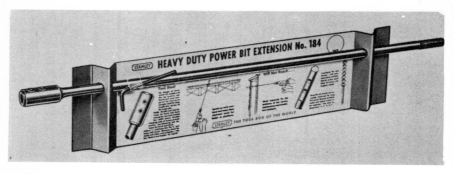

plate to run an electric cable in the wall. The extension bit has a ¼" diameter end which fits into the drill chuck. On the other end is a circular opening into which the bit it fitted. The bit is held in the extension bit by means of two Allen screws.

For exceedingly long holes and hard-to-reach places, it is possible to join more than one extension bit

An extension bit with Allen wrench to tighten the screws which hold the drill bit.

to a drill. However, a certain amount of wobble develops and this is neither good for the drill nor for the work. The hole will be larger than the bit used if there is a wobble.

Exterior Lighting

Wiring for lights and outlets outdoors requires bringing wires through the house foundation or exterior wall. The bringing of the current outdoors adds much enjoyment and increases the time you can spend in your outdoor living area by providing lights in the evening and a source of power for your radio or even television set.

See *Outdoor Lighting*.

Exterior Painting

Painting the outside of your home requires types of primers and paints which will withstand the elements and weather properly so as to be in good condition for periodic repainting. The technique, however, is the same as interior painting except for a few special requirements.

See *Painting*.

External Thread

The thread on the outside of a screw or bolt is technically called the external thread, as opposed to the internal thread of a nut.

Eyebolt

When a bolt has a hole or an eye at one end of the usual head, it is classed as an eyebolt. The eye is used to receive a pin, stud, rope or hook.

See *Bolts*.

An eyebolt has a hole or opening in one end and a threaded section with a nut at the other end.

F-Head Engine

This is a combination of an L-head and I-head engine. The intake valves are overhead while the exhaust valves are in the cylinder block. This style of engine is not used to any great extent today.

Cross-section view of an F-head automobile engine.

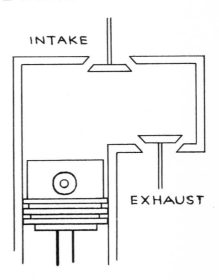

Facade

The front elevation or face of a building or structure.

Face

The term used to describe the long narrow side of a brick when it is exposed in a wall.

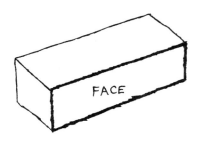

Facebrick

Better quality brick is often used on the exposed surfaces of a wall.

There are many types of decorative brick which can be used for this purpose.

The brick underneath or in less prominent places is often common brick. It is mainly for utility and has neither unusual nor attractive finish. See *Brick*.

Fall Seasonal Repairs

At the end of the summer, it's an excellent idea to start going over the house, its interior and exterior, and seing what repairs, renovations, or additions need to be made. Then, with the first cool days you can start, and have the jobs completed before the cold months set in. It is not necessary to do the work all at once; you can divide it over a period of four months, if that is better for you and more adaptable to the leisure time you have available for these house chores.

Do you need to repair, replace or clean out?

August, September

Bell, buzzer, or door chimes
Floor linoleum in any of the rooms
Squeaky or sagging floors
Clogged drain or pipes
Damaged wallpaper
Exterior house paint
Broken window pane or sash
Cracks in concrete walk
Soot in chimney and smokepipe

October, November

Weatherstripping around windows and doors

Furnace and hot water supply
Garden tools
Outside door weatherproofing
Paint on interior walls
Ceiling cracks
Basement leaks in floor or walls
Lawn slopes washed out

Of course these are general suggestions. The climatic and local conditions in which you live, and the type of residence, will determine what needs to be done. This, then, is the reminder that the early fall is the time to prepare for the winter, and to get a head start for the early spring, when you will be able to enjoy your house without needing to go into repairs at that time.

False Key

This is a round pin which is driven into a hole drilled one half in the end of a spindle or axle and the other half into a boss or wheel. It is used to prevent a wheel on an axle from slipping.

A false key is often used on wheels of hand lawn mowers and on the large drive wheels of 'walking' sprinklers.

A false key holds the wheel on the axle of this 'walking' sprinkler.

Fan Hanger Outlet

There are special electrical outlets and cover plates designed for use with electric fans mounted on the wall. This special unit, available in many hardware stores and all electrical supply outlets, has a special mounting bracket to which the fan can be attached.

Sketches courtesy of The Bryant Electric Co.

Fans for Cooling

Fans built into the house are often used to ventilate the kitchen and bathroom or to cool the entire house. There are many types of fans available today. Some can be mounted in a window with two simple screws; they are removed for the winter.

In other cases, fans are mounted permanently. Kitchen exhaust fans are commonly used and are set through the wall.

Attic fans are used widely in many sections of the country. These fans can be mounted in the attic floor or in the attic wall. However, some handymen prefer to use a window-mounted fan, the installation of which is easier and quicker.

Attic fans and their direct descendant, the window fan, have been used for many years in the South, where they seem to have developed more or less spontaneously. This contribution to good living has only recently come into use in the North, where it is making friends as rapidly as the Southern fried chicken that preceded it.

Basically, attic fans are nothing more than ventilating fans which have been used for years in restaurant kitchens, modified of course, for quieter operation and greater capacity. The average size is from 30″ to 36″ in diameter. Larger sizes are made, but are needed only for very large homes. The number of blades varies from 3 to 6 with a pitch of 30° to 40°. This permits the fan to move a large amount of air while turning at a fairly low speed, which is essential to quiet operation. Fans smaller than 30" are usually considered window fans, not because they are too small for use in attics but because they are about as large as can be mounted in the average window.

Now that we have introduced our friends, you may reasonably ask, just what can they do. Well, you remember how, even in the hottest weather, the air temperature drops several degrees after dark so that it is quite comfortable on the porch, or out on the lawn, but the house is still hot as an oven. Of course, the house finally cools off, but by that time the night may be too far gone for an adequate amount of sleep.

With an attic fan, you simply turn it on about sundown and it pulls out the hot air that fills the house, and permits the cooler outside air to take its place. This not only lowers the air temperature, but the cooler air actually absorbs the stored up heat in the walls and ceiling of the house. In the average house, the air is changed every two or three minutes. This rapid change is essential for good cooling, since the temperature differential is only a few degrees, and the greatest possible differential is essential to the rapid transfer of heat.

With a window fan, this warmed air is discharged directly outdoors, preferable on the side of the house away from the prevailing wind.

An attic fan discharges the slightly warmed air into the intensely hot interior of the attic, where daytime temperatures may reach 130° or more, forcing out this hot air and cooling the structural members of the house before escaping through the openings provided, which may be windows or louvres, or both. Since these openings should be screened against insects, the combined area should be at least 50% greater than the area of the fan—around 7½ square feet for a 30" fan, or about 12 square feet for a 36" fan.

It is preferable that the fan exhaust away from the principal outlet, to secure the maximum of turbulence, so there will be no isolated pockets of hot air to retard the cooling of the attic. This procedure assures that the house will be adequately cooled even by the children's bedtime.

If your situation is such that you cannot make an attic installation, a window fan will give you most of the benefits. You probably won't be able to turn it off at bedtime, as you usually can do with the attic fan, but even if it has to run all night, the cost will be low.

Attic Ventilation

The differences in the types of houses in the Northern and Southern climates must be considered in attic ventilation installations.

The great majority of homes in Northern climates have either open attic spaces or flat roofs with no attic spaces.

In homes with open attics, which are floored, the fan may discharge through a window or through an opening provided for ventilation, either in an end wall or in a dormer

Installation For Any Type Home

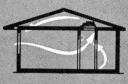

Low Pitched Roof

Vertical Discharge

Dutch Colonial

Suction Box

Attic Stairway

Attic Wall

Gable Installation

Basement

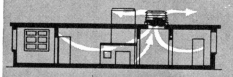

Flat Roof

Shed-Type Roof

placed in the sloping part of the roof. In both cases the air is discharged directly to the outside, the attic acting as a plenum chamber. This fan installation should be protected from the weather by either louvres or a rain hood.

For the houses with flat roofs, it is necessary to construct a penthouse or cupola which is connected directly to the finished ceiling opening by an air shaft.

In the Southern climates most of the houses have unfinished attic spaces, which make it possible to locate the fan unit near the ceiling opening to discharge air into the attic space and then outside through properly located and sized louvres.

LOCATION OF VENTILATING UNIT—The fans which must exhaust directly to the outside must be located so that they discharge with, and not against, the prevailing wind in your location.

Fans which exhaust into the attic from the space below should be located as centrally as possible from all the rooms to be ventilated. The discharge from the fan must be as far as possible from adjacent walls, chimneys, etc.

FAN UNIT CHARACTERISTICS—Quiet operation is the most desirable fan unit characteristic. It can be belt or direct-connected, be mounted in a substantial frame and be equipped with a resilient mounted motor or some form of shock and sound absorbing characteristic. The resistance against which the fan must operate is determined by the size of the air intakes and exhaust openings (louvres). If openings smaller than the recommended sizes are used, the resistance increases and the volume of air handled by the fan is reduced.

AIR CHANGES PER MINUTE—A definite figure cannot be set up for the number of air changes

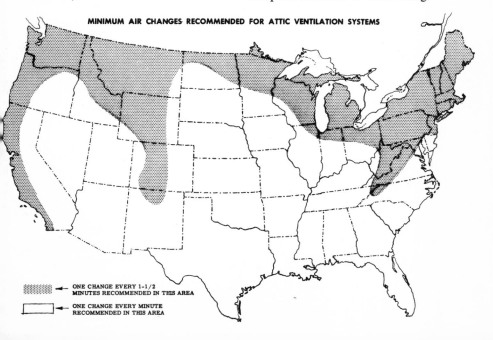

MINIMUM AIR CHANGES RECOMMENDED FOR ATTIC VENTILATION SYSTEMS

ONE CHANGE EVERY 1-1/2 MINUTES RECOMMENDED IN THIS AREA

ONE CHANGE EVERY MINUTE RECOMMENDED IN THIS AREA

per minute. The rate of air change depends not only on the climate and locality but upon the individual preference. Practice and past experience have determined that in 95% of the cases in the South a net air change of once a minute is satisfactory. For locations in parts of the North it is satisfactory and comfortable to change the air once every minute and a half.

FAN SELECTION—It is necessary to determine the cubic content of your house in order to select the right size fan to cool it. Only an approximate figure is needed; just multiply the width and depth of your home by the height. This will give you the approximate number of cubic feet in your home.

If you live in the Southern part of the United States (see *map showing air changes*), you will need a fan capable of changing the required number of feet every minute.

If you live in the northern section where an air change is needed every 1½ minutes, take two-thirds of the cubic content of your home. Buy a fan that will displace that cubic volume every minute.

It is better to buy a fan that will displace or move a somewhat greater amount than the actual cubic content of your home calls for. In this way, there will be less of a strain on the fan and you'll find yourself more comfortable on those especially hot and humid days.

AIR VELOCITIES THROUGH INLET GRILLE AND FAN UNIT—The air velocities through the ceiling grilles must not exceed 750 feet per minute, to keep air noise and static pressure as low as possible. The average velocity of the air leaving the fan ranges from 1200 to 1400 feet per minute. With this knowledge we can establish a rough ratio for ceiling grille area to fan orifice area at approximately two to one. This ratio is based on a

Typical Discharge Openings

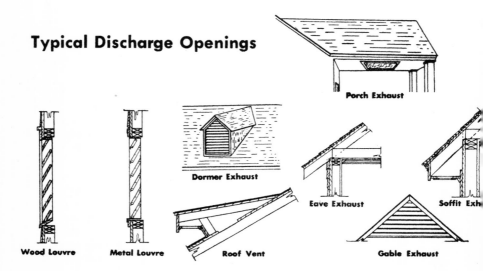

Porch Exhaust

Dormer Exhaust

Eave Exhaust

Soffit Exh

Wood Louvre

Metal Louvre

Roof Vent

Gable Exhaust

MINIMUM GROSS OUTLET AREAS FOR ATTIC FAN DISCHARGE VENTS

Areas	1 Minute Air Change	1-1/2 Minute Air Change
Wood louvres backed with 1/2" hardware cloth.	Not less than 1/40 of the gross floor area.	Not less than 1/60 of the gross floor area.
Metal louvres backed with 1/2" hardware cloth.	Not less than 1/50 of the gross floor area.	Not less than 1/90 of the gross floor area.
Other openings such as those in soffits, etc. Plain openings backed with 1/2" hardware cloth.	Not less than 1/65 of the gross floor area.	Not less than 1/100 of the gross floor area.

If louvres or openings are covered with No. 16 mesh screen, add a minimum of 100% of the gross louvre area. This may be done by:

a. Doubling the size of the louvre or opening.

b. Constructing a box-like frame behind the louvre or opening with a screened surface twice the area of the louvre.

net grille opening of 84% of the gross area.

ATTIC DISCHARGE VENTS (LOUVRES)—Correct area and location are the most important factors to be considered. There should always be a number of discharge vents rather than just one. A head wind from any single direction has little effect on the performance of the fan, if a number of openings are employed at different points of the compass.

All discharge vents must be covered with ½" hardware cloth to keep out birds.

INSTALLATION OF VARIOUS FAN TYPES—There are two types of fans, (1) fans which discharge horizontally; (2) fans which discharge vertically.

(1) Horizontal discharge fans are usually installed in an outside wall if the attic is finished, on the attic floor with a plenum chamber if the attic is unfinished, or in a penthouse or cupola if the building has a flat roof. A fan mounted in an outside wall or in a penthouse requires a tailor-made installation to meet the special conditions.

A fan installed in a prefabricated plenum chamber usually meets the requirements of the installation. Prefabricated plenum chambers are constructed of sound-deadening material supported on a skeleton wooden frame. The top of the plenum chamber may be horizontal or it may slope down from the fan.

In an automatic shutter installation, the vanes should open towards the fan in the same direction as the air flow. The shutters should cover the entire suction opening and be of such size as not to restrict the air flow.

The fan case must be mounted on rubber pads, springs, or on a sound deadening pad. The fan and plenum chamber installation consists of mounting the unit on a platform extending over the grille. The plenum chamber must be as nearly airtight as possible to get the utmost benefit of fan capacity in the area being ventilated rather than merely re-circulating the air.

(2) Vertical discharge fans are installed in the attic floor of unfinished attics or in the penthouse or cupola in buildings which have a flat roof. The plenum chamber is not necessary because the fan is mounted directly over the ceiling opening. A sound-isolating padding or other material must be placed between the fan and the supporting frame. Automatic or hand operated shutters are required below the fan to close the ceiling opening when the fan is not operating.

PROTECTION AGAINST WINTER HEAT LOSS—In the winter the openings, whether louvres, porch grilles, soffit outlets or others should have removable covers of insulation board. A similar cover should be provided for the grille opening or automatic shutter.

ELECTRICAL INSTALLATION—A separate circuit from the main service entrance panel should be provided to feed attic fan installations using motors of ⅓ H.P. and better. A fused disconnect switch in the hall or other easily accessible location must be provided. In the event of fire, an automatic method must be provided for cutting off the fan and closing the ceiling opening.

An attic fan mounted in the floor of the attic will draw the hot air out of the rooms in the house letting cool, fresh air come in through the windows.

Sketches courtesy of Propeller Fan Manufacturer's Association.

An attic fan is mounted to fit into an opening cut in the joists. Here the fan is mounted horizontally, but with a special box chamber, it can be mounted vertically in the chamber or even in an exterior wall in the roof.

The opening in the ceiling is covered by a special louvre grille. This protects fingers and other objects from getting in the way of the fan blades and also keeps the attic sealed closed when the fan is not in operation.

A fusible link, set to open at 135° F. is recommended for this purpose and is installed in the air stream. It is placed on the suction side of the fan to operate a cut-off switch in series with the fan.

Where the installation includes a trap door, the fuse releases it and closes the ceiling opening. In the automatic shutter installation, they are closed when the fan stops. The fan motors can be provided with automatic thermal cut-outs to prevent overheating of the motor. This precaution will prevent the motor from becoming a fire hazard as well as preventing the motor from burning out due to any overload.

OPERATING HINTS AND SUGGESTIONS—Check all bearings for lubrication. Oil the motor and fan bearings according to the manufacturers' directions.

Examine the belt for tension and alignment.

The fan will pull soot and dirt down the chimney if there is no other way for air to enter, so be sure to open a window before starting the fan.

During the initial operation of the fan check for noise sources, loose parts, and for loose floor boards on the attic joists.

After the fan has been operating for a few weeks examine the fan belt for tension. Make any necessary adjustments in accordance with the manufacturers instructions.

Make a note on your calendar to thoroughly examine and oil the fan every year.

How To Install an Attic Fan

After deciding upon the best size fan for your home, make certain that there is space for the unit in a convenient place where the fan will be able to draw air from all the rooms in about equal amounts. If the fan is located at one end of the house, it is likely to cool the rooms nearer to it rather than the rooms at the other end of the house.

Installing an attic fan is a simple job, but having a helper makes the

1. Locate the position of one of the ceiling joists and then mark the area to be covered by the fan. Try to cut as few ceiling joists as possible. This is done to reduce the amount of work; cutting even three joists (and this is not necessary with a home fan) usually will not affect the structure of the house. Actually, you will probably have to cut only a single joist, two at the most.

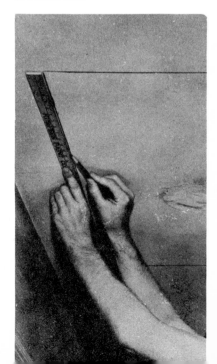

work easier; it also speeds the job. Here in photograph form is the step-by-step technique.

All you need in the way of tools —stepladder, ruler, compass saw, crosscut saw, brace and bits or portable electric drill, cold chisel, wood chisel, screwdriver and hammer, plus the tools for adding a new outlet and a switch to control the fan. A portable electric saw will be very useful, if available.

2. If the ceiling is made of plaster, score along the drawn line with a sharp cold chisel and then chop out the plaster, using a cold chisel and a hammer. Remember, do not try to chop the plaster out until you have made the score marks; otherwise, you may crack the ceiling outside the area to be removed for the fan.

Photographs courtesy of Robbins & Myers, Inc.

3. If you have a dry-wall material for a ceiling, you can use a portable electric or hand saw to do the cutting job. If you do not have the power tools, it is best to drill a 1" diameter hole at each corner and then remove the inside section by cutting with a keyhole or compass saw.

4. Remove the rest of the ceiling covering material and expose the joists overhead. Cut the joists with a crosscut saw or a portable electric saw as close to the outside edges of the opening as possible.

5. Use the cut pieces of the joists or wood of same thickness and width to join the cut edges of the joists on each side of the opening. Generally, you can use the cut pieces because the opening for most attic fans is cut in the shape of a square.

6. Get a helper to assist you and lift the entire fan unit into the attic through the cut opening. You will have to keep the fan at an angle so that it goes through easily.

Photographs courtesy of Robbins & Myers, Inc.

7. Check the opening nailed for the fan to see that it is the same size as the base of the fan unit. If it is, have your helper assist you in setting the fan assembly over the opening. It is best to glue some rubber cushioning material along the top edge of the opening, if such a cushion is not provided as part of fan mounting.

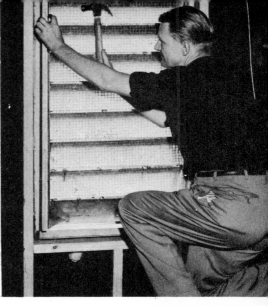

8. Install the louvre grille opening below. This comes in one piece, usually of metal, and is set in place with screws. If you use long screws, you will be able to drive them through the ceiling material into the joists overhead. Connect the fan motor wire to an outlet which is wired to a switch downstairs in the hallway or wherever the fan is located.

9. Check to see if you have adequate openings in the attic for the fan to operate properly. See the accompanying copy and table showing the size of openings needed. If the opening is too small, the fan will not operate at its maximum efficiency—there will be no place in the attic for it to force the air out of. Cover the opening to keep insects out.

Build Your Own Fan

Here's how you can build a 30″ fan that can be mounted in the attic or on a window at least 30″ wide.

Here are the parts you need:

One 4-arm fan spider, 30° pitch, ¾″ bore

Four ³⁄₁₆″ tempered hardboard fan blades

Two rubber cushioned bronze Oilite bearings, ¾″ bore

Basic parts of the fan kit—you can make your own window fan or attic fan with these parts. Here's an inexpensive way to keep your home cool in hot weather.

Photograph courtesy of Fan Kit Company

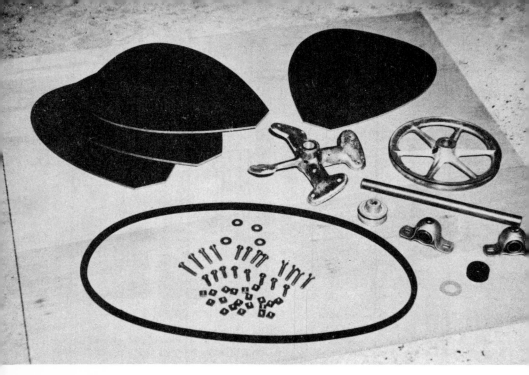

Window fan mounted in the window—the outside protective louver has been removed to show positioning of the motor, the drive wheel and belt operating this large window unit.

Photograph courtesy of Fan Kit Company

One ¾″ shaft collar and fiber thrust washer

One 11″ steel shaft, ¾″ diameter

One 8″ pulley for fan shaft, ¾″ bore

One 2″ motor pulley, ½″ bore

One ½″ V-belt, 54″ long.

The following ¼″ stove bolts and nuts: eight ¾″, four 1″, four 1¼″ round head and four 1¼″ flat head; four ¼″ washers.

Most of these parts can be purchased at any well-stocked hardware store, or they are available in kit form, complete with instructions from the Fan Kit Company.

MAKING THE FAN SPIDER —The toughest part to locate is a fan spider. If you can't find one and do not care to buy your parts in kit form, you can make one if you have the equipment. (See *Sketch 1*.) If you do not have the equipment you can have it made at a machine shop. It will be rather costly, though.

The spider itself is made from a 6″ square of ³⁄₁₆″ steel plate. After the indicated holes are drilled, cuts should be made on the heavy tines and the completed cross-shaped spider welded to the end of the hub. After welding, each arm is heated and twisted to an angle of 30° or 35°. The exact angle is not important, but should be exactly the same for each arm. Also, check each arm with a square to be sure all are at right angles to the shaft.

CUTTING BLADES — The

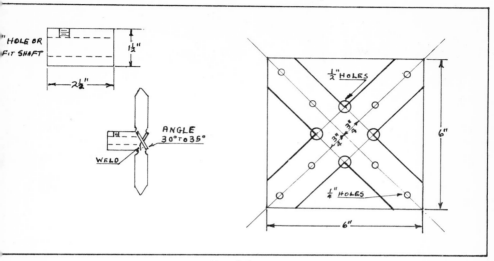

Sketch 1

blades can be cut from tempered hardboard, ³⁄₁₆″ thick. (See *Sketch 2*.) After they are cut, they should be tacked together and the edges sanded down so all blades will be exactly the same size. This is important and is necessary in order to get proper balance.

Here's the material you will need:

12 linear feet 1x12 wood

3 linear feet 1x5 wood

2 linear feet 1x4 wood

1 piece ³⁄₁₆″ x ¼″ plywood or hardboard 36″x36″

Nuts and screws

Sketch 2   1″ Squares

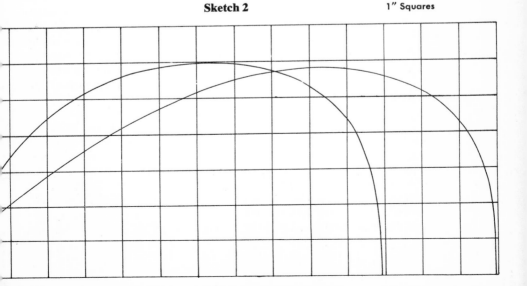

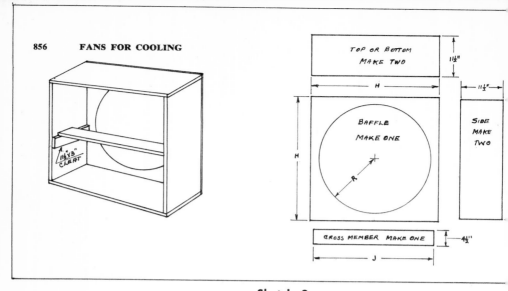

TOP OR BOTTOM
MAKE TWO

11¼"

11¼"

H

H

H

BAFFLE
MAKE ONE

R

SIDE
MAKE
TWO

CROSS MEMBER MAKE ONE

4½"

J

11 ½" CLEAR

Sketch 3

Table of Measurement			
	H	J	R
30" Fan	36"	34½"	15½"

¼ H.P. 1750 RPM motor

You can use either a ¼ H.P. or a ⅓ H.P. motor. In order to eliminate motor noise, the motor should have a resilient mount, or be mounted on a resilient material. If you don't have a motor, you should be able to buy a used appliance motor from any large appliance dealer or repair shop. If you want a new motor, just ask for a ¼ H.P. 1750 RPM split phase motor and a rubber mount.

CONSTRUCTION OF HOUSING—Essentially, the housing is a square box having one side covered with plywood, or wallboard, with a circle cut out for the fan. (See *Sketch 3*.) A horizontal cross member is mounted 1" below the center line and serves as a support for the fan shaft. The front edge of the cross member should be about 5"

from the circle. This cross member should not be heavier than 1" material, for it should have some spring, which contributes to quiet operation, as do rubber-mounted bearings.

With the housing completed, you are ready to assemble the fan. First of all, mount the blades on the spider. Tighten the bolts securely and mount the assembled fan on the shaft. Next in order is the shaft collar, with the smooth side away from the fan. Next, the fiber washer, then the other bearing and last of all, the large pulley. The whole assembly can now be placed on the cross member and shifted to bring the fan into the center of the round opening. When this has been done, the bearing should be lined up with the edges of the cross member and

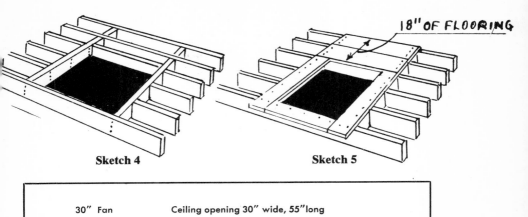

18" OF FLOORING

Sketch 4   **Sketch 5**

30" Fan	Ceiling opening 30" wide, 55" long

the location for the mounting holes marked. Drill ¼" holes and bolt the bearings in place.

Next, shift the fan until it operates half in and half out of the circle; the back edge of the blades should clear the cross member by at little over an inch. Push the shaft collar against the rear bearing and tighten the set screw firmly. Then push the large pulley against the other side of the bearing and tighten its screw. Turn the fan a complete revolution to make sure that everything clears and, if all is in order, you are ready to mount the motor.

If you have a rubber-mounted motor, simply put it in the lower right corner of the housing, put on the belt, shift it about to line up the pulleys and pull the belt tight, then mark the location of the bolt holes for the motor. Locate these at the right end of the slots in the motor base so that the motor can be shifted to tighten the belt, as it will loosen with use.

Before bolting the motor in place, check to see that it rotates counter-clockwise when facing the shaft. Be sure that the oil wells on the motor are filled, as some new motors have never been oiled. Oil the shaft bearings and you are ready to try it out.

MOUNTING FAN ON A WINDOW—The completed fan can be mounted either inside or outside a window, which should be at least as wide as the diameter of the fan blade. Four "L" shaped corner braces, about 1½" x 1½", from the hardware store provide the simplest method of mounting. If mounted outside, and not protected by a wide overhanging eave shed or awning, the fan should be protected by two or three coats of paint and sealed with spar varnish.

INSTALLING FAN IN ATTIC—If an attic installation is desired, a vent box will be required. (See *Sketches 4, 5,* and *6.*) This may be any sort of enclosure to connect the fan assembly to the opening through the ceiling below. This

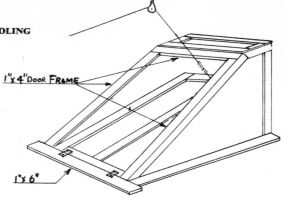

1"x 4" DOOR FRAME

1"x 6"

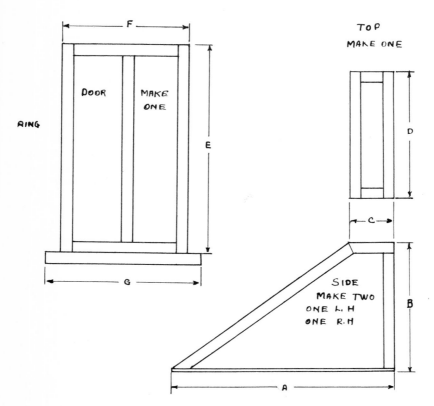

F

RING

DOOR   MAKE
ONE

E

G

TOP
MAKE ONE

D

C

SIDE
MAKE TWO
ONE L.H
ONE R.H

B

A

Sketches courtesy of Fan Kit Co.

Sketch 6

30" Fan	A	B	C	D	E	F	G
	60"	35"	12"	36"	58"	32"	44"

opening should be about 10 square feet in area, if a grille is used. (The sketch shows all essential details.) The trap door arrangement will not be needed if you use an automatic shutter, but only if a grille is used. This grille may be a piece of ½" mesh hardware cloth or expanded metal. The latter is preferable and should be used.

Those making an attic installation will need one 4'x8' sheet of fiber wallboard; about 50 linear feet of 1x4's; a pair of medium sized hinges; an awning pulley; a length of cotton clothesline; and about one pound of bill poster tacks. It is assumed that you already have an assortment of nails, hence these are not included in the listing.

In operation, one window should be raised about 6" in each room to be cooled, and the amount of air flowing through a given room is controlled by the distance the window is raised.

Now, all the above is based on the assumption that the temperature will drop after nightfall, and you may reasonably ask what about those nights when this doesn't happen. In this case, simply open the window in the part of the house where you are, and move your chair, or bed, so that you are in the path of the incoming current of air and you can keep quite comfortable; much more so than with an ordinary buzz fan, due to the larger volume of air being moved.

If the fan is used in the daytime, windows on the sunny side of the house should be closed and windows on the shady side should be opened, in order to bring in the cooler air.

It may require a few days for one not accustomed to using a window or attic fan, to discover the most effective combinations of opening windows and doors to gain the maximum cooling efficiency. During the cooler months, when most windows and doors are kept closed, a window or attic fan can be turned on for a short time to dispel cooking or any objectionable odor instantly.

Fascia

A broad band used in combination with moldings. Generally, this term is used to describe the special wood trim covering the joint between the exterior walls of the house and roof.

Fascia board outside a house is the finishing touch to the wall and roof joint.

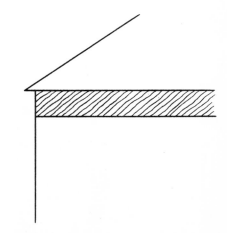

Faucets

Faucets generally used in homes are of three types: compression, Fuller ball, and ground-key.

The compression type of faucet is usually fitted with a lever or four-ball handle which offers firm resistance to efforts to turn down the spindle much beyond the point where the flow of water stops. The stem of the spindle may be seen to move in or out of the body of the faucet when the handle is turned. A self-closing faucet is usually of the compression type.

Fuller ball faucets are generally fitted with a lever handle and the stem does not move in or out of the body of the faucet when the handle is turned. When a Fuller ball is in good condition, the handle should require but one-quarter turn to open or close the flow opening.

The ground-key faucet is easily distinguished by the lever handle and plunger, which is made in one piece, and by the exposed nut or screw at the lower end which holds the plunger in place.

It is sometimes impossible to determine the type of faucet from the outside appearance. If so, the only way to find out will be to dismantle it. At the same time, the kind and size of washer or Fuller ball may be determined and the condition of the brass screw examined to see whether or not it needs replacing.

Compression

In the ordinary compression-type faucet the flow of water is regulated by turning a lever, T, or four-ball handle which is attached

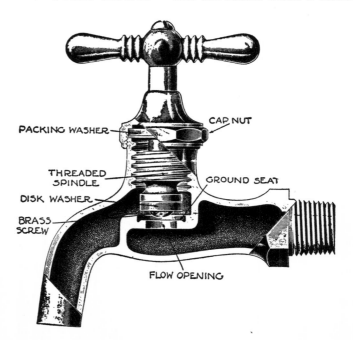

PACKING WASHER

CAP NUT

THREADED SPINDLE

GROUND SEAT

DISK WASHER

BRASS SCREW

FLOW OPENING

to a threaded spindle. When the spindle is turned down, the washer or disk attached to its lower end is pressed tightly against the smoothly finished ring or ground seat which surrounds the flow opening, thus shutting off the flow of water. If the washer and the seat do not make a firm contact at all points, water will leak through and drip from the faucet. A leak usually results from a wornout washer. If washers wear out rapidly, it may be because a poor grade of washer is being used, because the ground seat has become sharp and rough as a result of corrosion, or because the seat has become scratched or worn by grit.

Moderate force on the handle of a compression-type faucet in good repair should stop all flow and drip. If a leak develops, it may be caused by faulty washers which are not difficult to replace. It is important that faucets be tightly closed after they are used because dripping faucets tend to produce or aggravate leaks, waste water, and result in rust stains on porcelain surfaces. Soon after a hot-water faucet has been shut off and the water cools, contraction takes place which may cause a drip to develop. Should this occur, the spigot handle should be tightened without opening while the faucet is still cool.

The following tools and materials are needed: Wrench, screwdriver, fiber or special composition washers for compression-type faucets.

To avoid frequent renewals, a good grade of washer should be selected. The sizes most frequently used are $\frac{3}{8}''$, $\frac{1}{2}''$ and $\frac{5}{8}''$ and it is well to have a supply of each size on hand. Composition washers sometimes have one side flat and the other side slightly rounded. A good contact is made with this type of washer because, by fitting partly down into the seat of the faucet, it is subject to both horizontal and vertical pressure. Some faucets require specially shaped washers, the size and type of which should be d-termined for replacement.

To renew a washer, shut off the water directly below the fixture or in the main water supply pipe. If the water is shut off by the valve in the main pipe and there are fixtures located higher than the one in which the washers are to be replaced, the riser pipes to the higher fixtures should be drained before disassem-

1. Turn off the water going to the faucet to be repaired. Wrap some adhesive tape around the bonnet to prevent its being marred by the wrench.

bling the faucet. If this is not done, it may be impossible to control the flow of water issuing from the faucet when taken apart. If shut-offs located directly below the fixtures are used, this precaution will not be necssary. Then, with a wrench (using a cloth to protect the fixture from being marred), unscrew the cap nut of the faucet to allow the spindle to be unscrewed and removed. Carefully remove the brass screw that holds the washer to the bottom of the spindle, and replace the worn washer with a new one. If the head of the brass screw is badly worn, it will be difficult to remove and may be twisted off, unless handled carefully. A drop or two of kerosene and gently tapping the screw may help to loosen it in the stem. The screwdriver should have a good square edge and should be

turned with a strong steady pressure. If the head of the screw chips off or breaks so that it does not hold the screwdriver, the slot will have to be deepened, if possible by cutting into the head with a hack saw. A badly worn screw should always be replaced.

A worn or roughened washer seat can often be ground true and smooth with a faucet seat-dressing tool. Such a tool is inxpensive and will probably more than pay for itself within a reasonable time. One type consists of a stem with a cutter at the lower end and a wheel handle at the top to rotate the tool. It is fittted with a spiraled cone to be inserted into the body of the faucet and screwed down firmly for the purpose of centering and holding the cutter on the washer seat. When the tool is properly placed, it should

2. Take off the handle by removing the screw that holds it to the top of the spindle. There may be knurled nut or snap-on button over the screw head which must be removed first.

3. Remove the bonnet by turning counterclockwise with a wrench. The adhesive tape will protect the finish.

be carefully rotated back and forth several times with the wheel handle until the seat is ground free of irregularities. When the grinding is finished, all metal cuttings should be wiped out with a cloth before the faucet is reassembled. If the seat is in such bad condition that it does not respond to this treatment and continues to cut the washers, it will be necessary to substitute a new faucet.

If water leaks around the stem when the faucet is open, it may frequently be stopped by tightening the cap nut, but the nut should not be made so tight as to cause the faucet to bind. If tightening does not stop the leak, it is probable that the packing washers under the cap nut are worn out and need renewing. To put in new washers, remove the handle and cap nut and substitute

new washers for the old. To stop the leakage temporarily, wrap a small piece of oil-soaked candle-wicking or soft string around the stem, under the cap nut where the stem enters the body of the faucet.

Fuller Ball

In the Fuller ball faucet, a hard rubber or composition ball-like stopper, known as the Fuller ball, is fastened by a small nut or screw to a shaft with an eccentric end. When the faucet handle is closed, this ball is drawn firmly against the opening, shutting off the flow of water; when the handle is opened, the ball is pushed away from the opening, allowing the water to pass through. The best grade of Fuller ball should be used; the sizes range from ⅜" to 1".

To replace a Fuller ball, the

4. Slip spindle out of bonnet and remove washer by taking out the screw that holds it. Replace it with a washer of identical size made of fiber, rubber or plastic.

5. If the washer is chewed up, use the seat dresser to smooth the bottom of the inside of the faucet. Wipe inside to remove any metal chips.

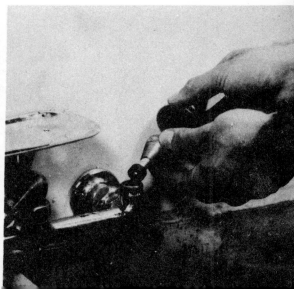

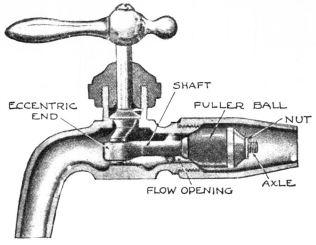

ECCENTRIC END

SHAFT

FULLER BALL

NUT

FLOW OPENING

AXLE

Cross section of a Fuller ball faucet.

water should be shut off and the faucet unscrewed and separated from the supply pipe. The nut or screw should be taken off with pliers or a screwdriver and the ball removed and replaced with a new one.

Sometimes the metal axle which holds the Fuller ball or the eccentric

part becomes worn, making it impossible to pull the ball tight against the seat, and allowing leakage between the ball and the seat. If this happens, it will be necessary to purchase new metal parts to replace the worn ones. If water leaks out around the stem when the faucet is open, repairs can be made in the

6. Slip bonnet over spindle and check packing. If worn, replace it by twisting on impregnated cord which you can buy at a local hardware store. Wind in clockwise direction from bottom to top.

7. Reset bonnet and spindle, but don't tighten spindle into seat. Tighten bonnet by turning clockwise until it's secure. Replace the handle, turn on the water and the job's done.

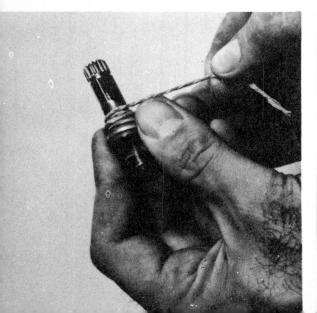

same manner as prescribed for similar leakage in compression-type faucets.

Ground-Key

The ground-key faucet has a tapered cylindrical brass plunger or plug which should fit snugly into a sleeve, bored vertically through the body of the faucet. The plunger, which is rotated by a handle, has a hole or slot bored horizontally through it, to coincide with a similarly shaped horizontal opening in the body of the faucet. When the handle that rotates the plunger is parallel to the body of the faucet, the two openings are in line with each other and allow the water to pass through. A short turn of the handle to the right or left throws the opening out of line and cuts off the flow.

The plunger or its sleeve may become grooved or worn by sand particles rubbing against the metal and allow the water to leak through. This requires repolishing of the rubbing surfaces. Also, the nut or screw at the bottom may become loose, permitting the plunger to move out of its proper position, allowing leakage. On the other hand, if the nut or screw is too tight, the plunger will bind and will be difficult to turn.

Noise in Faucets

Sometimes when a faucet is partly turned on or suddenly closed, a water hammer, tapping, or pounding noise is heard. In a compression-type faucet, this may be caused by a loose cap nut, a worn spindle, or a defective washer. In a Fuller ball faucet, the ball may become loose,

Ground-key faucet.

or the metal eccentric connecting the handle to the Fuller ball may become worn.

The following tools are needed: Wrench, screwdriver, and pliers.

To eliminate noise in a compression-type faucet, shut off the water and remove the spindle and washer so that they may be examined. If the washer is found to be loose, the brass screw should be tightened; if the washer is worn, the brass screw should be removed and a new washer attached. If the threads on the spindle or in the body of the faucet are badly worn, letting the spindle rattle, it will be necessary to purchase a new faucet.

If the faucet is of the Fuller ball type, shut off the water and tighten the small nut or screw which holds the Fuller ball; if the ball is badly worn it should be replaced. If parts of the eccentric are worn and tend to rattle, the faucet should be taken to a plumber. If the eccentric is beyond repair and new parts cannot be obtained, it wil be necessary to install a new faucet.

ABC's of Faucet Repairs

Most homes today have compression faucets—a washer moves

up and down over a "seat" or opening to control the starting and stopping of the water flow. These faucets develop two types of leaks:

a) dripping of water from underneath the handle or bonnet; this is caused by worn packing, and

b) dripping from the spout; this is often caused by a worn washer.

Changing a washer or replacing the packing is a simple task that takes but a few minutes. The one important thing to remember is to replace the washer with the same size as the worn one.

TOOLS YOU NEED—screwdriver and an open-end or monkey wrench. A seat dresser (available for a few cents with washers) is a useful accessory just in case the seat of the faucet is worn.

Faucet Outside Your Home

Having running water available outside your home is a great convenience. It's simple to attach a garden hose for watering the lawn or shrubs or washing the car.

Here's what you have to do to add a faucet for outside your home:

1. Decide upon the location of the faucet and make an opening for the pipe in the outside wall of your home.

2. If you have to go through a concrete block foundation wall, use a masonry bit with an electric drill or a star drill and hammer.

3. If you go through the wooden section of your house, use an expansion bit with a brace to make the opening through the wall for the pipe to pass through.

4. Find the nearest convenient

FAUCET PARTS

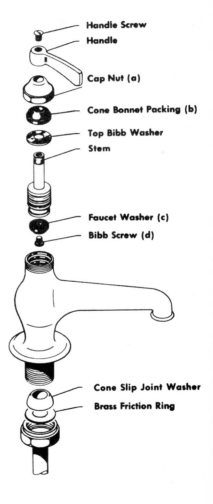

Handle Screw
Handle
Cap Nut (a)
Cone Bonnet Packing (b)
Top Bibb Washer
Stem
Faucet Washer (c)
Bibb Screw (d)
Cone Slip Joint Washer
Brass Friction Ring

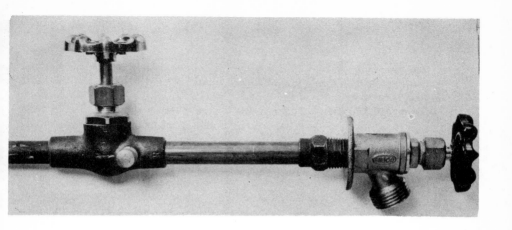

Hose cock installation showing the placement of the drainable valve on the inside of the house.

place to join this outside water pipe to the house line.

5. Shut off the main water or the branch line to be cut. It is best if you can avoid breaking into a line; if it is at all possible to hook in at a fitting, do so.

6. Insert a T-fitting in the line and connect pipe to the hole in the wall. See *Plumbing* for the how-to.

7. A drainable valve should be used inside the house to control the flow of water to the line. This valve has a special cap or screw opening to permit draining the water out of the line (between this valve and the outside hose cock), so that no water freezes during the cold weather and bursts the pipe.

8. Install the drainable valve so that the drain cap or screw is on the side toward the hose cock.

9. Attach a piece of pipe to this valve and through the wall.

10. A hose cock is attached on

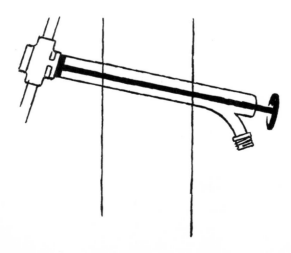

the other side of the wall. To keep the pipe steady, force a few wooden wedges between the pipe and the exterior wall and then calk the opening.

11. Now the main water valve or branch water line valve can be opened and the outside faucet is ready to use.

In the winter, when the outside faucet is not in use, shut off the drainable valve and then open the outside hose cock. After the water has dripped out of the pipe, open the drain cap or screw to let the remaining water trickle out. Keep this cap off and the hose cock open for the winter months.

If it is necessary to use water during exceedingly cold weather, you can obtain a hydrant-type valve.

This is a special valve where the seat or base is about 24″ or more away from the handle. Thus, when the water is shut off, there is little danger of it freezing and expanding to burst the pipe. Note that when installing this type of a valve, it should be pitched downward to permit proper drainage.

Normally, a compression type of faucet is used to control the flow of water outside the house. A hose cock is merely a special type of compression faucet with its end threaded to receive a hose coupling. However, if you live in an area with low water pressure, you should use a gate valve with a hose coupling adapter. The gate valve does not constrict the flow of water nor does it reduce the water pressure.

Feeder

Term used to describe the electrical wires which carry the current to a branch circuit.

See *Electrical Wiring*.

Feeler Gage

See *Gages*.

Fences and Gates

Conventional post and rail fence adds a distinctive touch to any property. It is easy to construct out of rough-cut logs or the parts can be purchased and set up on your property.

There are as many types of fences and gates, as there are houses. The fence should be built to conform to the style of the house and the size of the ground which it bounds, and it should be sturdy so that it fulfills its functional as well as decorative value.

Wood Fences

The rails may be bought ready-cut at a lumber yard. Or you may prefer to cut them yourself. Get the best quality wood you can afford as the fence must stand a long time; the wood needs to retain the paint, and you want to avoid replacement if possible. A durable, close-grained wood, therefore, is recommended.

Gate and Fence Posts

Special care must be given to the wood used for the posts, as they must be sturdy. The post ends, which go into the ground, should be treated with a modern wood preservative such as Woodlife, or creosote which is heated to about 200° F. may be brushed on to the wood ends. This acts as a decay preventative. The wood must be thoroughly dry and no pieces of bark must adhere to the posts. (Caution: creosote, if used, is flammable, so proceed with care when heating it!)

Fence Construction

It is impossible to go into the details of all types, as they range from the traditional picket fence to the modern ranch-style. Generally, however, the way to proceed is to measure off the distances at which the posts will be spaced. Then mark each post at the point where the horizontal top and bottom cross-rails will go. Cut out the notches on the posts for these cross-rails. Mark, measure, and cut the upright fence rails. If the fence is to be placed on ground which is not level, some of the posts and upright rails may need to be cut shorter or longer to accommodate uneven ground level.

Now dig out the holes for the posts. Set the first post in the ground, and pour in concrete or tamp the earth around it. (Concrete has the advantage of holding posts very firmly and is, of course, essential for iron fence supports. However, posts of any durable wood, if treated with a modern wood preservative, will last a long time in well-drained earth. In many cases, therefore, it is optional with the handyman which method he selects.) Follow the same method with the second post. Then nail the two horizontal rails across the two posts; or, if you do not use nails, insert the cross-rails into cut-out holes or notches (depending on the style you have chosen for your fence). Continue this process of setting posts and nailing or inserting cross-rails until they are all in place, and open space is left for the gate (if a gate is to be included).

Your next step is to nail the upright rails to the top and bottom cross-rails. You may prefer to nail the uprights as you work along; for instance between the first and second post; then when that is done, the cross-rails and the uprights between the second and third post. The rails may be spaced as far apart as you desire.

The nails and other hardware you use should, of course, be rust-proof and weatherproof.

You may want to leave the wood fence unpainted. However, if you paint it, be sure to use exterior paint.

Gate Hanging

You may find a ready-made gate at the lumber yard which fits the size and style of the fence. Otherwise, you could make your own gate, first building a framework, then proceeding with the rails to follow the general pattern of the fence. The gate is hung on the post with hinges which are durable and rustproof. A latch is attached to the opposite side of the gate and its adjacent post. The gate is then painted or left in its natural state, to correspond with the fence.

Brick Fence

This, of course, is not usually considered as informal as the wood fence. However, a brick fence is a solid wall for shrubs and vines if you want them for your garden. The color and design of the brick wall is a personal choice. The bricks are laid with mortar, as discussed in the section on *Brick*.

A wood gate is appropriate with

Modern basket weave fence is made of reinforced Fiberglas which comes in strips. The wood frame is made in the conventional manner and 1½" poles are used to weave the plastic strip. This fence provides privacy but it permits the light to pass through.

a brick fence. The gate may follow the general style of the house itself, and then be painted either the color of the brick or a dominant color used on the house exterior.

How To Set Fence Posts

To set wood or concrete posts, dig a hole from 1½′ to 3′ deep, depending upon the height of the post. The hole should be about 8″ to 12″ square at the top.

For best results, make the bottom of the hole somewhat wider than the top so as to resist any tipping effect on the post. Then pour about 4″ of concrete (ready-mixed saves you time if a large number of posts have to be set) into the bottom of the hole. Set the post into position and hold it securely by attaching a few 1x4 or 2x4 braces to it. Then pour concrete to fill the remainder of the hole, making certain to tamp the mixture down as you pour.

It is good policy to apply a coat of wood preservative over the base of the post before it is submerged in the concrete. A coating of asphalt is sometimes substituted.

If you use a metal post, it is not necessary to dig the hole as wide as for a wood post. In setting the metal post, however, it is advisable to sink the post about 6″ below the bottom of the hole before pouring in the concrete.

Always finish the top of the concrete off so that the water flows away from the post. A trowel is used for this job.

A wood pole (1″ or larger dowel) set in a metal sleeve in concrete. The pole can be removed while the sleeve remains imbedded in the concrete.

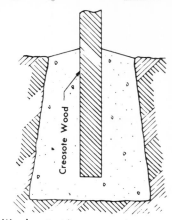

Wood post set in a concrete base.

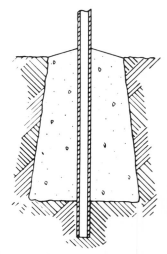

Pipe or metal post set in concrete.

Sketches courtesy of Sakrete, Inc.

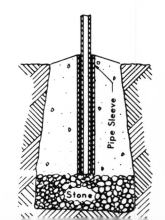

Planning a Picket Fence

Certain basic dimensions should be followed when making a picket fence. It has been found over the years that certain proportions and certain placement of parts produce the most pleasing effects. Here is a guide for building.

- Post should be made of 4x4 lumber and should extend about 36″ above the ground. Two feet should extend below ground level.
- The posts should be no more than 8′ apart unless you plan to use stringers of lumber heavier than 2x4's.
- The bottom stringer should be about 5″ above the ground level.
- When the pickets are mounted, the bottom edge should be about 2″ above the ground level.
- The pickets should be about 42″ long and extend about 6″ above the top stringer and 3″ below the bottom stringer.
- The space between the pickets should be the same as the width of the individual pickets.

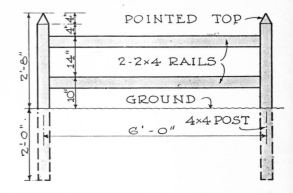

Details for a stretcher fence.

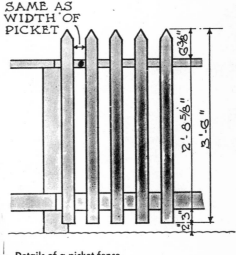

Details of a picket fence.

Patterns for picket tops.

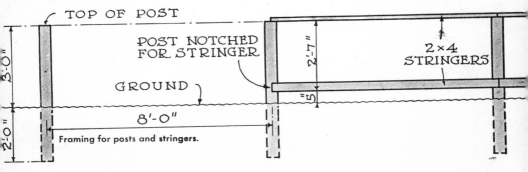

Framing for posts and stringers.

Ready-Made Fences

Many homeowners would rather not spend the time needed to make their own fence. They prefer buying ready-made fences and installing them around their property. Frequently, buying a ready-made fence is not more expensive than making your own. Before you build, if you plan a conventional fence, it pays to shop around. If there is not too much price differential and you prefer to spend your time doing other jobs, you might want a ready-made fence.

This attractive windbreak is made with triangle-shaped wood pieces and permits the air to pass through freely.

Photograph courtesy of Deltawood, Inc.

This attractive fence is made of heavy, prewoven hardwood veneer. The basket weave pattern combines smart ornamentation with privacy and with safety for small children and pets.

Photograph courtesy of Orchard Park Veneer & Container Corp.

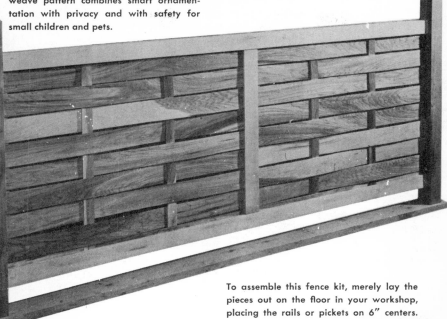

Photograph courtesy of Deltawood, Inc.

To assemble this fence kit, merely lay the pieces out on the floor in your workshop, placing the rails or pickets on 6" centers. Holding one piece with your foot, nail the other to it in the manner shown. Design blocks between the rails may be added if you wish. It is sometimes helpful to mark the design on the floor for quick, correct reproduction of the pattern.

The new triangle-shaped fencing is easy to put together and makes any fence a special eye-catcher on your property. Here the rails have been used with blocks. The pickets can also be used and the choice of the design is up to the man who builds the fence of the pre-cut material. Made of cedar, an 8' fence which is 4' high comes in a single package as a unit.

Distinctive Fences of Hardboard

Inexpensive tempered hardboard can be used to make unusual fences. Here are three patterns which you can easily make for your home by following simple fence construction techniques.

DOUBLE HEADER—This fence with 4x4 posts and 2x4's as stringers is covered with sheets of tempered hardboard. Note that the sheets are overlapped in a shadow wall effect. One sheet is nailed in place on one side of the stringers and the next sheet is set on the opposite side so that the edge overlaps slightly.

Sketch courtesy of Masonite Corp.

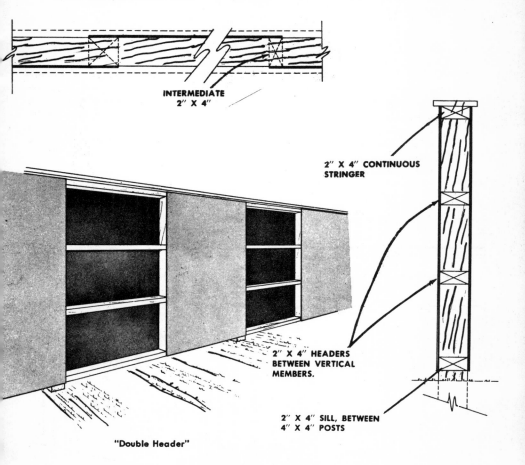

INTERMEDIATE
2" X 4"

2" X 4" CONTINUOUS STRINGER

2" X 4" HEADERS BETWEEN VERTICAL MEMBERS.

2" X 4" SILL, BETWEEN 4" X 4" POSTS

"Double Header"

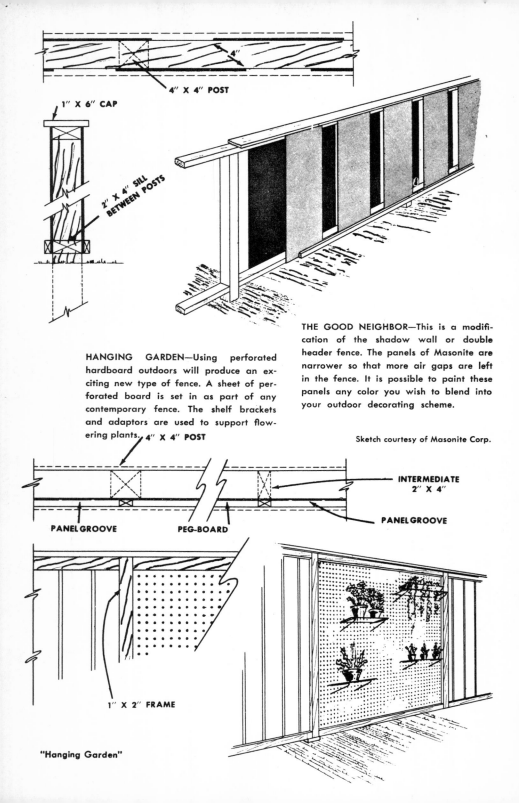

4" X 4" POST

1" X 6" CAP

2" X 4" SILL BETWEEN POSTS

HANGING GARDEN—Using perforated hardboard outdoors will produce an exciting new type of fence. A sheet of perforated board is set in as part of any contemporary fence. The shelf brackets and adaptors are used to support flowering plants.

THE GOOD NEIGHBOR—This is a modification of the shadow wall or double header fence. The panels of Masonite are narrower so that more air gaps are left in the fence. It is possible to paint these panels any color you wish to blend into your outdoor decorating scheme.

Sketch courtesy of Masonite Corp.

4" X 4" POST

INTERMEDIATE 2" X 4"

PANEL GROOVE

PEG-BOARD

PANEL GROOVE

1" X 2" FRAME

"Hanging Garden"

Woven fir plywood fence screens the back yard from wind, neighbors; it affords privacy on a small lot. It's an ideal project for the home handyman who wishes to add to the outdoor living area on his property or to shield a patio space.

Woven Plywood Fence

Exterior grade plywood can be used to make an attractive privacy fence which will still permit the breeze to come through. It is made with 4x4 posts set about 6' to 8' apart and a vertical separator set mid-point between the posts; this should be made of 2x2 stock.

Windscreen of woven plywood requires 4x4 posts and 2x2 separators to give you a fence of handsome wood and interesting patterned texture. Stressed construction around the posts takes maximum advantage of the plywood's strength.

Fir plywood, cut in 12" strips, is woven between the uprights to gain the overlapping shadowed texture in the windscreen fence. You can use 1/16" or 1/8" or 1/4" fir plywood and apply a sealer coat or paint the surfaces and edges of the entire fence.

Photographs courtesy of Douglas Fir Plywood Association.

Contemporary Fences with Reinforced Plastic Panels

You can give your home a new look, brighten up your lawn and garden and insure 'no trespassing' with a fence made with reinforced plastic panels. These panels are transluscent and shatterproof and can be sawed, nailed and drilled—just like wood. They are available in many different colors in flat or corrugated form.

These fences are incredibly strong, dentproof and rotproof. You admit the light with the transluscent panels but maintain privacy.

SCREENING FENCE—If you want complete privacy, here's the fence for you. With this tall screen-fence, you can close off your outdoor living area from your neighbors' view or hide unsightly burners, compost heaps and unattractive views.

Sketches courtesy of Monsanto Chemical Co.

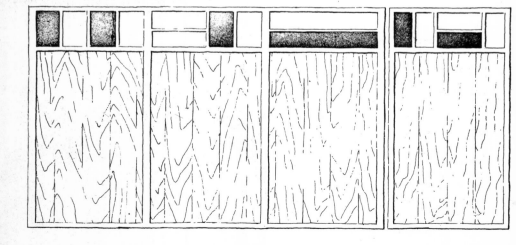

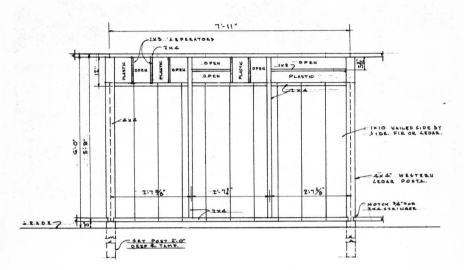

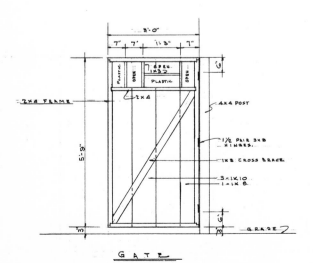

GATE

PROTECTIVE FENCE—This one gives you protection with a colorful design. It will keep children in the yard and keep frolicsome dogs out. The gate is sturdy and made in a contemporary design. The center reinforced plastic panel can be a colorful plaque for your home numbers.

Sketches courtesy of Honsanto Chemical Co.

DETAIL OF PLASTIC
INSTALLATION IN GATE

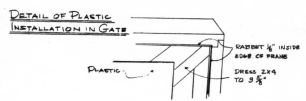

RABBET ⅛" INSIDE
EDGE OF FRAME

DRESS 2X4
TO 3⅝"

PLASTIC

2×4 STRINGER

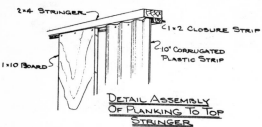

1×2 CLOSURE STRIP

10" CORRUGATED
PLASTIC STRIP

1×10 BOARD

DETAIL ASSEMBLY
OF PLANKING TO TOP
STRINGER

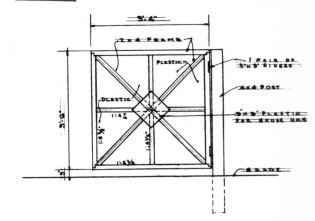

3'-4"

2×4 FRAME

PLASTIC

1 PAIR OF
3"×3" HINGES

4×4 POST

3"×3" PLASTIC
PER HOUSE MFG.

PLASTIC

3'-9"

1'-4½"

1'-4½"

1'-4½"

GRADE

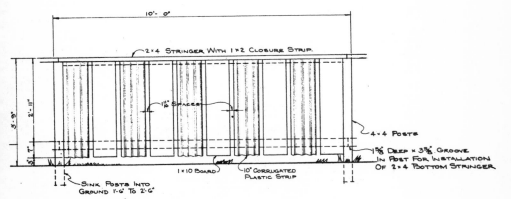

10'- 0"

2×4 STRINGER WITH 1×2 CLOSURE STRIP.

3'-9"

2'-11"

1⅛"
16 SPACES

4×4 POSTS

1⅝" DEEP × 3⅜" GROOVE
IN POST FOR INSTALLATION
OF 2×4 BOTTOM STRINGER

SINK POSTS INTO
GROUND 1'-6" TO 2'-6"

1×10 BOARD

10" CORRUGATED
PLASTIC STRIP

DECORATIVE FENCE—This fence outlines your property and accents the landscaping in your yard. It's low enough not to cut off the view, but high enough to invite trespassers to walk around.

Sketches courtesy of Monsanto Chemical Co.

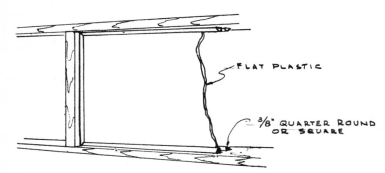

FLAT PLASTIC

3/8" QUARTER ROUND OR SQUARE

DETAIL ASSEMBLY SHOWING INSTALLATION OF PLASTIC

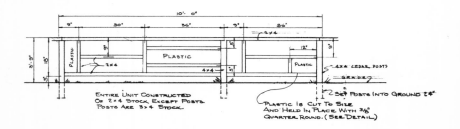

ENTIRE UNIT CONSTRUCTED OF 2 × 4 STOCK EXCEPT POSTS. POSTS ARE 3 × 4 STOCK.

PLASTIC IS CUT TO SIZE AND HELD IN PLACE WITH 3/8" QUARTER ROUND. (SEE DETAIL)

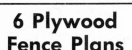

6 Plywood Fence Plans

On the following pages are detailed step-by-step plans for making a variety of fences out of exterior-grade plywood. There is one to meet your needs and the building style of your home.

Among the plans included are those for a:

1. Saw-tooth or Staggered Wall Fence, particularly useful as a privacy wall or sun shield.

2. Woven Fence made by interlacing 24" wide strips of plywood.

3. Closed Louver Fence which affords complete privacy and yet because of the louver setting of the panels gives the fence a lighter look.

4. Vertical Venetian Blind Fence for areas where you sometimes want the sun and at other times wish to shut it out.

5. Panel Fence for Carports which can be used to add a decorative finish to your carport and hide the car from view from your outdoor living area.

6. Framed Square Fence where construction is speeded by the use of large sheets of plywood, but the big areas are broken up by adding vertical and horizontal frames.

Finishing Details

After your fence has been completed, you should apply some finish to protect it from the elements.

The best paint for any wood to be exposed to the weather has proved best for exterior plywood as well. High grade exterior house paints of either titanium-lead-zinc or white lead and oil give excellent service on exterior plywood. Avoid paints which set to a hard, brittle film.

1. The initial or prime coat is the most important. This should be brushed on thoroughly as soon as possible after the fence is erected. Use a high grade exterior primer thinned with at least one pint pure raw linseed oil per gallon, or use a high grade aluminum primer.

2. Over the primer coat, following as closely as conditions permit, apply second and third coats according to paint manufacturer's directions, either brushed or sprayed on.

3. Paint both sides of the fence with equal coverage.

Saw-Tooth Fence

```
MATERIALS

    Exterior-type Douglas Fir
        plywood—4' x 8' x ⅜"
        thick
    Posts—4"x4"x10'
    Intermediate rails—2"x3"x
        8'
    Stops—⅜"x1⅛"
    Battens—1⅛"x2"x8'
    Galvanized nails
        4d for battens
        8d for nailing rails to
        posts
        16d for nailing top tail
        to posts
    Paint
    TOOLS
    Hammer
    Carpenter's square
    Saw
    Spirit level or plumb bob
    Shovel or post-hole digger
    Chalk line
    Brush
    Six-foot rule or steel tape
```

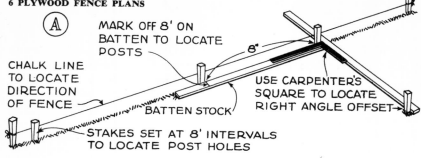

(A) MARK OFF 8' ON BATTEN TO LOCATE POSTS

CHALK LINE TO LOCATE DIRECTION OF FENCE

USE CARPENTER'S SQUARE TO LOCATE RIGHT ANGLE OFFSET →

BATTEN STOCK

STAKES SET AT 8' INTERVALS TO LOCATE POST HOLES

1. Indicated on Figure A is a method you can adopt for locating the fence. The plan shows a 4'x8' offset "step," but you can make this any length you wish by trimming the exterior plywood panels to the desired offset. Make a template out of the batten stock, as shown in figure A for locating the post holes. Posts should be redwood or cedar, although other materials may be used if treated or impregnated with wood preservative to assure long life while set in earth. Position each post, using spirit level or plumb bob to set to true vertical. Tamp dirt to pack tightly.

2. Edge-seal the exterior plywood panels with a thick lead and oil paint or other suitable compound. With 4d nails, nail the 1⅟₁₆" x2" battens horizontally on each side of the bottom of the panel, slightly recessing the panel as shown on Plan 3. Then cut four side stops to fit between batten and the top of the panel.

3. Mark a center line on the inside of each post to locate plywood panel in vertical position. Set the exterior plywood panel on blocks which raise it about 4" from the ground, positioning it between the posts. Hold panel in place verti-

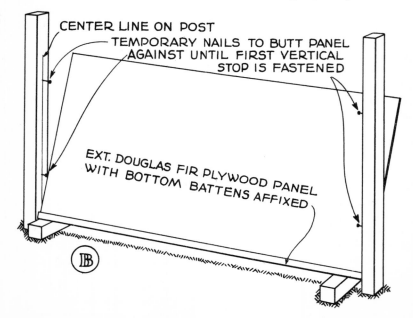

CENTER LINE ON POST
TEMPORARY NAILS TO BUTT PANEL AGAINST UNTIL FIRST VERTICAL STOP IS FASTENED

EXT. DOUGLAS FIR PLYWOOD PANEL WITH BOTTOM BATTENS AFFIXED

(B)

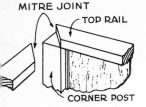

MITRE JOINT
TOP RAIL
CORNER POST

Fig. C

cally by setting temporary nails in the posts on one side of the panel. (Figure B.) Then nail one stop to each post as shown on Plan 5. Fasten panel to the stops. Remove temporary nails from other side of panel and fasten stops on that side.

4. Cut 2"x3"x8' intermediate rail. Cut two stops to fit this rail. With 8d nails, toe-nail rail to posts, flush with the top of the panel. Then nail the two stops in place as indicated on Plan 2.

5. Measure 12" above the 2"x 3" rail and mark each post with a square. Trim posts to this height. Plan shows a 12" open space. It can be more, or less, if you wish.

Cut and nail the top rail to the posts, with 16d nails. This rail should be centered on intermediate posts. For joining rail at corner posts, miter as shown on Figure C.

6. Nail 1¹⁄₁₆"x2" battens vertically in the center on both faces of the panel. Cut a spacer from the 2"x3" stock to fit between the cap and intermediate rails, then nail in place so it is lined up vertically with battens.

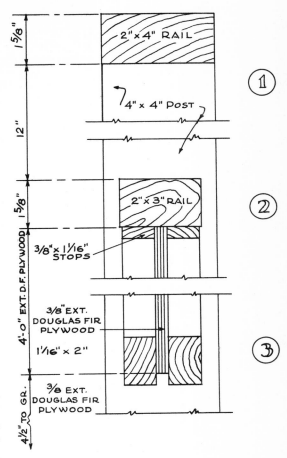

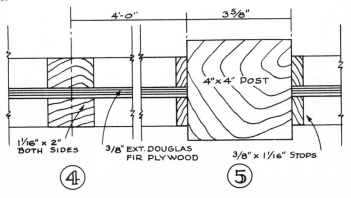

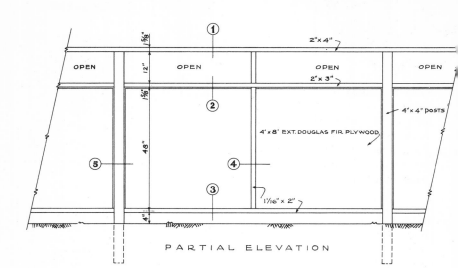

PARTIAL ELEVATION

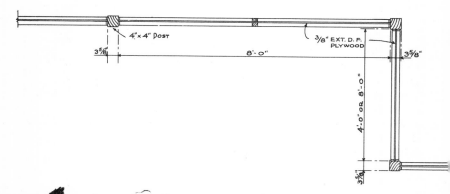

Woven Plywood Fence

MATERIALS

Exterior-type Douglas fir plywood (Fence is constructed of ¼" panels 2' x 8', cut from standard plywood sheets.)

Posts—4"x4"x10'

Divider posts—2"x4"x6'

6d galvanized casing nails

Paint

TOOLS

Hammer

Saw

Spirit level

Shovel or post-hole digger

Chalk line

Brush

1. Locate fence position by stretching chalk line between stakes. Dig the first hole (all holes should be at least 2' deep) and position the first post, using a spirit level or plumb bob to set it to true vertical. Tamp dirt around it to pack tightly.

All posts should be cedar or redwood, although other material may be used if treated or impregnated with wood preservative to assure long life while set in earth.

2. The first and last two posts in any direction are set on 7'9" centers so exterior plywood panels will line up flush with the outside edge of the first and last posts. Remaining posts are set on 7'11" centers. (Figure A.) Mark off and position as many posts as you will need, using a spirit level to set them to true vertical.

3. Mark a center line on the front and back faces of all the posts except the first or corner post. Nail small temporary battens to these lines. Edge-seal the plywood panels with a thick lead and oil paint or other suitable compound. Nail one panel flush with the edge of the first post, about 4" above the ground. Bend the panel so as to butt against the batten on the corresponding face of the second post, then nail it. (Figure B.)

4. Nail the second plywood panel flush with the edge of the first post, but on the opposite side from the panel just applied. The bottom of this panel rests on top of the first panel. Bend this panel in reverse direction to the first panel, so it butts against the batten on the second post, then nail.

5. Take the 6' divider post and nail vertically between the two panels at their centers as shown on the plans.

6. Position the top panel in the

same manner as the bottom panel and nail to the divider post to complete the section, using temporary battens or stops to hold panel in desired nailing position. (Battens are re-used and thrown away when fence is completed; they may be any scrap lumber.) Trim posts flush with the top plywood panel.

Repeat procedure on all remaining fence sections. Figure C shows typical corner detail.

NOTE: An attractive alternate design can be created by using ¼" exterior plywood panels cut to 16" widths. Four to six such widths could be woven into the posts, depending upon height desired. Post and divider lengths would naturally have to be altered to fit planned height.

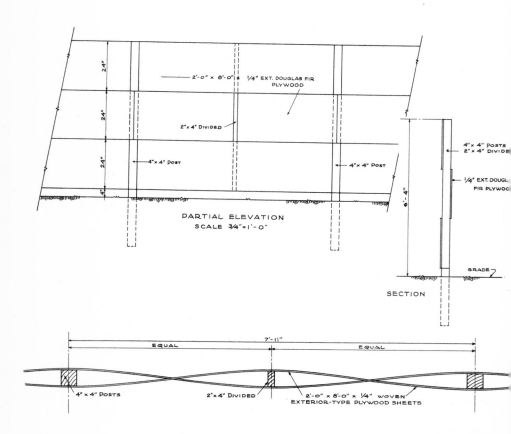

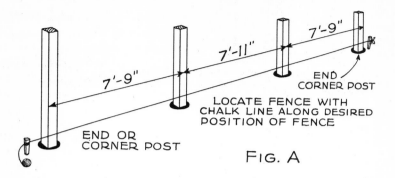

7'-9"   7'-11"   7'-9"

END
CORNER POST

END OR
CORNER POST

LOCATE FENCE WITH
CHALK LINE ALONG DESIRED
POSITION OF FENCE

FIG. A

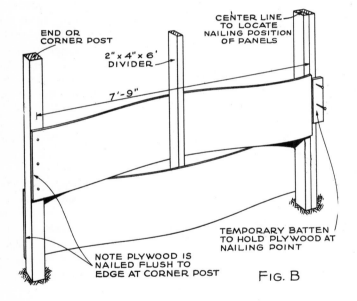

END OR
CORNER POST

CENTER LINE
TO LOCATE
NAILING POSITION
OF PANELS

2"x 4"x 6'
DIVIDER

7'-9"

NOTE PLYWOOD IS
NAILED FLUSH TO
EDGE AT CORNER POST

TEMPORARY BATTEN
TO HOLD PLYWOOD AT
NAILING POINT

FIG. B

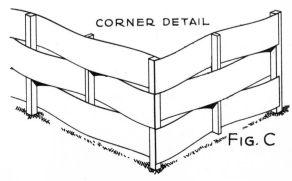

CORNER DETAIL

FIG. C

Closed Louver Fence

MATERIALS

Exterior-type Douglas fir
  plywood—2'x6'x⅜"
Posts—2"x6"x10'
Intermediate posts—1"x6"x
  6'
Side rails for base—1"x6",
  random lengths
Base cap, and cap rail—
  1"x8"x14'
Quarter round—¾"
Galvanized nails—4d and
  8d
Paint

TOOLS

Hammer
Saw
Bevel gauge
Spirit level
Shovel or post-hole digger
Square
Chalk line
Brush

1. See Figure A. First, lay out and cut one section of 1"x8" base cap to use as a template to space the posts in the ground, as well as to set them at the proper angle. On this piece actually lay out in pencil, one length of a complete panel assembly consisting of posts, intermediate posts, and three exterior-type plywood panels, as indicated on the plans. Cut this piece of stock on the angles at the inner edge of each 2" guide for setting the posts accurately. As shown on Figure B, marking a center line will be helpful in lining up the template and posts.

2. Locate the fence by stretching a chalk line between two stakes. This line will act as a guide for the back or front of the fence, whichever you prefer. Dig the first hole. All post holes should be at least 2' deep.

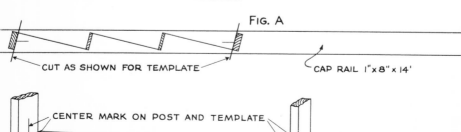

FIG. A

CUT AS SHOWN FOR TEMPLATE

CAP RAIL 1"x8"x14'

CENTER MARK ON POST AND TEMPLATE

POSITIONING POST WITH TEMPLATE

FIG. B

Posts should be cedar or redwood, although other material may be used if treated or impregnated with a wood preservative to assure long life while set in earth.

Take your template and line it up lengthwise with the chalk line, allowing one end of the template to extend a little beyond the inside edge of the post hole. Butt the post to the angle end of the template. Tamp the dirt, holding the post in position. Use a spirit level to set the post vertically.

3. Replace your template again with one end butted to your first positioned post. Dig the next hole at the end of the template for the second post. Center your second post at the angle of the template; fill in the dirt and tamp. Again, use the spirit level to set the post vertically.

4. Now that you have set the first two posts, proceed with the rest of them, using the template for spacing and setting the posts at the correct angle. If you need a corner, cut the 1"x8" base as shown in Figure C and use it to position the first post in the other direction. Then position and set the remaining posts with the first template.

5. Apply the rails to the base of the fence. Rails are 1"x6" stock, random lengths, with scab joints as indicated on Figure D. Nail the rails temporarily, with one nail in each post, so you can do some adjusting later if necessary. Nail the first rail to the front posts about 4" above the ground. Because the posts are set at an angle, the rails will touch on the corner of each post. Nail another rail to the back of the posts

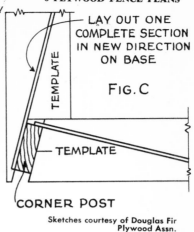

LAY OUT ONE COMPLETE SECTION IN NEW DIRECTION ON BASE

FIG. C

TEMPLATE

TEMPLATE

CORNER POST

Sketches courtesy of Douglas Fir Plywood Assn.

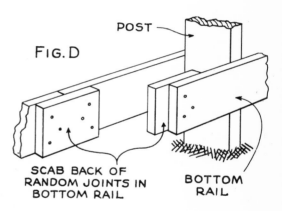

POST

FIG. D

SCAB BACK OF RANDOM JOINTS IN BOTTOM RAIL

BOTTOM RAIL

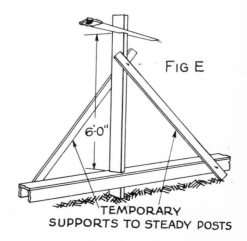

FIG E

6'-0"

TEMPORARY SUPPORTS TO STEADY POSTS

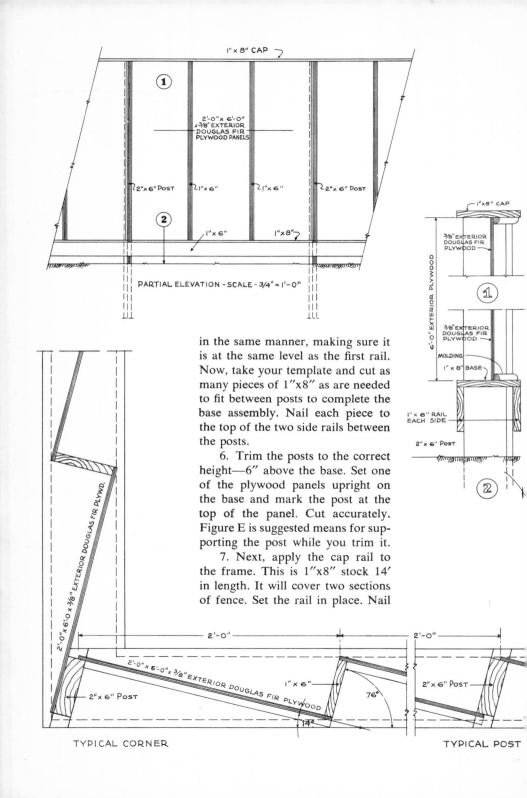

I" x 8" CAP

①

2'-0" x 6'-0"
x 3/8" EXTERIOR
DOUGLAS FIR
PLYWOOD PANELS

②

2" x 6" Post   1" x 6"   1" x 6"   2" x 6" Post

1" x 6"   1"x 8"

PARTIAL ELEVATION - SCALE - 3/4" = 1'-0"

I"x8" CAP

3/8" EXTERIOR
DOUGLAS FIR
PLYWOOD

①

6'-0" EXTERIOR PLYWOOD

3/8" EXTERIOR
DOUGLAS FIR
PLYWOOD

MOLDING

I" x 8" BASE

I" x 6" RAIL
EACH SIDE

2" x 6" Post

②

in the same manner, making sure it is at the same level as the first rail. Now, take your template and cut as many pieces of 1″x8″ as are needed to fit between posts to complete the base assembly. Nail each piece to the top of the two side rails between the posts.

6. Trim the posts to the correct height—6″ above the base. Set one of the plywood panels upright on the base and mark the post at the top of the panel. Cut accurately. Figure E is suggested means for supporting the post while you trim it.

7. Next, apply the cap rail to the frame. This is 1″x8″ stock 14′ in length. It will cover two sections of fence. Set the rail in place. Nail

2'-0" x 6'-0" x 3/8" EXTERIOR DOUGLAS FIR PLYWD.

2'-0"   2'-0"

2'-0" x 6'-0" x 3/8" EXTERIOR DOUGLAS FIR PLYWOOD

1" x 6"

2" x 6" Post   2" x 6" Post

76°

14°

TYPICAL CORNER   TYPICAL POST

it temporarily to the first post, allowing the end of the cap rail to extend a little beyond the first post. Place your template under the cap rail between the first and second posts to adjust the correct distance at the top. Temporarily nail the cap to the second post. Again, place the template under the cap rail to measure the distance between the second and third rail. Then trim the cap rail on angle at center of third post and temporarily fasten in place.

8. Trim the 1"x6" intermediate posts to the same height as the plywood panels. Edge-seal the plywood with a thick lead and oil paint or suitable compound. Nail the panels to the intermediate posts as indicated on the plans. This unit consists of three plywood panels and two intermediate posts. Position this unit between the base and cap rail. Nail the first plywood panel to the center of the first post; then nail the third plywood panel to the center of

the second post. You now have a section in place, and the remaining sections are handled in the same manner.

9. Now that the units fit snugly between the posts, nail quarter-round molding to the cap rail and also the base, flush with the face of the plywood panels. This holds the panels at top and bottom so you can toe-nail them to the cap rail; toe-nail them to the base. Now, permanently nail all frame parts and proceed to the next section.

Alternate Panel Arrangements

If you wish your fence 8' high, simply cut each 4'x8' panel of plywood into two 2'x8' pieces and provide 12' posts for the necessary height. Figure F shows an alternate treatment for a 6' fence, using an intermediate rail and 4'x8' plywood panels. Here, cut the 4'x8' panels into 2'x8' pieces for the bottom and 2'x2' for the top portion of each fence section.

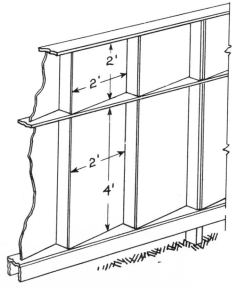

Vertical Venetian Blind Fence

> **MATERIALS**
>
> Exterior-type Douglas fir
>   Plywood—4'x8'x⅜" thick
> Framing Material—2"x3"
> Galvanized casing nails
> Hardware as shown
> Waterproof-type glue
> Mastic
> Paint
>
> **TOOLS**
>
> Carpenters' square
> Rule
> Brace and bits
> Miter-box
> Saw, hammer
> Sandpaper, brush

1. First you will have to figure the opening you wish to fill with the movable screen sections. Then divide the total space to determine how many sections will be needed, remembering that the total width of any one section will be a maximum of 4'2", the total height a maximum of 8'4¼".

2. After dividing the opening to determine the total number of sections needed, construct the framework for the sections. Framing is 2"x3", rabbeted to accommodate the plywood panel (⅜" wide and ⅝" deep) as shown on Figure A. Size of the opening will naturally determine the size of each section.

3. Miter frame corners as shown in Figure B. Glue and nail the corner joint. Fit panel into the rabbeted frame and toe-nail with 6d galvanized nails. Seal edges of the plywood panels with a thick lead and oil paint or other suitable compound. Set the bottom panel—frame joint in mastic to prevent water from entering joint and injuring paint finish.

4. Mark off center of each door frame, top and bottom, for pivots upon which door will swing. Figure shows a simple pivot you can construct with ½" threaded pipe. It is suggested that a foot-type door stop be used for holding each door at any desired position.

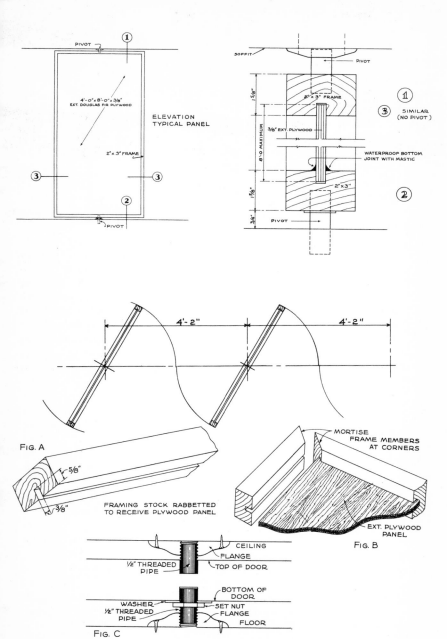

PIVOT

ELEVATION
TYPICAL PANEL

4'-0" x 8'-0" x 3/8"
EXT. DOUGLAS FIR PLYWOOD

2" x 3" FRAME

PIVOT

SOFFIT

PIVOT

5/8"

2" x 3" FRAME

3/8" EXT. PLYWOOD

8'-0 MAXIMUM

WATERPROOF BOTTOM
JOINT WITH MASTIC

1 5/8"

2" x 3"

3/4"

PIVOT

① ③ SIMILAR
(NO PIVOT)

②

4'-2"   4'-2"

FIG. A

5/8"

3/8"

FRAMING STOCK RABBETTED
TO RECEIVE PLYWOOD PANEL

MORTISE
FRAME MEMBERS
AT CORNERS

EXT. PLYWOOD
PANEL

FIG. B

CEILING
FLANGE
TOP OF DOOR

1/2" THREADED
PIPE

BOTTOM OF
DOOR

WASHER
1/2" THREADED
PIPE

SET NUT
FLANGE
FLOOR

FIG. C

Carport Fence

MATERIALS

Exterior-type Douglas fir
    plywood panels—4"x8'x
    ⅜"
Posts—4"x4"
Horizontal rail strips—1"x2"
6d Galvanized nails
Steel tape or rule
Paint

1. If your carport is already supported by posts you can of course apply the exterior-type plywood panels horizontally to these posts, cap the top and place the rail at the bottom as shown above. If your port is a wide soffit or overhang, or has supports only at the extreme corners, you will need to place posts properly on 4' center as outlined in step 2.

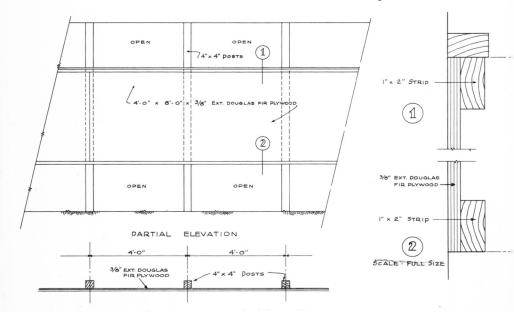

OPEN   OPEN

4" x 4" posts ①

4'-0" x 8'-0" x ⅜" EXT. DOUGLAS FIR PLYWOOD

②

OPEN   OPEN

PARTIAL ELEVATION

4'-0"   4'-0"

⅜" EXT. DOUGLAS
FIR PLYWOOD   4" x 4" posts

1" x 2" STRIP

①

⅜" EXT. DOUGLAS
FIR PLYWOOD

1" x 2" STRIP

②

SCALE - FULL SIZE

2. Intermediate posts to support the plywood panels are best set on concrete blocks, shimmed to proper height so post can be nailed to framing member on underside of the carport roof. Set posts on 4' centers.

3. Seal edges of the plywood panels with a thick lead and oil paste or other suitable compound. Place the standard 4'x8' panels on the posts, midway between the ground and the underside of the carport roof-line. Panels are nailed to posts with 6d galvanized nails.

4. When panels are in place, nail a 1"x3" batten flush with the top of the panel as shown on Drawing 1 of the plans. Do the same with the bottom of the panel, as shown on Drawing 2.

5. Across the top of the panel and the top batten just applied, nail another 1"x2" batten, allowing it to extend beyond the first batten. (See Drawing 1.) This carries out a horizontal effect and gives a finished appearance to the job.

ALTERNATE DESIGN ARRANGEMENTS

You can vary the basic suggested design in many ways to create individual, distinctive effects. Here in sketch form are five additional ideas for panel arrangement and decorative treatment.

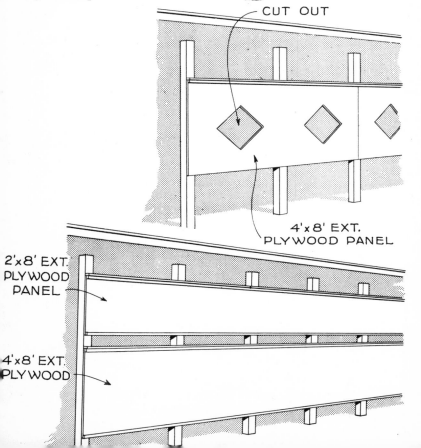

CUT OUT

4'x8' EXT. PLYWOOD PANEL

2'x8' EXT. PLYWOOD PANEL

4'x8' EXT. PLYWOOD

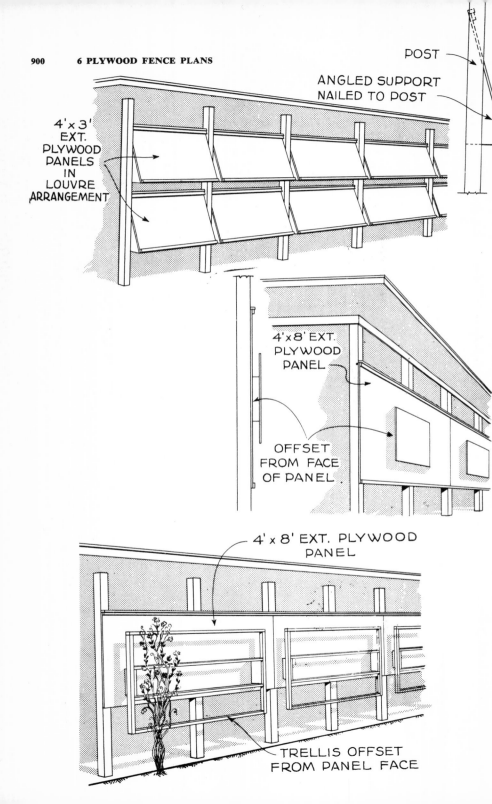

POST

ANGLED SUPPORT
NAILED TO POST

4' x 3'
EXT.
PLYWOOD
PANELS
IN
LOUVRE
ARRANGEMENT

4' x 8' EXT.
PLYWOOD
PANEL

OFFSET
FROM FACE
OF PANEL

4' x 8' EXT. PLYWOOD
PANEL

TRELLIS OFFSET
FROM PANEL FACE

Framed Squares

1. Locate fence by stretching a chalk line between two stakes, then dig your post holes at least 2′ deep, spaced 4′ apart. Posts should be cedar or redwood, although other material may be used if treated or impregnated with wood preservative to insure long life while set in earth.

2. As indicated on plan, 2″x4″ intermediate posts will have a 2″x4″ scab nailed on them, from ground line down. Seal between post and scab with thick lead and oil paint, aluminum paint, or high-grade exterior house primer. This gives added protection against deterioration. Cut a 2″x4″ four feet long to use as a spacer to position each post. Tamp the dirt tightly around the post. Use a spirit level or plumb bob to set post on true vertical. (Figure A.)

3. Edge-seal the plywood panels with a thick lead and oil paint or other suitable compound. Nail 1″x2″ batten horizontally on both sides of the panel at the bottom, slightly recessing the panel as shown in Figure B. Cut four 1″x1″ stops to fit between this batten and the top of the panel.

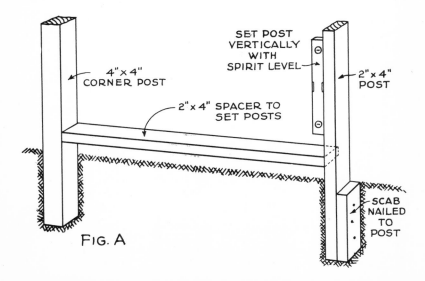

FIG. A

4. Find center of each post and draw two lines, each ³⁄₁₆″ from this center line, which will show nailing position of panel on post. Position the panel between posts by setting it on blocks which will hold it about 4″ above ground line. Set the panel in place, using temporary nails as stops on one side until the vertical 1″x1″ stop is in place on opposite side. (See Figure C.) Remove temporary nails and nail opposite stop to post, then to panel.

5. Trim posts flush with top of the panel. Cut and nail the top rail to the posts. Top rail should be flush with the outside of the first and last post. Joints in top rail should be planned to come on center of any

intermediate post, depending on length of top rails used. For joining rail to 4″x4″ corner post, miter as shown in Figure D.

6. Cut two more 1″x1″ stops. Position them to hold the plywood panel in place under top rail. (See Plan 1.) Nail 1″x2″ battens to quarter the panel faces on both sides. (See Plan 2.)

NOTE: If one section of fence is to be used for shelves, as suggested, these shelves can be made from ¾″ exterior-type plywood. Decorative shapes can easily be cut with a jigsaw, if desired. If valances are wanted (as shown in Figure E), these may be cut from ⅜″ exterior plywood.

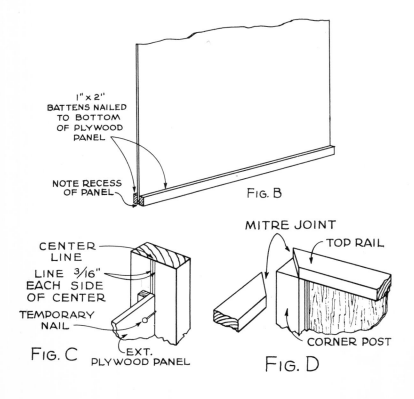

1″ x 2″ BATTENS NAILED TO BOTTOM OF PLYWOOD PANEL

NOTE RECESS OF PANEL

FIG. B

CENTER LINE

LINE 3⁄16″ EACH SIDE OF CENTER

TEMPORARY NAIL

FIG. C   EXT. PLYWOOD PANEL

MITRE JOINT

TOP RAIL

CORNER POST

FIG. D

MATERIALS

Exterior-type Douglas fir plywood. Fence is constructed
of ⅜″ thick panels 4′x6′,
which should be cut from
standard plywood sheets.
Corner posts—4″x4″x10′
Extra 2″x4″ for below
ground scabs on posts
Intermediate posts—2″x4″x
10′
Stops—1″x1″
Battens—1″x2″
Galvanized nails—
16d for top rail
8d for bottom rail
4d for battens and stops
Paint

TOOLS

Saw
Shovel or post-hole digger
Chalk line
Plumb bob or level
Brush

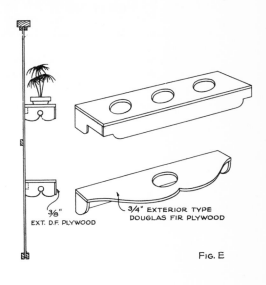

⅜″
EXT. D.F. PLYWOOD

¾″ EXTERIOR TYPE
DOUGLAS FIR PLYWOOD

FIG. E

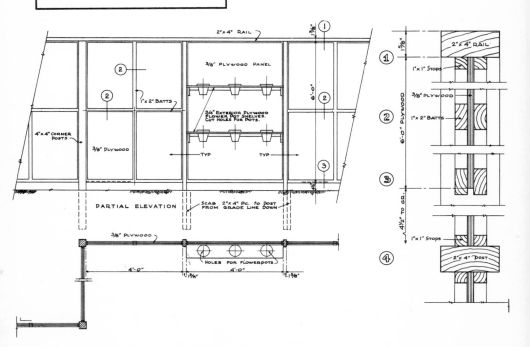

PARTIAL ELEVATION

HOLES FOR FLOWERPOTS

Ferrule

The metal part which holds the bristle to the handle of the paint brush is called the ferrule. Try to keep this part of the brush free of paint. If any paint gets on during painting, wipe it clean with a cloth dipped in turpentine and then dry the metal. It is important that this metal part does not rust.

Note the ferrule, the metal part, of the paint brush; it holds the bristles together and joins them to the handle.

Fertilizers

Materials

For convenience and adequate turf nutrition, use a complete fertilizer; that is, a fertilizer containing all three of the major fertilizer materials. The law requires that every package of fertilizer be labelled to show the guaranteed minimum percentages (or grade) of the three important fertilizer nutrients. For example, a 10-6-4 fertilizer contains at least 10% nitrogen, 6% phosphoric acid, and 4% potash. Many grades of complete fertilizer are available.

Most complete fertilizers are composed of simple chemicals quickly absorbed by plants. These inorganic fertilizers are the least expensive, but they require some care for safe application during the growing season. Natural organic fertilizer (such as activated sludge, processed tankage, and vegetable meals) release their nutrients somewhat more slowly. They are more expensive but they will not burn growing grass even if they are applied carelessly. Otherwise, the effect of the two types of fertilizer is similar, especially where clippings are left on the lawn.

Barnyard manure is not a good lawn fertilizer, for it is relatively low in nutrients and usually contains large numbers of weed seeds. Weed-free fertilizers are to be preferred, even when manure can be had without cost. Commercially dried manures are relatively expensive for the benefits received.

Liquid fertilizers may be more convenient to apply than dry fertilizers under certain circumstances. This is their only advantage over

Dry fertilizers, which can be applied by hand, are best applied to the lawn with a spreader.

Photograph courtesy of O M Scott & Sons

equivalent amounts of the more economical dry fertilizers.

Fertilizing Established Turf

If yours is an average lawn in good condition, fertilize it in early fall. If your soil is poor, repeat the application in early spring. Even on good soils this second application will do no harm.

Rates To Use

The fertilizer recommendations given here are in terms of pounds of 5-10-5 or its equivalent, only because 5-10-5 is widely available at competitive prices and often is at hand for other purposes. Some other complete fertilizer may be more economical for you, depend-

ing upon your local market conditions; or perhaps you will choose a natural organic fertilizer or a combination organic-inorganic fertilizer because it is safer to apply to growing grass and stimulates the grass somewhat more gradually. So far as the benefit to the grass is concerned, any of the many common grades of complete fertilizer will be satisfactory so long as you use it at the proper rate.

To determine the proper rate for a single application of any fertilizer, consider only the first figure (nitrogen) of the grade you have chosen. Then find the rate for 1,000 square feet as listed in the table.

How To Apply

Apply fertilizers evenly, or your lawn will have dark and light streaks. A mechanical spreader is best for this work. You may apply a natural organic fertilizer at any season without danger of burning your grass. Inorganic fertilizers will not burn if you spread them in early spring before growth starts. Inorganic fertilizers are entirely practical during the growing season, also, but take these precautions against burning: be especially careful about even distribution; spread fertilizer only when the grass is completely dry; and sprinkle the lawn thoroughly to wash the fertilizer from the grass blades to the ground.

Amount of Fertilizer To Use

If the first figure of the grade is	For 1,000 square feet of area	
	of established lawn	of new seed-bed or lawn to be renovated
	Pounds	Pounds
4	25	50
5	20	40
6	17	33
7	14	28
8	12½	25
9	11	22
10	10	20

How To Use Liquid Fertilizers

If you want to grow big plants fast, you can't beat the new soluble fertilizers. Because they are liquid, they get to the plant in less time and produce results more quickly. You can sprinkle them right onto the leaves—dry fertilizer would "burn" if applied that way—for fastest action, or you can pour them on the ground around the plant. They work

fine on everything from African violet house plants to lawns and shade trees.

Besides making your garden grow faster, liquid fertilizers are a lot more convenient to use. You can save work by combining fertilizing with other spraying or sprinkling chores. Lawns and many flowers can get their feedings as part of a regular watering.

If you spray fruit trees with DDT, you can mix fertilizer into the insecticide solution and feed the tree while you kill the bugs.

Several brands of ready-to-dissolve fertilizers are on the market, but you can reduce the cost by mixing your own. You need three chemicals: potassium nitrate (saltpeter), monoammonium phosphate and urea. All three of these chemicals supply nitrogen, while the ammonium phosphate also supplies phos-

Three Formulas for Mixing Soluble Plant Foods

	1-lb. batch	10-lb. batch
Balanced fertilizer		
(Approx. analysis, 20-20-20		
Potassium nitrate	7 oz. (¾ cup)	4¼ lb. (7½ cups)
Urea	4 oz. (⅔ cup)	2½ lb. (7 cups)
Monoammonium phosphate	5 oz. (⅔ cup)	3¼ lb. (6½ cups)
High-nitrogen fertilizer		
(Approx. analysis, 24-17-16)		
Potassium nitrate	5½ oz. (⅝ cup)	3½ lb. (6⅛ cups)
Urea	6 oz. (1 cup)	3¾ lb. (10¼ cups)
Monoammonium phosphate	4½ oz. (⅝ cup)	2¾ lb. (5½ cups)
High-phosphorus fertilizer		
(Approx. analysis, 19-23-17)		
Potassium nitrate	6 oz. (⅔ cup)	3¾ lb. (6½ cups)
Urea	4 oz. (⅔ cup)	2½ lb. (7 cups)
Monoammonium phosphate	6 oz. (¾ cup)	3¾ lb. (7½ cups)

Note: The analysis figures indicate approximate percentages of nitrogen, phosphorus and potassium, respectively, in the fertilizer mix. To mix, use the equivalent volume of each ingredient if you don't have a scale.

---

phorus and the potassium nitrate gives potassium.

You can buy these chemicals from laboratory- or chemical-supply houses in most cities. Ask for "technical" or "fertilizer" grades which are cheaper.

How To Mix

Different plants require different proportions of the three plant-food elements—leafy plants need lots of nitrogen, root crops don't. Formulas for three common mixtures are given in an accompanying table (the numbers indicate the percentages of nitrogen, phosphoric oxide and potassium oxide, respectively). Other ratios are easily obtained. Equal `volumes will give a 21-21-18 fertilizer, while equal weights make a 23-20-15 fertilizer. If you have no scale for weights, measure by volume (see table).

The actual mixing is best done by dumping the dry chemicals onto newspaper and turning the stuff over and over with your hands. It must be completely and evenly mixed because you will later want to scoop out a spoonful or cupful of properly proportioned fertilizer. Another way is to dissolve the dry chemicals—unmixed—into a concentrated solution.

How To Apply

You have to dissolve the dry mix in water before using. It is concentrated and will burn your plants if applied dry.

The standard-strength solution

Sprinkle, pour or spray it—you can choose among three ways of applying liquid fertilizer. When it is sprinkled, leaves absorb some. Pour solution (center) into the ground when transplanting. The hose attachment (right) feeds a lawn while it is being watered.

To feed a tree, punch holes in the ground in the pattern shown at right, pour in liquid fertilizer and then fill the holes with soil.

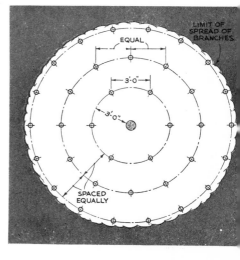

takes ⅛ pound (¼ cup) of mixed fertilizer to a 12-quart pail of water. For larger or smaller amounts of the standard-strength solution, use these proportions: one teaspoon to one quart of water; one heaping table-spoon to a gallon; ¼ pound (½ cup) to six gallons; one pound (two cups) to 25 gallons.

For garden plants—flowers, vegetables and shrubs—sprinkle the standard-strength solution directly onto the leaves from a watering can, applying it about every two weeks. Large garden areas can be treated with one pound of the fertilizer (25 gallons of solution) per 1,000 square feet. On potted plants and window boxes, substitute the ferti-lizer solution for the regular water-ing once every two weeks.

Some house plants, such as Afri-can violets and gloxinias, are too delicate for leaf-feeding. Instead, apply a half-strength solution to the soil around the plant every two weeks in place of the regular water-ing.

For transplanting, use a double-strength solution, but do not apply it directly to the plants. Use it to satu-rate the soil around the roots. Fol-low with supplemental leaf-feedings of standard-strength solution every two weeks or so if shrubs look sickly after they have been transplanted.

Trees can be fed with standard-strength solution shortly after they have leafed out. Pour the solution— a gallon or more, depending on the size of the tree—into holes poked in the ground. The holes should be an inch or two in diameter, about 12 inches deep, and spaced two or three feet apart from the trunk to the outermost spread of the branches. After the fertilizer has soaked in, fill the holes back up with earth.

Lawns are almost shamefully easy to feed with liquid fertilizer— attachments for your garden hose let you fertilize and water at the same time. One type of attachment is an "aspirator," a long tube that sucks fertilizer solution from a pail and mixes it with the sprinkling water. Another type works much the same way but takes the fertilizer solution from a small jar connected to a nozzle that you fit to the end of your hose.

Since the fertilizer is greatly di-luted when mixed with sprinkling water, you can use an extra-strong solution: one pound of dry mixture to 10 or 12 quarts of water. This is too concentrated to be applied di-rectly to the lawn and should be used only with a hose attachment.

Use about one pound of ferti-lizer for each 2,000 square feet of lawn, applying it every two or three weeks. New lawns will require more feeding—say once a week—to get started. In hot, dry weather ferti-lize less often.

Fiber Rug, Painting

To freshen up the color of a fiber rug if it has faded, and to add longer wear, it may be painted with a canvas or awning paint. First make sure the rug is thoroughly clean, on the underside as well as the top. As the paint might seep through, especially if the rug has a loose weave, it is wise to put a waterproof sheeting or some layers of newspaper under the rug before you start painting.

Use a stiff paint brush, cover about a square foot area at a time, and see that the paint gets into all the crevices in the woven rug. Be sure the rug is completely dry before it is walked upon.

- -

Fiberboard

See *Walls*.

- -

File Card

This is a small wire brush used to clean metal filings which fill in the grooves of a file. The small wire bristles do an efficient cleaning job when the brush is worked either in the direction of the file grooves or at right angles to it.

A file card is used to clean files.

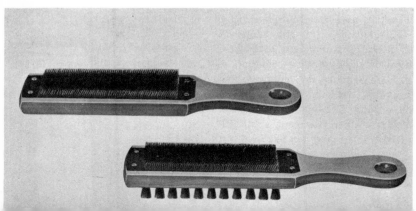

Files

Files and rasps have three distinguishing features:

(1) Their length, which is always measured exclusive of the tang.

(2) Their kind (or name), which has reference to the shape or style.

(3) Their cut, which has reference to both the character and the relative degrees of coarseness of the teeth.

Length—The length of the file is the distance between its heel (or part of the file where the tang begins) and the point (or end opposite). The tang (or portion of the file prepared for the reception of the handle) is never included in the length. In general, the length of files bears no fixed proportion to either their width or their thickness, even though the files be of the same kind.

Kind—By kind is meant the various shapes or styles of files, as distinguished by such technical names as Flat, Mill, Half Round, etc. These are divided, from the form of their cross-sections, into three general geometrical classes: Quadrangular, Circular and Triangular. From them are derived, further, odd and irregular forms or cross-sections which are classified as Miscellaneous. These sections, in turn, are sub-divided, according to their

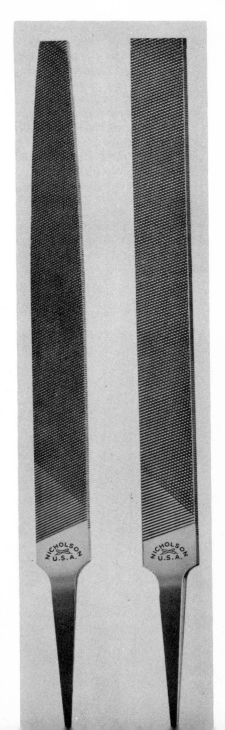

Photographs courtesy of Nicholson File Co.

general contour or outline, into *taper* and *blunt*.

• *Taper* designates a file, the point of which is more or less reduced in size (both width and thickness) by a gradually narrowing section extending from one-half to two-thirds the length of the file, from the point.

• *Blunt* designates a file that preserves its *sectional size throughout,* from point to tang.

Cut—The cut of files is divided, with reference to the character of the teeth, into single, double, rasp and curved; and with reference to the coarseness of the teeth, into coarse bastard, second and smooth cuts.

Single cut files are usually used with a light pressure to produce a smooth surface finish, or a keen edge on a knife, shears, saw-tooth or other cuttting implement.

Double cut files are usually used, under heavier pressure, for fast metal removal and where a rougher finish is permissible.

Rasp cut is a series of individual teeth produced by a sharp, narrow, punch-like cutting chisel. It is an extremely rought cut and is used principally on wood, leather, aluminum, lead, and similarly soft substances for fast removal of material.

Photographs courtesy of Nicholson File Co.

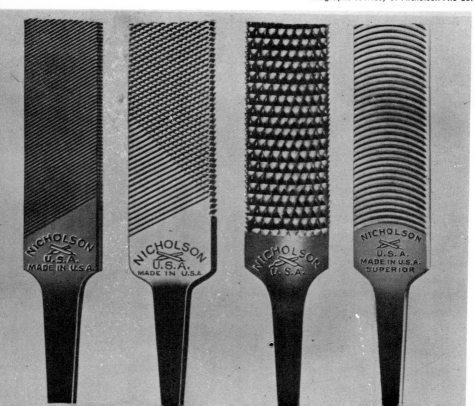

Mill Files

Mill files are so named because they are widely used for sharpening mill or circular saws. These files are also useful for sharpening large crosscut saws and mowing-machine knives; for lathe work, drawfiling; for working on compositions of brass and bronze; and for smooth-finish filing in general.

Mill files are single cut and are tapered slightly in width and thickness for about a third of their length. Usually made with two square edges, with cuts thereon as well as on sides. Also made with one and two round edges—to prevent causing sharp corners or edges in the gullets of crosscut saws. The Mill Blunt is likewise used for crosscut saws (and often for bucksaws) as well as for general filing.

The accompanying illustration shows a typical range of coarseness of tapered and blunt mill files. These also apply approximately to the triangular and other shapes of saw files.

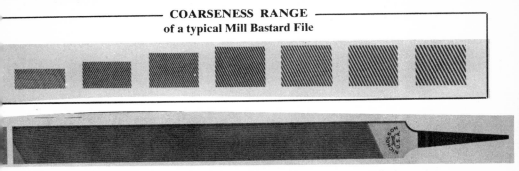

COARSENESS RANGE
of a typical Mill Bastard File

Mill File (Tapered) with square edges. Also made with one or two round edges for filing the gullets between saw teeth.

Mill File (Blunt) or Special Crosscut with square edges.

Triangular Saw Files (Tapered) are made for filing all types of saws with teeth of 60° angle. Various thicknesses; taper, extra slim taper, double extra slim taper.

Photographs courtesy of Nicholson File Co.

Triangular Saw Files (Blunt) are frequently preferred by carpenters and other expert filers of 60° hand-saws. Various thicknesses. Cantsaw File is used for sharpening saws with less than 60 angle teeth—for many types of circulars and also for crosscuts with "M" teeth.

Crosscut File is used for sharpening a great variety of crosscut saws. Rounded back is used to deepen gullets of saw teeth; sides for filing teeth themselves.

Pruning Saw File is specially designed for use on needle point pruning saws. Single cut on edges and both faces of one side; other side uncut.

Rasp

The rasp cut differs from both the single and double cuts of files in the respect that the teeth are individually formed and disconnected from each other. In the wood rasps the curved side is similar to that of the half round file, but in the cabi-

net and the patternmakers' rasps, the radius is larger. Rasps are also made in flat and round shapes.

Rasps have long been an important tool of cabinetmakers and handymen working on relatively soft substances requiring the fast removal of material.

Wood rasps are used by wood workers, wheelwrights and plumbers. Made in flat, half round and round shapes.

Cabinet rasps, used by cabinetmakers and woodworkers, are half round and round, and in same style of cut as wood rasps, but with relatively smaller degrees of coarseness.

Horse rasps come in plain and tanged types and flat section. Plain horse rasps are double ended; all have rasp teeth on one side and file teeth on the other.

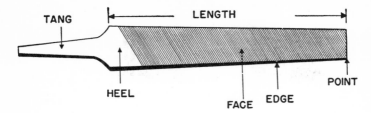

Use the Right File

Actually there are thousands of kinds, cuts and sizes of files. That is because there are thousands of different filing jobs, each of which can be done better by using the right file for the job.

Therein lies the first rule on how to get the most out of files. The right file enables the job to be done properly, whereas the wrong one does not—and may, in fact, ruin the work.

The right file saves time, because it performs correctly, and usually faster, on the kind of metal or work for which it is designed.

The right file permits a greater number of efficient filing strokes—per file and per file cost. Sum up all these advantages and they represent a big item of savings in a day's filing and production costs.

Many factors enter into the selection of the right file for the job. In general, it may be said that different files are required:

(1) to file a flat or convex surface

(2) to file a curved or concave surface

(3) to file an edge

(4) to file a notch, a slot, or a square or round hole.

But these factors can immediately become complicated by:

(1) the kind of metal or other material to be filed

(2) the kind, shape and hardness of the object or part to be filed

(3) the location, size and character of the surface, edge, notch, slot, or hole to be filed

(4) the amount of metal to be removed—and the practical time permitted for removing it

(5) the degree of smoothness or accuracy required.

All these conditions have a bearing on the kind, size and cut of file which will best attain a particular objective. Calculate the number of possible combinations of such conditions, and selecting exactly the right file for any combination thereof would seem to be a sizable task for any one person.

Experience is a good guide—but a slow teacher. But with proper information, no file user need ever be far off the track to the right file

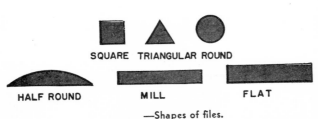

—Shapes of files.

File Terminology

Back—The convex side of Half Round, Cabinet, Pitsaw, and other files of similar cross-section.

Bastard Cut—File coarseness between "Coarse" and "Second Cut."

Bellied—Used to describe a file having a fullness in the middle.

Blank—A file in any process of manufacture before being cut.

Blunt—Used to describe a file with parallel edges and sides; i.e., one which preserves its sectional size throughout from point to tang.

Broach—Jewelers' steel-wire files of many gages.

Cabinet (File or Rasp)—Used by cabinetmakers and woodworkers.

Coarse Cut—Coarsest of all cuts.

Crosscut — A file for sharpening crosscut saws.

Curved Cut—File teeth which are made in curved contour across the file blank.

Cut—The character of a file's teeth with respect to coarseness (Coarse, Bastard, Second, Smooth) or their type (single, double, rasp, curved, special).

Dead Smooth Cut—The finest of the standard cuts of regular files.

Double Cut—A file tooth arrangement formed by two series of cuts—the overcut, followed, at an angle, by the upcut.

Double Ender—A saw file cut from the points toward the middle—for filing from either end.

Filing Block—A piece of hard, close-grained wood having grooves of varying sizes upon one or more of its sides. Used for holding small rods, pins, etc., in the jaws of the vise while being filed. Also a block of zinc, copper or other fairly soft metal, as one of a pair of protectors placed between the vise jaws to prevent work from becoming damaged while being held for filing.

Float—sometimes used to refer to the coarser grades of single-cut files when cut for very soft metals (like lead) or for wood.

Handsaw—A triangular file (see *Slim Taper*) for sharpening handsaws.

Hopped—A term used among file makers to represent a very wide skip of spacing between file teeth.

Knife — A file whose cross-section resembles the blade of a knife—thick at one edge, thin or sharp at the other.

Mill—A single-cut (tapered or blunt) file which acquired its name from its early use in filing mill or circular saws.

Needle—Files of many shapes, used by tool and die makers, and also by watch and clock makers.

Overcut—The first series

of teeth put on a double-cut file.

Point—The front end of a file.

Rasp Cut—A file tooth arrangement under which teeth are individually formed, one by one, by means of a narrow, punchlike chisel.

Re-cut—A worn-out file which has been re-cut and re-hardened after annealing (softening) and grinding off the old teeth. (Similar to re-grooving as applied to automobile tires.)

Safe Edge (or *Side*)—Used to denote that a file has one or more of its edges or sides smooth or uncut, so that it may be presented to the work without injury to that portion or surface which does not require filing.

Scraping—As applied to machine shops, the process of removing an exceedingly small portion of the wearing surfaces of machinery by means of scrapers, in order to bring such surfaces to a precision fit or finish not attainable by ordinary filing means.

Screw Head—A file for clearing out the slots in the heads of screws.

Second Cut—File coarseness between *Bastard* and *Smooth*.

Section (or *Cross-section*)—The end view of a file if cut off squarely at the greatest width and thickness from its tang.

Set—To blunt the sharp edges or corners of file blanks before and after the overcut is made, in order to prevent weakness and breakage of the teeth along such edges or corners when file is put to use.

Single Cut—A file tooth arrangement formed by a single series of cuts.

Slim Taper—Triangular file, slenderer than the regular *Taper,* used mainly for hand-saw sharpening. Also *Extra Slim Taper* and *Double Extra Slim Taper.*

Smooth Cut—A file cut of less coarseness than *Second Cut.*

Swiss Pattern—A large series of files of various shapes and a range of cuts of their own, designed principally for precision work in the jewelry, die-making, silversmithing, clock-making, watch-making and other industries.

Taper—Used to denote the shape of a file, as distinguished from the *Blunt.* Custom has also established it as a short name for the Triangular Handsaw File. Graded variations are *Slim Taper, Extra Slim Taper,* and *Double Extra Slim Taper.*

Upcut—The series of teeth superimposed on the overcut, and at an angle to it, on a double-cut file.

Warding—A file named after its original or most common use, filing ward notches on keys and locks.

WRONG   **RIGHT**

for the job. This, at any rate, is true as to the kind or type of file for the object and metal or other material to be filed. The filer's own survey of the conditions will help further to determine the right size and cut of file.

Use the Right Filing Method

There are three fundamental ways in which a file can be put to work:

1. Straight filing, which consist of pushing the file lengthwise—straight ahead or slightly diagonally—across the work (since all files, with the exception of a few machine operated files, are designed primarily to cut on the forward stroke).

2. Drawfiling, which consists of grasping the file at each end and pushing and drawing it across the work.

3. Lathe filing, which consists of stroking the file against work revolved in a lathe.

Place Work at Proper Height for Filing

Most work to be filed should be held in a vise. For general filing, the vise should be about elbow height. If a great deal of heavy filing is to be done, it is well to have the work lower. If the work is of a fine or delicate nature, it should be raised near to the eye level.

For work which is apt to become damaged by pressure when held in a vise, it is well to provide a pair of protectors—pieces of zinc, copper, or other fairly soft metal for placing between the jaws and the work to be held. For holding varying sizes of round pieces—such as small rods and pins—a block of hard, close-grained wood with a series of varying-sized grooves is sometimes used where a lot of filing of such pieces required.

Grasping the File

With files intended for operation with both hands, one of the

most generally accepted ways of grasping the handle is to allow its end to fit into and bring up against the fleshy part of the palm below the joint of the little finger—with the thumb lying parallel along the top of the handle and the fingers pointing upward toward the operator's face.

The point of the file is usually grasped by the thumb and the first two fingers of the other hand. The hand may then be held so as to bring the thumb, as its ball presses up on the top of the file, in line with the handle when heavy strokes are required.

When a light stroke is wanted and the pressure demanded becomes less, the thumb and fingers of the point-holding hand may change their direction until the thumb lies at right angle, or nearly so, with the length of the file—the positions changing more or less as may be needed to increase the downward pressure.

In holding the file with one hand, as in filing pins, dies and edged tools not held in a vise, the forefinger—instead of the thumb—is generally placed on top and as nearly as possible in the direction of its length.

"Carrying" the File

The most natural movement of the hands and arms is to "carry" (stroke) the file across the work in curved lines. This tends toward a rocking motion and, consequently, produces a convex surface where a level surface is desired.

For the usual flat filing, the operator should aim to carry the file

Use protective jaws on vise to protect the work to be filed.

Drawfiling consists of grasping the file firmly at both ends and alternately pushing and pulling it sidewise across the work.

Photograph courtesy of Nicholson File Co.

forward on an almost straight line—changing its course enough to prevent "grooving."

Keep the File Cutting

One of the quickest ways to ruin a good file is to use too much pressure—or too little—on the forward stroke. Different materials, of course, require different touches; but, in general, just enough pressure should be applied to keep the file cutting at all times. If allowed to slide over the harder metals, the teeth of the file rapidly become dull; and if they are "overloaded" by too much pressure, they are likely to chip or clog.

On the reverse stroke it is best to lift the file clear off the work, ex-

Brass is a difficult metal to file and you should use a special file for the job.

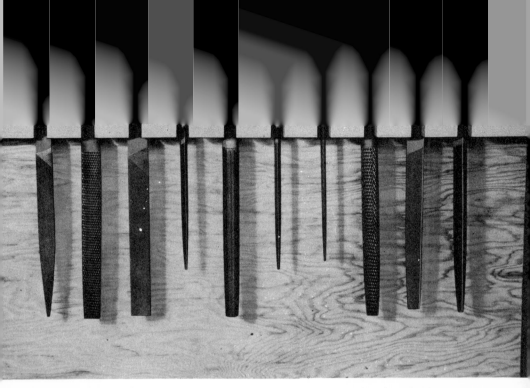

Files should never be stacked against each other. Keep them separate—standing with their tangs in a row of holes or hung on a rack by their handles as shown.

Photograph courtesy of Nicholson File Co.

cept on very soft metals. Even then the pressure should be very light— never more than the weight of the file itself.

Filing Aluminum

Because aluminum is a soft, ductile and malleable metal, it is difficult to file with ordinary files because the file teeth soon become clogged—even under moderate pressure.

The filing of aluminum can be divided into three general classifications: (1) filing the roughness from aluminum castings; (2) filing sheet and bar aluminum; (3) filing aluminum alloys.

For fast, rough metal removal, a special aluminum rasp is often used. But for cutting aluminum rap-

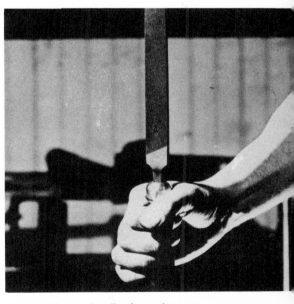

To set a file in a handle, do not hammer the file! Set end into handle and pound on bench.

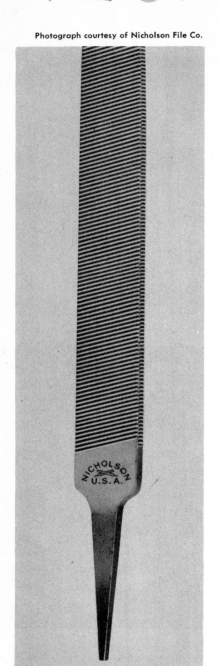

idly, yet leaving a good finish, the aluminum "Type A" file is a recent file-manufacturing development. Its special tooth construction is very effective in eliminating clogging. The upcut is deep with an "open-throat"; the overcut fine, producing small scallops on the upcut which break up the filings, allow the file to clear itself, overcome chatter and prevent taking too large a bite.

By using this file with a shearing stroke toward the left, a good finish can easily be obtained.

Filing Brass

With a structure all its own, brass is a difficult metal to file. While softer than steel, brass is tough and ductile. These characteristics demand file teeth that are sturdy, very sharp, and cut at an angle that prevents "grooving" and running the file off the work. Still more important, the file must not clog.

In addition to a short upcut angle, the brass file (like the aluminum "Type A") has a fine, long-angle overcut — producing small scallops which break up the filings and enable the file to clear itself of chips. With a little pressure, the sharp, high-cut teeth bite deep; with less pressure, their short upcut angle produces a smoothing effect.

Filing Lead

Extra-soft metals, such as lead, babbitt and pure copper, present filing conditions distinct from any others herein before described. The metal removal in normal filing jobs is virtually a "shaving" or "floating" principle, as the design of this lead

Clean your files immediately after you've finished working—don't put them away dirty!

float file indicates. Its course, short-angle single-cut teeth are virtually a series of stubby blades which shear away the metal rapidly under ordinary pressure. Light pressure produces the smooth effect.

Lead float files are used largely on lead pipe fittting, solder joints and on soft bearings, shims and molded parts.

The Care of Files

File life is greatly shortened by improper care as well as by improper use—and improper selection. Files should never be thrown into a drawer or tool box containing other tools or objects. They should never be laid on top of or stacked against each other. Such treatment ruins the cutting edges of their teeth. Keep them separate—standing with their tangs in a row of holes or hung on a rack by their handles. Keep them in a dry place so rust will not corrode their teeth.

It is also of great importance to keep files clean of filings or chips, which often collect between the teeth during use. After every few strokes the good mechanic taps the end of the file on the bench to loosen these chips. And he always has on hand a file card or brush. The teeth of the file should be brushed frequently with this type of cleaner, and always before putting the file away. Oil or grease on file should be removed with chalk.

Fillers

See *Crack Fillers*.

Fillister

This term is used to describe a special type of head used on screws and bolts. It is cylindrical with a slot for a screwdriver.

Fillister head bolt.

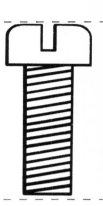

Finger Joint

Technically, a joint with five tongues or fingers on each piece often used on table brackets. The fingers interlock to form the joint.

It is described completely in the section on *Dovetail Joint*.

A modified finger joint—several tongues or fingers are used in place of the normal five.

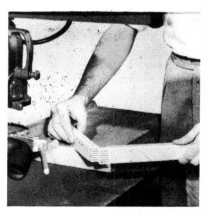

Photograph courtesy of DeWalt, Inc.

Fire Protection

Any discussion of protection against fire should start with the best way of preventing a fire from getting started. The following sug-gestions are intended as a general guide for the prevention of fire in the home:

1. Keep matches out of the reach of young children. Teach children the dangers of playing with fire.

2. Do not throw away cigars, cigarettes, and matches without first

making sure they are extinguished.

3. Do not allow accumulations of combustible waste materials in or near the house. Without them fires from carelessly discarded materials would be less frequent.

4. Keep chimneys and stove-pipes clean with all joints and connections tight. Provide separate metal cans for ashes and rubbish. Never mix the two.

5. Place substantial fire-resist-ant guards in front of all woodwork close to sources of heat.

6. Keep greasy and oily rags in tightly closed, preferably metal, containers provided for the purpose.

7. Avoid the filling of lighted kerosene and gasoline lamps. Avoid the use of kerosene to start fires in stoves, etc.

8. Do not use gasoline, naptha, or benzine for cleaning. Choose some of the safer solutions now obtainable, and use these, in any considerable quantity, only out-of-doors and during the day.

9. Keep all open flames away from gas leaks. Explosive mixtures of gas and air are quickly formed in enclosed places, and they only need a lighted match or a spark to cause disastrous results.

10. Avoid hanging curtains and other draperies near gas jets or other open flames. Remember that the draft from nearby windows may cause fires to spread and make them difficult to extinguish.

11. Use decorative wax candles with caution. Each year some deaths of children and adults are due to placing candles on Christmas

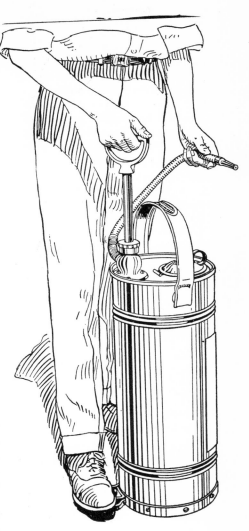

WATER AND ANTI-FREEZE SOLUTION
Place foot on the foot rest at bottom of tank. The pump stroke need not be more than 6″ or 8″ in length. Direct stream at base of flames. Follow flames and work around fire if possible.

trees or using them near flammable materials.

12. Avoid placing articles made of celluloid, pyralin, xylonite, fiberoid, viscoloid, and similar materials, such as combs, toilet articles, etc., upon or near sources of heat, as they are very likely to catch afire. Also remember that articles of these materials should not be worn in the hair as they may readily catch fire and seriously burn the wearer.

13. Permit only experienced persons to install or repair electrical fittings and appliances.

14. Never leave unattended lighted heating or cooking appliances, particularly kitchen ranges and stoves, flatirons, toasters, waffle irons or other equipment of a similar nature.

15. Make sure that when you burn refuse that you do so out-of-doors in a metal container well away from any building. Also be sure that when you leave you have extinguished all smoldering embers.

Fire Extinguishers

Fire-fighting equipment for the ordinary dwelling will usually be limited, by practical considerations, to portable hand apparatus. Principal reliance for extinguishing fires which have gained any appreciable headway must, of course, be placed on outside aid. When a fire occurs, the fire department, if one is available, should always be summoned without delay.

It is, however, true that most household fires start from a small beginning and can in the majority of cases be readily extinguished before they have gained headway and

before any considerable damage has been done or risk of personal injury has developed, if the proper means is right at hand and can be promptly applied. The immediate application of a little water or the use of blankets may readily extinguish a small

CARBON DIOXIDE
The extinguisher is removed by grasping the handle with the left hand. It should be carried to the fire by means of the handle and the valve opened by turning counter-clockwise to release the gas.

blaze which might later have developed into a disastrous blaze. A partially filled pail of water may often be used effectively. A broom can be used to apply the water in a finely divided state, which is often satisfactory for extinguishing a fire, and also may be used to bring within reach burning draperies or to beat out a small blaze. An ordinary garden hose with nozzle, kept where it can be quickly attached to a water faucet, is also an effective fire-extinguishing device for the area over which its length will permit its application. But water should not be used to combat oil, grease, or electrical fires.

Portable Extinguishers

There are on the market portable hand extinguishers which are specially designed for first-aid firefighting, the effectiveness of which

has been demonstrated by years of experience. They are much more effective than improvised means, and have the added advantage that, since they are intended for one purpose only, they can be kept in assigned places where they will be available when needed. It is, therefore, distinctly worthwhile to have one or more good portable fire extinguishers in every household.

In providing first-aid fire-fighting devices for the protection of the household, it is of prime importance that the devices purchased be reliable, and designed and constructed in accordance with recognized standards with regard to safety and performance, such as are defined in Federal specifications or those set up by the Underwriters' Laborato-

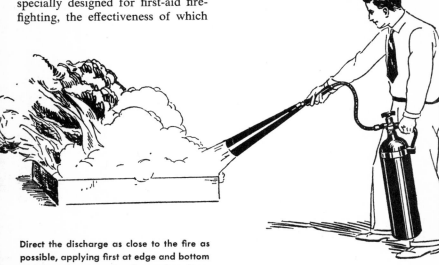

Direct the discharge as close to the fire as possible, applying first at edge and bottom of fire and progressing forward and upward, moving discharge horn slowly from side to side. Continue discharge even after the fire has been extinguished to cool liquid and prevent possible reflash.

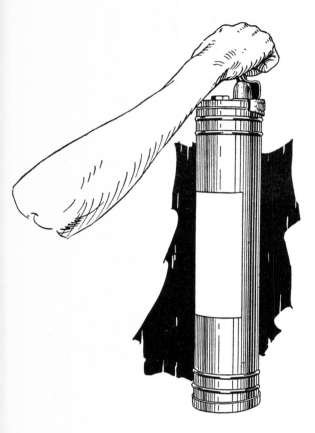

VAPORIZING LIQUID
Remove extinguisher from wall bracket
by grasping handle and pulling outward.

ries, or other recognized authorities. Since it is usually not feasible for the householder to make adequate examination and tests, he will have to rely on the results of tests and approval made by others, as evidenced by inspection labels, certifications, or other forms of guaranty.

In the case of Underwriters' Laboratories each extinguisher of a type which has been approved is marked with a distinctive inspection label. This label is usually in the form of a small brass plate attached to the extinguisher near the name plate or forming a part of the name plate itself. This does not mean that all fire-fighting devices which do not bear the Underwriters' Laboratories label are improperly designed and constructed, but that the presence of this label does assure the purchaser that a given extinguisher has been built in accordance with recognized standards.

Portable fire extinguishers are suitable for combating three classes of incipient fires in the home. According to the National Board of Fire Underwriters, those classes of fires are as follows:

(a) Class "A" fires—in ordinary combustible materials (such as wood, paper, textiles, rubbish, etc.) where the quenching and cooling effects of quantities of water or solutions containing large percentages of water is of first importance.

(b) Class "B" fires—in flammable liquids, greases, etc., where a blanketing effect is essential.

(c) Class "C" fires—in electrical equipment where the use of a nonconducting extinguishing agent is of first importance. The following table gives various types of available fire extinguishers, the kinds of fires they can be used on, and how they are started and how far they will operate.

There has been a good deal of controversy about the toxic effect of the carbon tetrachloride used in the vaporizing liquid type of hand fire extinguishers. It is recognized that carbon tetrachloride vapor has an

| SODA ACID | PUMP | GAS CARTRIDGE | FOAM |

Fire Extinguisher Facts

TYPE	KINDS OF FIRE	HOW TO START	DISCHARGE
Soda Acid	Class A	Turn over	
Water Pump	Class A	Pump by hand	For 2½ gal. size
Gas Cartridge	Class A and small Class B	Turn over and pump	30'–40' 50–55 sec.
Foam	Class A and Class B	Turn over	
Carbon Dioxide	Class B	Pull pin and open valve	6'–8', about 42 sec. (15-lb. size)
	and		
Vaporizing Liquid	Class C	Turn handle, pump by hand	20'–30' 45 sec. (1-qt. size)
Dry Chemical	and sometimes Class A	Pull pin and open valve (or press lever), then squeeze nozzle valve	About 14' 22–25 sec. (30-lb. size)

Note: Do not use water-base extinguishers on electrical fires.

| CARBON DIOXIDE | VAPORIZING LIQUID | DRY CHEMICAL |

anaesthetic effect and if subjected to high temperatures decomposes to some extent, forming toxic gases, including hydrochloric acid and phosgene. The standards of the National Board of Fire Underwriters

contain the following caution:

"In using extinguishers of this type, especially in unventilated spaces, such as small rooms, closets, or confined spaces, operators and others should take precautions to avoid the effects which may be caused by breathing the vapors or gases liberated or produced."

Location of Fire Extinguishers

Since no one type of extinguisher is equally effective against all types of fires, it is best to use one which is effective against oil, grease, and electrical fires, and partially effective against rubbish, wood and paper fires. These include carbon

On way to fire, unlock handle by turning. If device is of air pump type, hold finger over nozzle and pump up pressure.

Direct stream at base of flames and work around fire rapidly. If fire is in a container or tank, direct stream against inside opposite wall above level of burning liquid.

tance, provide separate extinguishers for the different areas.

In the garage, if there is a water faucet nearby, have a 25-foot length of garden hose ready for immediate use. Buckets of sand should also be kept here for use against small spill fires.

Fire Alarms

A small home fire alarm can give the first warning of a fire. Since a large proportion of all fires start in the basement, this would be a good

Vaporizing Liquid (carbon tetrachloride)—to be used against Class B (oil, grease, paint, gasoline) and Class C (electrical) and has some effect on Class A (wood, paper and textiles). This pressurized can is small enough to be kept easily available in even the smallest apartment.

Water Pump Tank—to be used against Class A fires (rubbish, paper, and wood, etc.) To prevent freezing and to make sure that the extinguisher will work at temperature as low as 40° below 0, mix antifreeze into the water.

dioxide, vaporizing liquid, and dry chemical. However, in a large house, for specific locations, other types should be included.

In the basement, add a water pump tank since this is the area where rubbish and papers are usually collected and become a fire hazard. Also keep two buckets of clean sand, one near the furnace and one near the entrance to the basement for use against small spill fires of flammable liquid.

In the kitchen, in an easily available place, have one of the three types recommended for general use, but be sure it is light enough for a woman to handle easily. Here the dangers are rubber, grease and electrical fires.

In a two-story or split-level house, or one that rambles a dis-

Photograph courtesy of
Richmond-Electron Corp.

place to install one. Of course, other parts of the house can be similarly protected.

There are three types of alarms: the manual wind-up, battery operated, and electrically operated. The manual wind-up is least subject to failure. The electrically operated alarm will not work during power failures or electrical failures on the line it is wired on. For one model, its effective area can be extended by simply adding more wire with fire sensitive elements.

This automatic unit operates on a thermostatic principle; power is supplied by two flashlight batteries. If heat or flame reach a dangerous level, the alarm sounds a warning.

What To Do in Case of Fire

Each member of a household should understand how to send in a fire alarm to the fire department. In many cities the fire alarm may be sent in by telephone or from a street fire-alarm box. Some cities require that the alarm be sent in by telephone, and others require that a fire-alarm box be used. Seconds count at the time of a fire, so the proper method should be definitely known, and used.

If sending in a fire alarm by telephone is required or permitted, the telephone number of the fire department should occupy a conspicuous and permanent place at each telephone or telephone extension in the home. In giving information about a fire over the telephone, one should carefully consider what he is doing. What the fire department wants and should know is (a) the number of the house, (b) the name of the street or road, (c) the nearest street corner, and (d) the number of the telephone from which the call is made. A few seconds lost in giving this information are not wasted.

If sending a fire alarm from a fire-alarm box is required or permitted, the location and method of use of the nearest fire-alarm box should be definitely known. Also, if such a method is employed, someone should be stationed in the vicinity of the fire-alarm box or along the route of the responding fire department company to direct it to the fire.

Saving the lives of the occupants of a building on fire should receive first consideration. Many lives have been lost in attempts to put out fires or to save personal belongings.

In case of fire:

1. Collect your thoughts. Keep

your mind on what you are doing. Act quickly.

2. Unless you are very sure that you can handle the fire without help, notify the fire department or have someone else do this. Many have been sure until too late.

3. Summon help if anyone is within calling distance.

4. If the blaze is small and you think you can put it out by devices which are available, either

(a) use a suitable fire extinguisher, or

(b) use a woolen blanket or rug to smother the fire. Keep the air from the fire. Or

(c) throw water from a garden hose on the fire if such a hose is available. If it is not, throw water from a pail, using a dipper or a broom. Do not use water on an oil or grease fire; use sand or earth from flower pots. Water, especially in small amounts, will cause spattering of burning grease.

(d) Beat down any draperies, curtains, or light materials causing the blaze, using a wet broom or a long pole. Using the bare hands may result in serious burns.

5. Tie a wet towel or any other material (preferably of wool) over the mouth and nose if you are fighting the fire and are exposed to smoke or flames. More people lose their lives by suffocation than through burning.

6. Place yourself so that you can retreat in the direction of a safe exit without passing through the burning area. Unless you can do something worthwhile, get out of the building.

7. If necessary to go through a room full of smoke, keep close to the floor and crawl on the hands and knees, having covered the mouth and nose with a wet cloth. The drafts and currents cause the smoke to rise and the air nearest the floor is usually the purest.

8. If you have to retreat and all occupants are out of the building or burning portion thereof, cut off the draft by closing doors and windows.

Carbon Dioxide—to be used for Class B fires (oil, gasoline, paint, grease) and Class C (live electrical equipment). These extinguishers also have some effect on Class A fires (wood, paper, textiles, etc.) This type of extinguisher smothers the fire by cutting off the oxygen.

9. Do not jump from a high window unless into a life net. To use a rope or life line, twist the rope or life line around one leg and, holding the feet together, regulate the speed of descent. Otherwise the hands may be painfully injured by friction with the rope or life line, especially if the height is great. Sheets and other articles of bedding will often provide a life line if knots are carefully made so that they will not slip. An extra loop in the knot may avoid this danger. Tie the rope or life line to a bed or other article of furniture which will not pull through the window. The rope or life line should not be thrown out of the window until the instant it is needed. Getting out from an upper story onto a porch or veranda has saved many lives. Such action also affords temporary relief from smoke and heat and also attracts rescuers.

Other information on the subject of fires is included in the sections and on *Accident Prevention* and *Electrical Hazards.*

PERSONS WITH CLOTHING AFIRE—When a person's clothing catches fire, the first consideration is that the flame or hot gases should not be inhaled.

If your clothing is on fire do not run, as running fans the flames and makes conditions worse. Smother the flames by wrapping yourself in a rug, blanket, portiere, or woolen coat and roll on the floor. While rolling on the floor call for help. If the article of clothing which is on fire can be easily stripped off, this should, of course, be done. If a shower bath or pail of water is handy, use it and then roll in the spilled water.

If the clothing of another person takes fire, use the same measures. If the person is excited because of fear caused by the blazing clothing, it may be necessary to trip him to make him lie down. Then, if water or a fire extinguisher is handy, apply it at once, being careful not to direct the stream from the extinguisher on the face.

After the flames of a person's burning clothing are extinguished and the clothing has been drenched with water, do not remove the clothing from burnt skin until an ointment is available to apply to the burn. Avoid tearing the skin.

Fire Stop

A fire stop is usually a piece of material placed in any passage or cavity within a wall through which flames might travel. While it is best to make the fire stop of an incombustible material, a piece of lumber is often used. Its purpose is to prevent or delay flames from leaping through the wall trough; it acts principally as a fire retarder.

Fire Wall

A fire-resistant transverse bulkhead to set the engine apart from the rest of the automobile. The wall directly below and behind the dashboard in a car is a fire wall to protect the rest of the car if a fire breaks out in the engine.

Within the home, a fire wall serves the same purpose—to retard the spreading of a fire. It is made of an incombustible material—Sheetrock, brick or concrete—and is used:

(a) when the garage is part of the house, to provide a fire-resistant wall between the garage and house; and

(b) when a basement is finished, to set the section around the furnace off from the rest of the basement.

Firebrick

This is a special type of brick which is capable of withstanding the effects of great heat. It is used to line the inside of a furnace and often used to line the inside of a barbecue built outdoors.

Fireplaces

A fireplace is ordinarily considered appropriate to a living room, dining room, and bedroom; however, basement and porch fireplaces are gaining in favor with the householder.

All fireplaces should be built in accordance with a few simple essentials of correct design if satisfactory performance is to be real-

Prefabricated fireplace is easily added in any room of the house and can be installed with a few hand tools. It comes with its own chimney, thereby eliminating expensive masonry work.

Photograph courtesy of Uni-Bilt Division, Vega Industries, Inc.

This fireplace is covered with plastic-finished hardboard in a wood grain pattern, which is also used as a wainscot around the rest of the room.

Photograph courtesy of Marsh Wall Products, Inc.

ized. They should be of a size best suited to the room in which they are to be used from the standpoint of appearance and operation. If too small, they may function properly but do not throw out sufficient heat. If they are too large, a fire that would fill the combustion chamber would be entirely too hot for the room and would waste fuel.

The location of the chimney, which determines the location of the fireplace, is too often governed by structural considerations only. A fireplace suggests a fireside group and a reasonable degree of seclusion and therefore, especially in the living room, it should not be near doors to passageways of the house.

Characteristics

The principal warming effect of a fireplace is produced by the radi-

ant heat from the fire and from the hot back, sides, and hearth. In the ordinary fireplace practically no heating effect is produced by convection, that is, by air current. Air passes through the fire and up the chimney, carrying with it the heat absorbed from the fire; at the same time outside air of a lower temperature is drawn into the room. The effect of the cold air thus brought into the room is particularly noticeable farthest from the fire.

Modified Fireplaces

The Franklin stove is a type of modified fireplace. There are also modified fireplaces manufactured as units of heavy metal, designed to be set into place and concealed by the usual brickwork or other construction, so that no practical change in mantel design is required by their

use. The modifications are built-in standard parts of the fireplace—only the grilles show.

One advantage claimed for modified fireplace units is that the correctly designed and proportioned firebox, manufactured with throat, damper, smoke shelf, and chamber, provides a form for the masonry, thus reducing the risk of failure and assuring a smokeless fireplace. However, there is no excuse for using incorrect proportions; and the desirability of using a foolproof form, as provided by the modified unit, merely to obtain good proportions should be considered from the standpoint of cost. Even though the unit is well designed, it will not

operate properly if the chimney is inadequate; therefore, the rules for correct chimney construction must be adhered to with the modified unit as well as with the ordinary fireplace

Manufacturers claim labor and materials saved tend to offset the purchase price of the unit; also that the saving in fuel justifies any net increase in first cost. A minimum life of 20 years is claimed for the type and thickness of metal commonly used today in these units.

Field tests have proved that, when properly installed, the better designs of modified-fireplace units circulate heat into the cold corners of rooms and will deliver heated air

This simple fireplace has ceramic tiles around the fireplace opening. Many varieties of these tiles are available.

Photograph courtesy of The Mosaic Tile Co.

Inviting and warm, a fireplace and wood mantel add to this room's decorating scheme.
Photograph courtesy of Superior Fireplace Co.

through ducts to adjoining or upper rooms. For example, heat could be diverted to a bathroom from a living-room fireplace.

The quantity and temperature of the heated air discharged from the grilles were measured to determine the merits of the convection features. These measurements showed that very appreciable amounts of convected heat are produced by the modified unit when properly installed and operated. Discharge-air temperatures in excess of 200°F were attained from some of the units tested. The heated air delivered from the discharge grilles of some of the medium-sized units represented a heating effect equivalent to that from nearly 40 square feet of cast-iron radiation of the ordinary hot-water heating system, or sufficient to heat a 15' by 18' room built with average tightness to 70°F. when the outside temperature is 40°F. Additional convected heat can be produced with some models by the use of forced-circulation fans.

However, the nature of operation, with the unavoidably large quantity of heated air passing up the stack, makes the inherent overall efficiency of any fireplace relatively low. Therefore, claims for an increased efficiency of modified fireplaces should be understood merely as constituting an improvement over the ordinary fireplace and not over stoves or central heating plants.

Selecting a Fireplace

When a fireplace is being selected the kind of fuel to be burned should be considered; also, the design should harmonize with the room in proportion and detail.

In Colonial days, when cordwood was plentiful, fireplaces 7′ wide and 5′ high were common, especially when used in kitchens for cooking. They required large amounts of fuel and too frequently were smoky.

Where cordwood (4′ long) is cut in half, a 30″ width is desirable for a fireplace; but, where coal is burned, the opening can be narrower. Thirty inches is a practical height for the convenient tending of a fire where the width is less than 6′; openings about 30″ wide are generally made with square corners. The higher the opening, the greater the chance of a smoky fireplace.

In general, the wider the opening, the greater should be the depth.

A shallow opening throws out relatively more heat than a deep one of the same width but accommodates smaller pieces of wood; thus it becomes a question of preference between a greater depth which permits the use of large logs that burn longer and a shallower depth which takes smaller-sized wood but throws out more heat.

In small fireplaces a depth of 12″ will permit good draft if the throat is constructed as explained above, but a minimum depth of 16″ to 18″ is advised to lessen the danger of brands falling out on floor.

As a rule, fireplaces on the second floor are smaller than those on the first floor and it is well to follow this practice because the flue height is less for second-floor fireplaces.

In this modified fireplace air enters the inlet, a, from outside and is heated as it rises by natural circulation through the back chamber, c, and the tubes, t, being discharged into the room from the register, b. Air for supporting combustion is drawn into the fire at d and passes between the tubes up the flue. A damper is also provided to close the air inlet.

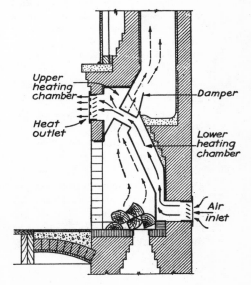

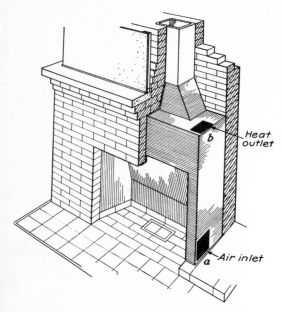

In this fireplace the air is not drawn in directly from outdoors but through the inlet by contact with the metal sides and back of the fireplace, rises by natural circulation, and is discharged back into the room from the outlet, b, or to another room on the same floor or in the second story. The inlets and outlets are connected to registers which may be located at the front of the fireplace. The registers may be located on the ends of the fireplace or on the wall of an adjacent room.

Unless a fireplace 6' wide is fully 28" deep, the logs will have to be split, and some advantage of the wide opening will be lost.

Screens of suitable design should be placed in front of all fireplaces.

A fireplace 30" to 36" wide is generally suitable for a room having 300 square feet of floor. The width should be increased for larger rooms, but all other dimensions should be taken from the table "Rec-

ommended Dimensions for Fireplaces."

Units providing for burning gas are often built in to resemble fireplaces.

Pleasing designs result from exercising good taste in use of materials and mantels that suit the room. The essentials for safety and utility, however, should not be sacrificed for style.

Construction

The ordinary fireplace is constructed generally with these essentials: (1) that the flue have the proper area, (2) that the throat be correctly constructed and have suitable damper, (3) that the chimney be high enough for a good draft, (4) that the shape of the fireplace be such as to direct a maximum amount of radiated heat into the room, and (5) that a properly constructed smoke chamber be provided.

Dimensions

The table, "Recommended Dimensions for Fireplaces," gives recommended dimensions for fireplaces of various widths and heights.

If a damper is installed, the width of the opening will depend on the width of the damper frame, the size of which is fixed by the width and depth of the fireplace and the slope of the back wall.

The width of the throat proper is determined by the opening of hinged damper cover. The full damper opening should never be less than the flue area. Responsible manufacturers of fireplace equipment give valuable assistance in the selection of a suitable damper for a given fireplace. A well-designed and well-installed damper should be regarded as essential in cold climates.

When no damper is used, the throat opening should be 4 inches for fireplaces not exceeding 4 feet in height.

Prefabricated Fireplace

To fill the need for a low-cost fireplace that eliminates expensive masonry construction, a completely prefabricated fireplace and chimney have been developed. The unit, complete with chimney, can be installed in four to six manhours, according to the manufacturer who developed the Uni-Bilt.

This ready-made fireplace, which meets Underwriters' Laboratory requirements, can be mounted flush with the wall or recessed into it. The cantilever designed hearth, which is 15″ above the floor, burns wood up to 27″ long. The outer shell

of the fireplace is steel with stainless steel trim. The firebox itself is formed of high-impact ceramic material.

Except for the trim, the complete unit is prime coated and ready to paint with any interior paint to harmonize with the room decorating scheme. A flexible hearth screen comes with the fireplace to prevent sparks from flying out of the fireplace into the room.

Preformed Firebox

Fireplace construction is an exacting art. While some handymen would like to build a fireplace from scratch, others undoubtedly will be content to install a prefabricated fireplace and chimney while others would like to eliminate the compli-

A shallow fireplace, with a copper hood, throws out considerable heat after the hood gets hot. The wall should be of fire-resistant masonry.

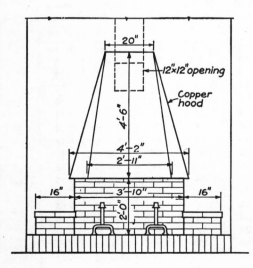

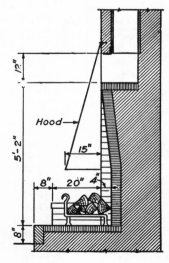

cated firebox construction and do the rest of the work themselves. A preformed metal unit, Heatform, will enable the handyman to eliminate the complicated planning and building of the firebox.

The units are available in different styles so that you can build any type of fireplace—Colonial to Contemporary—around the basic frame. Heatform is a double-walled metal unit consisting of a firebox, throat, dome and heat control damper. It forms a guide around which masonry walls of the fireplace can be built easily and economically.

For those who wish to build a complete unit themselves, there are full details in the remainder of this section.

Hearth

The hearth in conventional fireplaces should be about flush with the floor, for sweepings may then be brushed into the fireplace. When there is a basement, an ash dump located in the hearth near the back of the fireplace is convenient. The dump consists of a metal frame about 5″ by 8″ with a plate, generally pivoted, through which ashes can be dropped into a pit below.

In buildings with wooden floors the hearth in front of the fireplace should be supported by masonry trimmer arches or other fire-resistant construction. Hearths should project at least 16″ from the chimney breast and should be of brick, stone, terra cotta, or reinforced

Recommended Dimensions for Fireplaces

Opening Width	Height	Depth	Minimum back (horizontal)	Vertical back wall	Inclined back wall	Outside dimensions of standard rectangular flue lining	Inside diameter of standard round flue lining
Inches	Inches	Inches	Inches	Inches	Inches	Inches	Inches
24	24	16–18	14	14	16	8½ x 8½	10
28	24	16–18	14	14	16	8½ x 8½	10
24	28	16–18	14	14	20	8½ x 8½	10
30	28	16–18	16	14	20	8½ x 13	10
36	28	16–18	22	14	20	8½ x 13	12
42	28	16–18	28	14	20	8½ x 18	12
36	32	18–20	20	14	24	8½ x 18	12
42	32	18–20	26	14	24	13 x 13	12
48	32	18–20	32	14	24	13 x 13	15
42	36	18–20	26	14	28	13 x 13	15
48	36	18–20	32	14	28	13 x 18	15
54	36	18–20	38	14	28	13 x 18	15
60	36	18–20	44	14	28	13 x 18	15
42	40	20–22	24	17	29	13 x 13	15
48	40	20–22	30	17	29	13 x 18	15
54	40	20–22	36	17	29	13 x 18	15
60	40	20–22	42	17	29	18 x 18	18
66	40	20–22	48	17	29	18 x 18	18
72	40	22–28	51	17	29	18 x 18	18

concrete not less than 4" thick. The length of the hearth should be not less than the width of the fireplace opening plus 16". Wooden centering under trimmer arches may be removed after the mortar has set, though it is more frequently left in place.

Wall Thickness

The walls of fireplaces should never be less than 8" thick, and if of stone they should be at least 12" thick. When built of stone or hard-burned brick, the back and sides are often not lined with firebrick, but it is better to use firebrick laid in fire clay. When firebricks are laid flat with the long edges exposed there is less danger of their falling out. They are generally placed on edge, however, forming a 2" protection, in which case metal ties should be built into the main brickwork to hold the 2" firebrick veneer in place. Thick metal backs and sides are sometimes used as lining. When a grate for burning coal or coke is built in, firebrick at least 2" thick should be added to the fireplace back unless the grate has a solid iron back and is only set in with an air space behind it.

Jambs

The jambs should be wide enough to give stability and a pleasing appearance; they are frequently faced with ornamental brick or tile. For an opening 3" wide or less, a 12" or 16" width is generally sufficient, depending on whether a wood mantel is used or the jambs are of exposed masonry. The edges of a wood mantel should be kept at

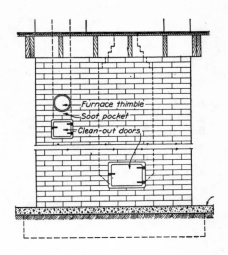

The ashpit should be of tight masonry and should be provided with a tightly fitting iron clean-out door and frame about 10" by 12". A clean-out for the furnace flue as shown is sometimes provided.

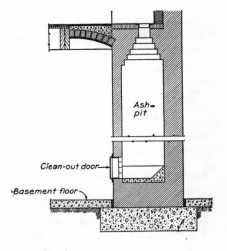

least 8″ from the fireplace opening. For wider openings and large rooms, similar proportions should be kept.

Lintel

Lintels of ½″x3″ bars, 3½″x 3½″x¼″ angle irons, or damper frames are used to support the masonry over the opening of ordinary fireplaces. Heavier lintel irons are required for wider openings.

Where a masonry arch is used over the opening, the jambs should be heavy enough to resist the thrust of the arch. Arches over openings less than 4′ wide seldom sag, but sagging is not uncommon in wider fireplaces, especially where massive masonry is used.

Throat

The sides of the fireplace should be vertical up to the throat, or damper opening. The throat should be 6″ to 8″ or more above the bottom of the lintel and have an area not less than that of the flue and a length equal to the width of the fireplace opening. Starting 5″ above the throat, the sides should be drawn in to equal the flue area.

Proper throat construction is necessary to a successful fireplace and the builder must make certain that the side walls are carried up perpendicularly until the throat is passed and that the full length of opening is provided.

Smoke Shelf and Chamber

The smoke shelf is made by setting the brickwork back at the top of the throat to the line of the flue wall for the full length of the throat. Its depth may vary from 6″ to 12″

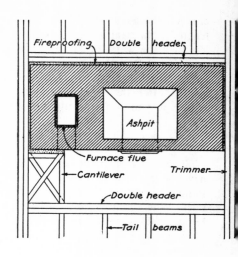

Where a header is more than 4′ in length, it should be doubled, as shown. Headers supporting more than four tail beams should have ends supported in metal joists hangers. The framing may be placed ½″ from the chimney because the masonry is 8″ thick.

or more, depending on the depth of the fireplace.

The smoke chamber is the space extending from the top of the throat up to the bottom of the flue proper and between the side walls. The walls should be drawn inward 30° to the vertical after the top of the throat is passed and smoothly plastered with cement mortar not less than ½″ thick.

Damper

A properly designed damper affords a means of regulating the draft and prevents excessive loss of heat from the room when the fire is out. A damper consists of a cast-iron frame with a lid hinged so that the width of the throat opening may be

Notice the beautiful pattern and texture of the stone work in this Model "A" Heatform fireplace, and note too that the stones have been spaced for inlets and outlets. This is recommended provided sufficient open space is left for the free flow of air. Here, also, the owner has used a few antique accessories with a modern design.

Photograph courtesy of Superior Fireplace Co.

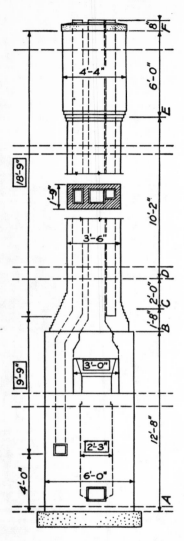

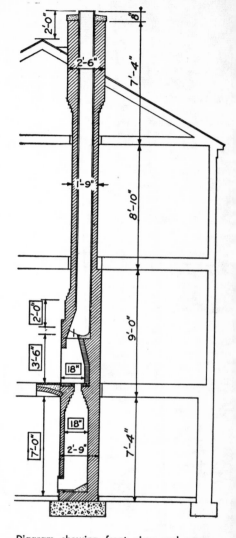

varied from a closed to a wide-open position. Various patterns are on the market, some designed to support the masonry over the opening, others requiring lintel irons.

A roaring pine fire may require a full-throat opening, but slow-burning hardwood logs may need only 1″ or 2″ of opening. Regulat-

Diagram showing front view and cross section of an entire chimney such as is commonly built to serve a furnace, fireplace, and kitchen stove. Two sets of dimensions are given; those in rectangles refer to the approximate sizes of the voids or openings, the others refer to the outside dimensions of the brickwork. These are used in estimating the quantities of brick required.

ing the opening according to the kind of fire prevents waste of heat up the chimney. Closing the damper in summer keeps flies, mosquitoes, and other insects from entering the house down the chimney.

In houses heated by furnaces or other modern systems, lack of a damper in the fireplace flue may interfere with uniform heating, particularly in very cold windy weather, whether or not there is a fire on the hearth. When air heated by the furnace is carried up the chimney there is a waste of the furnace fuel, but a damper partially open serves a slow fire of hardwood without smoking the room or wasting heated air from the main heating system.

Flue

The area of lined flues should be a twelfth or more of the fireplace opening, provided the chimney is at least 22′ in height, measured from the hearth. If the flue is shorter than 22′ or if it is unlined, its area should be made a tenth or more of the fireplace opening. A fireplace which, for instance, has an opening of 7.5 square feet, or approximately 1,080 square inches, needs a flue area of approximately 90 square inches; a rectangular flue, 8½″x18″, outside dimensions, or a round flue with a 12″ inside diameter might be used, as these are the nearest commercial sizes of lining. It is seldom possible to obtain lining having exactly the required area, but the inside area should never be less than that prescribed above. A 13″x13″ flue was selected for convenience when combining with the other flues. If the flue is built of brick and is unlined,

Sizes of Fireplace Flue Linings[1]

Area of fireplace opening	Outside dimensions of standard rectangular flue lining	Inside diameter of standard round flue lining
Square inches	Inches	Inches
600	8½ × 8½	10
800	8½ × 13	10
1,000	8½ × 18	12
1,200	8½ × 18	12
1,400	13 × 13	12
1,600	13 × 13	15
1,800	13 × 18	15
2,000	13 × 18	15
2,200	13 × 18	15
2,400	18 × 18	18
2,600	18 × 18	18
2,800	18 × 18	18
3,000	18 × 18	18

[1]Based on a flue area equal to one-twelfth the fireplace opening.

its area should be approximately one-tenth of the fireplace opening, or 108 square inches. It would probably be made 8″x16″ (128 square inches) because brickwork can be laid to better advantage when the dimensions of the flue are multiples of 4″.

The Table, "Sizes of Fireplace Flue Linings," is convenient in selecting the proper size of flue or for determining the size of fireplace opening for an existing flue. The area of the fireplace opening in square inches is obtained by multiplying the width by the height, both measured in inches.

Refer to *Chimney Construction* also *Chimney Repairs*.

This common red brick fireplace is built around the Model "A" Heatform and has a raised hearth. Split bricks have been spaced for the inlet and outlet grilles to allow maximum warm air passage.

Smoky Fireplace

When a fireplace smokes, it should be examined to make certain that the essential requirements of construction have been fulfilled. If the chimney is not stopped up with fallen brick and the mortar joints are not loose, note whether nearby trees or tall structures cause eddies down the flue. To determine whether the fireplace opening is in correct proportion to the flue area, hold a piece of sheet metal across the top face of the fireplace opening and then gradually lower it, making the opening smaller until smoke does not come into the room. Mark at the lower edge of the metal on the sides of the fireplace. The opening may then be reduced by building in a metal shield or hood across the top so that its lower edge is at the marks made during the test. The trouble can generally be remedied in another way by increasing the height of the flue.

Soot Removal

Refer to the section on *Chimney Repairs.*

Cleaning Brickwork

When the brickwork around the fireplace becomes soiled, it may be scrubbed with a brush dipped into a solution of 1 tablespoonful of tri-sodium phosphate to a gallon of water. Rinse off with clear water, and then dry with a cloth.

But if the bricks are stained, they may need to be bleached. For

Colorful flagstone adds to the appearance of this fireplace. Both the cool air inlets and warm air outlets if the preformed fireplace unit have been located on the return sides of the fireplace.

An attractive brick fireplace. Note the cool air inlets and warm outlets are formed right into the masonry of the fireplace.

Photographs courtesy of Superior Fireplace Co.

this purpose use about 1¼ lbs. of oxalic acid crystals in a gallon of warm water, adding sufficient lime or whiting to form a soft paste. (Caution: oxalic acid is a poison,

Cement blocks were used as a building medium in this modern fireplace built around a 38 Model "S" Heatform. The raised hearth provides informal seating capacity, as well as a permanent place for the television. The designer preferred to form the cool air inlet and warm air outlet of the masonry used in the fireplace and wall. Good judgment was exercised in placing the cool air inlet at floor level, which assures a greater volume of warm air circulation and warmer floors.

Photograph courtesy of Superior Fireplace Co.

and it must be handled carefully!) Use a broad knife or spatula to spread this paste over the stained parts of the brickwork. Let it remain about 15 minutes, then scrape off the paste. Wash the bricks with clear water, then dry with a cloth.

Should the cleaning or bleaching not remove the dirt or stains from the bricks, try putting a thin oil stain over them, choosing the same or perhaps a little darker color than the bricks. This will give them a uniform dark appearance.

Hearth Tiles

To keep the hearth looking its best, wash the tiles with warm, soapy water, then rinse with clear water. When completely dry, rub a coat of wax over them. This not only adds to their good appearance but makes the tiles more dirt-resistant.

When Fireplace Is Unused

During the warm months when the fireplace is left unlighted, instead of the open, gaping space you may want to camouflage it in a decorative manner. Here are some suggestions: Build a wood trellis to stand in front of the fireplace; place two or three small potted foliage plants in front of the trellis and train the leaves over it. Or, without the trellis, place three or four large pots of upright foliage plants in front of the fireplace; these will cover the open space. (Refer to the section on *Plants for the Home* for a choice of foliage plants.) Or you may use a small decorative straight or folding screen in front of the unused fireplace.

Fireplace, Outdoors

See *Barbecue.*

Fishtape

Fishtape or an electrical snake is used to fish wires through a wall, floor, pipe or conduit. It is light and flexible, but must be strong. When purchasing fishtape in a hardware store, get a 50′ or 100′ roll.

When using fishtape, lubricate it with soapstone or talcum powder to make it easier to handle. The end of the tape is shaped into a hook and the wires attached to it.

To fish a wire cable through a wall, floor, pipe or conduit, push the wire completely through and connect the cable to the hook at one end. Then slowly pull the cable through by pulling on the tape. It is important to form a perfect knot with the cable or else it will come loose as it is fished through.

An open hook at the end of a fishtape.

A closed hook at the end of the tape.

How both wires of a cable or conductor are secured to a closed hook when being fished through a wall, floor, pipe or conduit.

Fixture Splice

A special type of joining between the main electric wires and the wires from the electrical ceiling or wall fixture. Frequently, the main electric wire is solid whereas the fixture wire is stranded.

Both can be joined with a solderless connector. However, many handymen prefer to twist the wires together, solder and then tape them. Here's how to make a fixture splice:

1. After removing the insula-

tion from both wires, make certain that the wires are clean.

2. Twist the stranded wire of the fixture tightly around the solid wire of the main electrical line.

3. Then bend the solid wire over with a pliers to hold the two together firmly.

4. Heat the wires and solder them.

5. Cover the splice with rubber tape followed by friction tape, or use plastic tape.

See *Electrical Wiring.*

A fixture splice to join an electrical fixture wire, usually stranded, to the main electrical wires, usually solid.

Flagstone

Flagstone can be used to make a decorative patio and garden walk. Here the flagstones are combined with brick to make an outdoor living and play area.

Flagstone and slate are large slabs of limestone, shale or sandstone, which come in varying widths and lengths in thicknesses ranging from about ¾" to 2". Generally, they are irregular in shape although they can be bought cut and matched.

Available in a broad range of colors—red, pink, gray, buff, orange, slate and charcoal—these stones are used for patios, terraces, walks, exterior walls, occasionally floors, and around fireplaces.

Flagstones can be set on a con-crete base or when used outdoors, set on gravel or sand. However, unless the flagstone is set on concrete, it should be at least 1½" thick to withstand wear and tear in normal use.

The handyman can cut the stone to size himself. A mason's hammer does an effective job, if you have one handy, or you can use a cold chisel and hammer, holding the flagstone over a solid base, such as a steel I-beam.

See *Patios*.

Flagstone can not only be set over concrete to make a decorative walk but used for outdoor steps as well.

Cutting flagstone with a mason's hammer.

Flange

This is a flat rim on the end of an iron pipe fitting with holes in it to permit the bolting of the unit to a surface or another flange. It is often used when making handrails on stairways, or when making awning frames out of pipe.

A flange is a plumbing fitting.

Flange Nut

A special nut with a flange as an integral part is called a flange nut. It is used instead of a separate washer and a nut. The flange end of the nut is set flush against the surface to be held.

A flange nut.

Flaring Tool

Copper tubing joined with flared fittings requires a special tool to spread or flare the ends. The flaring tool comes in several forms. There are individual flaring rods made to fit specific size tubing, or adjustable flaring tools which can be used with several different sizes of tubing.

See *Plumbing*.

An adjustable flaring tool is used to spread the end of different diameter copper tubing for use with flared fittings.

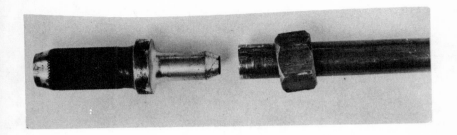

The flaring tool shown in this photograph can be used only with the one diameter tubing. There are several sizes made and it is necessary to have a few of these for any extensive work with copper tubing.

Flash Point

This is the temperature at which an oil gives off vapor in sufficient quantity to ignite if a spark or flame is present. An open can of paint placed in the sun or next to heat is a fire hazard if the oil in the can reaches the flash-point level.

Flashing

By means of a lap joint, flashing may be used to make watertight the angle where a roof meets an intersecting surface. Flashing is installed at junctions between roof and walls, chimneys, skylights, and similar places, and in valleys or depressions where two planes of a roof join. Flashing around walls, chimneys, or other vertical surfaces is designed to shed water from the joint, causing it to seek lower levels; flashing in valleys is intended to conduct the water to the gutters. Corrosion-resistant flashing material should be used wherever possible.

For further information on flashing, see the section on *Chimney Construction,* also section on *Roof.*

Methods of Application

Several materials (cut in strips or pieces) such as tin or terneplate, galvanized iron, slate, sheet copper, soft lead sheets, sheet aluminum, or flashing felt are used for flashing. The methods of applying the different materials vary according to conditions, and recommendations by manufacturers of roofing materials should be followed if furnished.

There are several different methods of fastening the upper edge of flashing places against a vertical surface, depending upon the material in the vertical surface. When

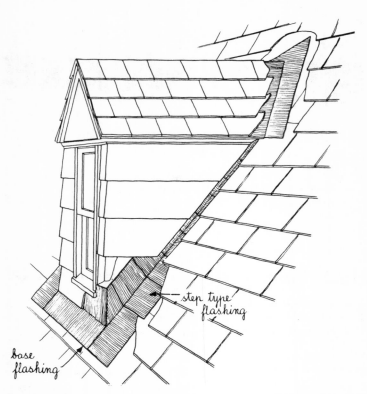

step type flashing

base flashing

placed against a brick or other masonry surface, the upper edge is usually bent and inserted into a groove or joint in the masonry, and the crack is sealed with flashing cement.

Sometimes two pieces of flashing are used in connecton with masonry walls. The first is bent in the middle and the upper half is nailed to the vertical surface of the wall; the lower half is then nailed over one thickness of roofing and covered by another thickness. The second piece, known as counterflashing, is hung over the first to form an apron. It is suspended by bending the upper edge and inserting it into a joint in the vertical surface of the masonry.

Since the two pieces of flashing are independent of each other, they are not likely to break if parts of the building settle or shrink.

Against stucco or other plastered walls, the upper edge of the flashing may be inserted behind the lath or fastened in such a way that it will be covered by the plaster when it is applied. In frame construction, the upper edge of the flashing is generally run up behind the siding or shingles.

Where the vertical surface intersects another surface in a horizontal line, as at the face of a chimney near the eaves or at a horizontal roof line at the base of a wall, flashing is generally extended down over

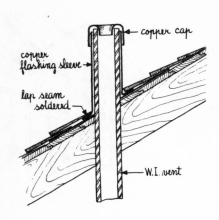

copper cap

copper flashing sleeve

lap seam soldered

W.I. vent

ing are generally employed. The base and cap flashing means that, working upward on the roof, each succeeding piece of flashing extends from the vertical surface down over a shingle on the roof and is then covered by the next higher shingle course. This course is then covered by the next higher piece of flashing and so on up the slope. For an intersection where roll roofing is used, it is either turned up under the side wall material or the flashing is nailed over it, with flashing cement between to seal the joint.

At the up-slope face of a chimney which protrudes through a sloping roof a so-called cricket or saddle is usually constructed in the roof's surface. As the name "saddle" indicates, it is a small ridge formed behind the chimney to divide the water running down the roof and throw it to each side away from the chimney instead of allowing it to dam up back of it. Water accumulating back of the chimney might eventually result in leakage at that point. The joint between the chimney and cricket is also flashed.

Both open and closed valleys are used in roof construction. In an open valley the flashing is applied before the roofing is laid. The roofing material is then extended over

the top or next to the top course of roofing and nailed down after the space to be lapped has been coated with flashing cement to make a tight joint. Similarly, when a roof covered with roofing or other flat roofing material meets a vertical surface in a horizontal intersection, the flashing from the vertical surface usually extends down and is sealed and nailed on top of the roofing.

However, where a roof meets a vertical surface in a sloping line, such as along the sides of a chimney on a sloping roof, and the roofing consists of shingles or similarly lapped material, base and cap flash-

check flashing for:
tightness of joints
wrinkles or buckles
holes or breaks
width

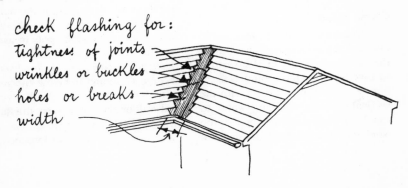

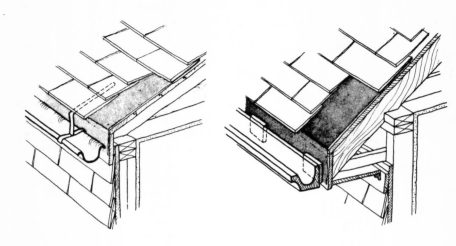

the flashing to make a lap joint. The center portion of the flashing is visible for the entire length and the open space is usually wider at the bottom than near the ridge to accommodate the increasing volume of water as it nears the eaves. In the closed valley, the flashing is inserted by the base and cap flashing method to make an unbroken surface which is generally considered more pleasing in appearance. The flashing material in either case should be wide enough to extend under the roofing material a sufficient distance to insure good protection.

Causes of Leakage

Occasionally metal wall flashing may warp and be drawn out of the groove or joint in the vertical surface or, when roll roofing is used, it may break at its junction with the vertical surface, allowing water to run down behind it. The force of the wind may tear flashing loose from the face of the roofing and water will enter during heavy rains. Valley flashings, if too narrow, may allow backed-up water to find its way under the roofing. This seeping sometimes occurs when the valleys are dammed up with snow and ice. Flashing material in valleys may corrode or break, causing cracks or holes through which water may enter and drip through the joint below.

To Make Repairs

The approximate location of leaks in flashing may often be determined by looking for wet spots on the walls or ceiling of the house. Carefully examine the flashing above and near such spots to ascertain the exact location and cause of leakage if possible. If the leak is near a chimney or below the junction between the roof and a vertical wall or similar surface, the flashing should be inspected to see whether it has become loosened. It

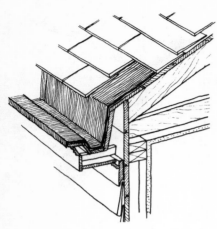

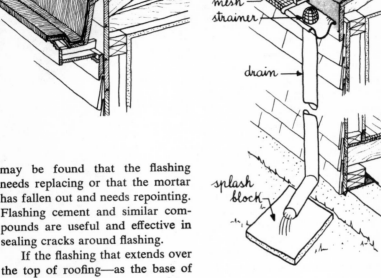

may be found that the flashing needs replacing or that the mortar has fallen out and needs repointing. Flashing cement and similar compounds are useful and effective in sealing cracks around flashing.

If the flashing that extends over the top of roofing—as the base of a vertical surface—becomes loosened, it should be nailed down after the underside of the lap has been well coated with flashing cement. The flashing cement serves to seal the spaces around nails and the cracks along the edges which otherwise might allow leakage. It is also best to use short nails in order to avoid penetration of roof boards.

When exposed metal flashing shows signs of rusting, it should be cleaned with a wire brush and painted with a good metal paint to preserve it from further corrosion. This paint coat should be examined at regular intervals and renewed when it shows signs of wear.

To make valley flashing watertight, it is advisable to cover the portion to be overlapped with flashing cement immediately before applying the roof covering. This should seal the space between the flashing and roof and prevent water from backing up over the edge of the flashing.

If the flashing in a valley is too narrow or if it is corroded or broken, it will probably be necessary to replace it with new pieces of metal. This is not difficult in an open valley but is rather troublesome in a closed one.

In a closed valley covered with shingles, it is quite difficult to repair leaks in the flashing unless the metal pushed under the shingles to cover the leaky spots is folded into a wedge-shaped point. Folding makes it easier to push the sheets past obstacles such as nails. If nails interfere too much, they can be cut off under the shingle or pulled with a sharp cold chisel or nail ripper and later replaced with new nails. The size of the sheets to be used for flashing depends upon the pitch of the roof and the exposure of the shingles to the weather.

Insert a piece of flashing under top layer of first course of shingles at the eaves and over the top of the old flashing and slide it up until the upper point of the sheet is at least 2″ above the butts of the second course of shingles. Then insert another sheet under the second course of shingles, pushing it up on top of the old flashing. The lower point of this piece will show below the butts of the second course of shingles. Continue this process until the top of the valley has been reached or until all broken flashings have been

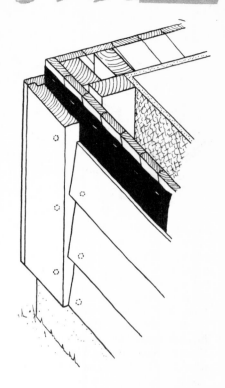

covered. If good material is used, this method makes a permanent repair and covers the cracks or holes that have rusted out in the angle of the original flashing.

Method of repairing valley flashing.

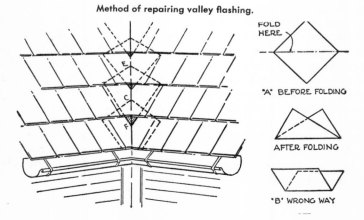

FOLD HERE

"A" BEFORE FOLDING

AFTER FOLDING

"B" WRONG WAY

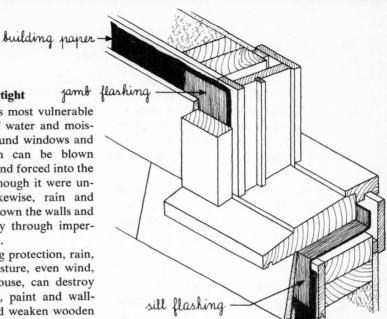

building paper

jamb flashing

sill flashing

building paper

Make Walls Watertight

The wall joints most vulnerable to the entrance of water and moisture are those around windows and doors. Here, rain can be blown against the joints and forced into the house almost as though it were under pressure. Likewise, rain and melted snow run down the walls and can find their way through imperfectly sealed joints.

Without lasting protection, rain, melted snow, moisture, even wind, can enter your house, can destroy plaster, insulation, paint and wallpaper, can rot and weaken wooden framework, can cost you many times over the small sum you pay for the lasting protection of durable flashing.

Window Head Flashing

Steps 1 to 5 illustrate a proper and simple method of forming window head flashings.

In brick or stone veneer construction the flashing should be carried the full length of the lintel and at the ends it should turn up ½″.

Where windows are wider than 44″, use two sheets, lapping the ends a minimum of 3″.

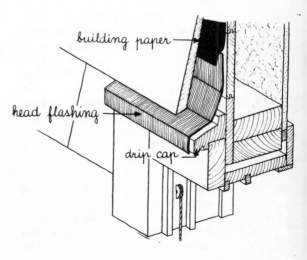

building paper

head flashing

drip cap

1. Cut a section of flashing 4″ longer than the width of the window casing.
2. Flashing will extend horizontally out over window casing. When clapboard siding is used, flashing will extend vertically on wall a minimum of 4″. When shingles are used, flashing will extend vertically on the wall 2″ above the butt line of the succeeding course. Bend flashing lengthwise

to form necessary vertical leg.

3. The flashing is held in place by nails along its upper edge. The outer edge of the horizontal leg is bent down over front of casing to form a drip.

4. At side edges of casing, the metal should be slit to form tabs which are bent over the ends of the casing. First fold back the lower tabs, then fold down the upper tabs to cover them.

5. This procedure insures weathertight flashing, which is applicable to door heads as well as windows. For the sake of appearance, it is important to paint the exposed parts of such flashing.

Protect the Joints

1. Mark a full size sheet of flashing lengthwise down the middle. Then mark it crosswise into sections 9″ long.

2. Cut along these lines to obtain pieces each 9″ square.

3. Bend each piece lengthwise into a right angle along a line 4″ from one edge (5″ from the opposite edge).

4. The 5″ legs will be placed on the roof, and the 4″ legs will lie against the vertical wall.

5. Cut-away section—In laying the flashing, start at the eave line and work up. The separate pieces of flashing are set in between each course of shingles. Secure each piece to the roof boarding with a nail.

Flathead

This term, or flush head, is used to designate the head of a screw or bolt which can be set into a countersunk hole so that the top of the head rests level with the surface into which it was sunk.

Frequently, flathead screws are set so that the head is slightly below the surface. In this way, the cavity can be filled with wood filler or wood putty, which is sanded flush when dry. The final effect is the almost complete concealment of the screw head.

While it is possible to drive a flathead screw in soft wood so that its head is flush with the surface by

using only a screwdriver, it is better to countersink the hole. In this way, there is less danger of cracking the head of the screw or splintering the wood.

See *Countersink*, *Bolts* and *Screws*.

A flathead bolt.

Flemish Bond

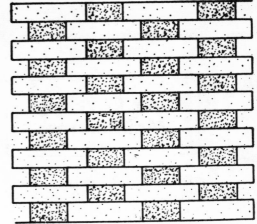

This is a form of bricklaying and consists of alternate headers and strechers in every course. Each header is centered on the strechers in the courses above and below.

See *Brick*.

Float

A flat board or sheet of metal with a handle attached, used for concrete or plaster work. It is used to spread the concrete or plaster and to smooth the surface.

See *Concrete*.

Wood and steel floats are used for finishing concrete. The steel float produces a fine, smooth surface while the wood float produces a somewhat rougher texture.

Float Valve

Sometimes called a float, this is generally a hollow ball inside a toilet tank which controls the flow of water into the tank. The hollow ball floats on top of the water and, as the water rises, the ball connected to a control arm shuts the valve through which the water flows to fill the tank.

In recent years, the copper float has been displaced in some homes by floats made of polystyrene. In addition, inflated polystyrene in the shape of a block has been used as a float valve.

See *Drainage Systems* and *Toilet Tank Repairs*.

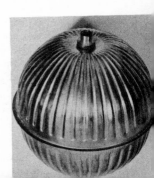

Float valve is part of the toilet tank water system controlling the inflow of water.

Floor Coverings, Maintenance

Both wood and concrete floors may be covered with linoleum, asphalt tile, and similar materials. Such coverings should be installed and maintained in accordance with the manufacturer's instructions, which usually include thorough cleaning and the application of protective wax coatings. Available in an almost limitless range of colors, these floor coverings will serve as a starting point for remodeling or changing the color scheme of a room.

Linoleum

Linoleum, whether for floor coverings, kitchen counter tops, walls, or other inside surfaces, will stay attractive longer and wear better if waxed and polished. A few simple rules for its care will be found useful: (1) dust daily; (2) use water sparingly; (3) clean with special linoleum cleaner, mild soapsuds, or mild detergent solution; (4) apply wax in a thin, even film; (5) rewax only as needed, usually not oftener than once a month; and (6) never use harsh abrasives other than fine steel wool to take off spots that are hard to remove.

No matter what type of wax is used, always start with a clean surface before waxing. There are some excellent linoleum cleaners which may be diluted with water in accordance with the manufacturer's directions. In using them, clean only a few square feet at a time, going over that area with a fresh cloth wrung out with clear, lukewarm water, and permit the surface to dry thoroughly and the wax to spread evenly.

Waxes that protect linoleum are essentially of two types: paste and liquid waxes with a volatile-solvent base, and self-polishing waxes with a water-emulsion base. They should be applied in very thin coats to avoid making the floor slippery.

Volatile-solvent waxes may be abtained in either paste or liquid form. The liquid is somewhat easier to apply than the paste because of the large proportion of solvent. Both paste and liquid are suitable for linoleum as well as for wood or concrete floors.

Paste wax should be applied with a slightly dampened soft cloth or with a wax applicator and allowed to dry, after which it should be polished to a lustrous finish. Liquid wax should be spread evenly over the cleaned surface with a lamb's-wool applicator in straight, parallel strokes. After drying for 30 minutes, it should be polished to a lustrous finish. Waxes of the organic-solvent type must not be used on asphalt tile because they soften and mar the surface of the tile.

Self-polishing or water-emulsion base waxes will give a protective coating if used on linoleum, rubber tile, cork, asphalt tile, mastic, and other flooring. The wax should be spread as thinly and evenly as possible with a lamb's-wool applicator or soft cloth mop in straight, parallel strokes. If properly applied it should dry to a hard,

Photograph courtesy of Red Devil Tools, Inc.

lustrous film in less than 30 minutes. Although not required, the gloss may be increased by a slight buffing after the wax becomes thoroughly dry.

A weighted floor brush or electric polishing machine does an excellent job with little effort. If a polisher is not part of the household equipment, it may be rented in many communities at nominal cost by the hour or the day. For a very hard surface, the linoleum should be given two or three coats of wax, making sure to let each coat dry for at least 30 minutes before polishing.

Care should be taken not to flood linoleum surfaces with water, since any water that seeps through the edges of seams may affect the cementing material and cause the backing to mildew or rot and edges of the linoleum to become loose and curled. Wiping up water as soon as it is spilled on waxed linoleum will keep light spots from appearing. Grease and other spots should be cleaned as quickly as possible, with a soft cloth or sponge wrung out of mild lukewarm soapsuds or mild detergent solution. Rinse by using a clean cloth wrung out of clear, lukewarm water. Floor oils and sweeping compound containing oil should not be used on linoleum, because these materials may leave a film of oil on the surface to collect dust and dirt.

Asphalt Tile

Asphalt tile may be used to cover both new and old concrete or wood floors and may be obtained in colors suitable for any room in the house. Impervious to water, the tiles are especially suitable for floors on which water is likely to be spilled, such as kitchens, laundries, and bathrooms; they also prove attractive and satisfactory for basement recreation rooms and enclosed porches.

When installing this type of flooring, always obtain a few extra tiles for replacement or testing, because it may be difficult to match them exactly later on. Missing tiles or those that have become broken or marred should be replaced by cementing new ones into place.

Mastic floor covering of the asphalt type has asphalt, bitumen, or resin as the base and will give excellent service if given proper care. There are some "do's" and "don'ts" which are very important. Cleaners and polishes containing abrasives, oils, or organic solventts, such as gasoline, turpentine, or carbon tetrachloride, should not be used to clean asphalt-base coverings. Never use unknown cleaning preparations on asphalt tile without testing them first, unless they are recommended by the manufacturer of the flooring.

To test a cleaning or polishing preparation for use on asphalt tile, moisten a white cloth with the preparation and rub over the surface of a spare tile. If the color of the tile shows on the cloth, the preparation has acted as a solvent, dissolving the surface of the tile, and is not safe to use.

Asphalt tile floors may be washed with neutral soap and lukewarm water in much the same manner as linoleum, except that water will not harm the tile unless permitted to stand and seep under edges enough to loosen them from the floor. After cleaning and drying, the care of asphalt tile floors is similar to that recommended for linoleum with one very important exception: Never use paste wax or liquid wax that has a solvent base on asphalt tile—these waxes will soften the tile and mar the surface.

Water-emulsion or self-polishing waxes that are free from oils are suitable and safe for asphalt tile. They should be spread as thinly as possible on the surface of the floor with lamb's-wool applicator. Use straight, parallel strokes in one direction only. In a short time, approximately 30 minutes, the wax should dry to a hard, lustrous finish. While these waxes are self-polishing to a degree, the appearance of the floor will be improved by a light buffing. Before polishing, however, the wax should be completely dry.

Wax should be renewed at intervals, depending upon the severity of wear, but it is not necessary to rewax as long as the floor responds to polishing. Daily dusting and occasional machine polishing will eliminate the need of mopping and extend the life of the wax coating.

Photograph courtesy of Red Devil Tools.

Floors

Photograph courtesy of Mastic Tile Corp.

Floors, like walls, are extensive and not easy to change. When finishing a new addition to your home—extra bedrooms in the attic, a family recreation center in the basement or a garage converted into a den—you should choose your floor material carefully and wisely. Floors are meant to be walked on, less often to be run, jumped or danced on. They must also support the weight of furniture as well as provide comfort.

What are the attributes of a 'good' floor?

1. It should be durable, able to take the daily punishment without cracking, disintegrating or wearing noticeably.

2. It should be easy to maintain. It should not be necessary to re-finish frequently because of scratch marks, or to scour daily to remove shoe prints.

3. It should be resilient; in other words, have a bounce when you walk on it. A 'stiff' floor without some spring is very tiring if you stand on your feet on it for any prolonged period or do considerable walking to and fro as the home-maker must in her kitchen.

4. It should be sound-absorbing in that it should deaden noise; although walls and ceilings offer better possibilities for absorbing noise, the floor should help and not hinder.

This section is confined to hard-surface flooring as opposed to soft floor coverings (carpets and rugs). Here are some of the hard-surface

Standard wood flooring comes in unfinished tongue-and-groove boards. Here, however, the ranch plank boards (note pegs near boards ends as covers for countersunk screws) come prefinished with false pegs. These planks are glued to the subfloor.

Prefinished laminated wood blocks make an attractive floor covering in any home. These squares are ½" thick and are held to the subfloor with an adhesive.

Photograph courtesy of E. L. Bruce Co.

Vinyl-asbestos tiles in spatter pattern can be installed below grade as well as on ground level and suspended floors. These are rugged blocks able to withstand the use and abuse in a child's room.

Photograph courtesy of Armstrong Cork Co.

Old fashioned linoleum is given a new look with the addition of bright metallic chips. Large cocoa and black squares combine to make a high style room.

Photograph courtesy of Mastic Tile Corp.

flooring materials for use in the home.

ASPHALT TILE—It can be used directly over concrete or wood floors and generally comes in 9"x9" squares although other sizes and shapes are available. These tiles are easy to maintain but too often are noisy. Furthermore, they become brittle in cold weather and soft with heat. They cannot be used where they come into direct contact with the elements.

CONCRETE—This is the least expensive of all flooring materials but is not too attractive. It is generally covered with another surface: wood, asphalt tiles, cork tile or carpets and rugs. It is exceedingly durable but cold unless radiant-heated.

It has no resiliency.

CORK—Although expensive, these tiles have a long life if maintained properly. They are very resilient and can be used in any room of the home. However, for kitchen and bathroom use, or in areas where subject to strains or splashing, the vinyl-surfaced cork tiles should be used.

LEATHER—Attractive richlooking pigskin leather is available in floor tiles in 4½"x9" with beveled edges. These tiles come with some slightly lighter than others. They can be laid in any pattern.

LINOLEUM—Available in rolls and in squares, this floor covering material is moderately easy to main-

Another unusual treatment given ordinary asphalt tiles. A parquet effect is obtained by the scored lines in each block and with the blocks set at right angles to one another.

Photograph courtesy of Mastic Tile Corp.

Attractive and different are the flagstone tiles which are laid as individual pieces. A neutral grid used with the colorful flagstone pieces resembles a pointed mortar bed. Here is one way to add a touch of outdoors inside the house.

Photograph courtesy of Armstrong Cork Co.

Floors—Tiles

Floor tiles are easy for the handyman to install. Today, there are tiles made of many different materials which can be used in every room of the house. There are, however, limitations on certain types of tiles which cannot be laid below ground (that is, below ground level) while others are not recommended for areas where the tiles are likely to be stained (for example, in the kitchen).

Asphalt tiles, rubber tiles, cork tiles, vinyl tiles, and vinyl-asbestos tiles can be used for any do-it-yourself project. There are many different colors, patterns and sizes available.

Before you lay any tiles, it is necessary to prepare the floor surface. Tiles set over uneven floors may crack or show ridges where the floor is uneven. Therefore, follow preparation steps carefully so that your job, when completed, is worth the effort.

Among the tools you will need are: a serrated paste spreader, a sharp flooring knife, chalk and chalk-line, ruler or yardstick, a steel straight edge to guide the cutting knife, dividers, trowel for spreading the adhesive and a carpenter's square. You will also need a hammer and a nail set if a felt lining is needed under the tiles you are laying.

Among the materials you will need are tile adhesive and tiles. In some instances, you will also need felt lining and linoleum paste to adhere this lining to the original floor.

Using different colored tiles to form unusual patterns adds to the decorative effect of a tile floor.

Photograph courtesy of Rubber Manufacturers Association.

Photograph courtesy of B. F. Goodrich
Koroseal.

Dramatic floor treatment is all that it takes to make even an entry way of postage-stamp proportions say a big welcome to your home.

Photograph courtesy of Armstrong Cork Co.

The outdoors is moved into the home with this new flagstone asphalt tile. It comes in three color combinations in plain, straight grain and swirl marbelized pieces.

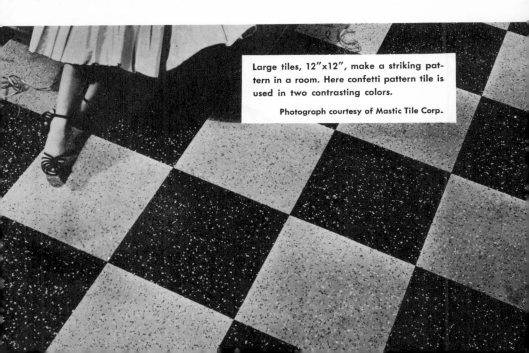

Large tiles, 12"x12", make a striking pattern in a room. Here confetti pattern tile is used in two contrasting colors.

Photograph courtesy of Mastic Tile Corp.

tain. To increase the wear life and maintain the appearance of linoleum, it is necessary to wax fairly frequently.

RUBBER—This highly durable flooring material is very resilient and easy to maintain. It comes in a wide range of colors and is greaseproof. Generally, the handyman uses rubber in tile form although roll goods are available.

VINYL-ASBESTOS — This composition tile can be used anywhere asphalt tile is used in the home. It is highly durable and easy to maintain. It has more resilience than asphalt and is not as easily affected by cold and heat.

VINYL—This floor covering usually comes in tile form and can be purchased in many different colors and textures. It is very easy to maintain and particularly practical in kitchens and bathrooms.

WOOD—The standard floor covering found in practically every home is available as individual, unfinished tongue-and-groove boards or in prefinished blocks or boards. In some instances, it is possible to use plywood or hardboard as flooring material. Wood is resilient and warm.

FLAGSTONE—Used in the proper setting, flagstones make attractive and durable entrance halls and foyers.

How To Install Floor Tiles

1. It is best to center the floor tiles by starting in the middle of the room. Mark center line down the length of the room and another at right angles to it across the room. When you start the tiles afterwards, lay the tiles at the intersection of the two center lines.

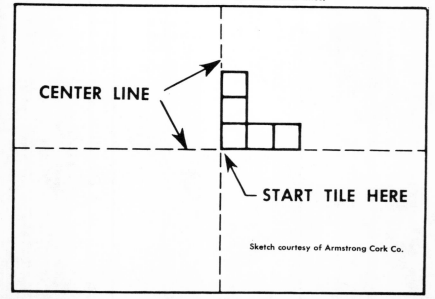

CENTER LINE

START TILE HERE

Sketch courtesy of Armstrong Cork Co.

No matter what type of floor tile you plan to use, the technique for laying the tiles is practically the same. Certain tiles require special adhesives and it is, therefore, best to follow manufacturers' instructions, using the following as a guide.

If tiles are to be placed on concrete, it is necessary to have a perfectly smooth surface. There are special mastics which are spread over the floor and evened-off so that all indentations are filled. The tiles can be laid directly over the concrete.

On wooden floors, however, it is usually necessary to lay a felt lining over the boards to prevent the board edges from eventually showing through the tiles. Unless the wooden floor is perfectly smooth and all the joints between the boards properly filled, a felt lining is recommended for under the tiles. Certain tiles require this lining no matter how smooth the floor. Therefore, check the manufacturers' literature before starting your floor project.

Furthermore, when laying tiles in a room with a baseboard, it is best to remove the shoe mold (See *Baseboard*) by prying it off with a floor or glazier's chisel so that the edges of the tile can be concealed afterwards when the molding is replaced.

2. The center lines are best made with a chalk line. If you don't have a chalk line (a useful, inexpensive accessory available in any store selling floor tiles or hardware), you can use string with marking chalk. Tack the two ends in place and snap the cord; this will leave a chalk line where you want it.

Photograph courtesy of Rubber Flooring Division, Rubber Manufacturers Association.

3. Here is a chalk line across the room and down the length of the room on a concrete floor in the basement. This smooth concrete requires no further preparation; the tiles can be laid directly over it. If it were uneven, however, it would be necessary to use a special mastic filler to make the flloor level and smooth.

4. When working on a wooden floor, a felt lining is frequently necessary. Linoleum adhesive is spread over the floor with a notched trowel and the cut sheets of felt are laid over the adhesive.

6. The tiles are then set over the adhesive starting with the first tile aligned with the two center lines. Continue laying the tiles so that the edges abutt the center line, which is used as a guide.

5. After the center lines have been marked. start in one segment of the room and apply the tile adhesive over the floor. Spread the adhesive evenly so that there are no bare spots or lumps anywhere in the work area.

7. Always work from the uncovered portion of the floor. Place each tile in position; don't slide them. This will prevent the adhesive from oozing up between the tile joints. If, however, any adhesive does ooze up, wipe it off immediately with a clean, damp cloth.

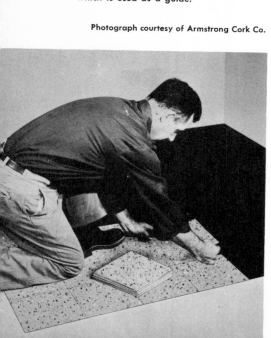

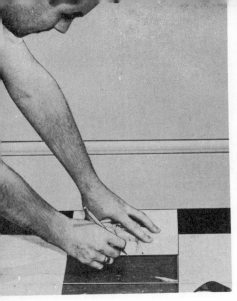

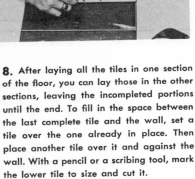

8. After laying all the tiles in one section of the floor, you can lay those in the other sections, leaving the incompleted portions until the end. To fill in the space between the last complete tile and the wall, set a tile over the one already in place. Then place another tile over it and against the wall. With a pencil or a scribing tool, mark the lower tile to size and cut it.

10. Around door frames and other projections in the room, you might find a pair of dividers exceedingly helpful in determining the exact size and shape to cut the tiles. Mark the location of the last full tile

9. Cut the tile to size with a flooring knife and a steel straight edge. Set the tile on a piece of wood for cutting so that you don't mar the floor. If you have an assistant, you can cut the tiles to size while your assistant marks them.

Photograph courtesy of the Rubber Flooring Division, Rubber Manufacturers Association.

on the floor and then measure the amount needed for the filler tile. Transfer measurements from floor with dividers to the tile and then cut to shape.

Photograph courtesy of Armstrong Cork Co.

11. Asphalt tile is easier to cut if heated slightly. You can use a sun lamp or heat lamp to warm the tiles.

12. A blowtorch, used carefully, is another way to heat the asphalt tiles before you cut them to shape and size.

13. Special cutting is often necessary to fit a tile around a pipe or other object protruding from the floor, such as a sink leg which cannot be removed. It is best to make a paper pattern and then trace this onto a tile. Thin tiles can be cut with scissors.

Photograph courtesy of Armstrong Cork Co.

14. It is sometimes best to heat the tile after it has been cut so that it will be easier to bend around an immovable object. Heating the tile for a few seconds over the kitchen range makes the tile pliable and easier to bend.

Photograph courtesy of The B. F. Goodrich Co.

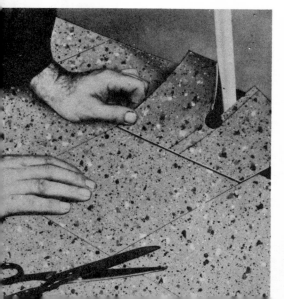

15. Twist the heated tile and slide it around the object so that the straight-cut side is nearest the wall where it won't be easily seen. Replace the shoe mold (see **Baseboard**) after the tiles have been set in place.

Photograph courtesy of The B. F. Goodrich Co.

Laying Self-Adhesive Tiles

To make life simpler for the handyman or the handywoman, there are floor tiles available which come already prepared with adhesive. This speeds the floor tile laying job and, when a felt lining is not needed, eliminates part of the mess sometimes encountered.

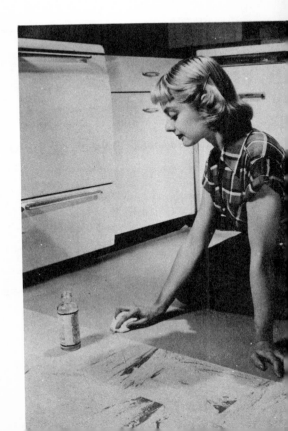

1. Clean the floor surface with a cleaning fluid, such as carbon tetrachloride. This is not flammable but must be used in a well-ventilated room. This is done to remove all the dust and to activate the adhesive on the back of the tile.

2. Strip the plastic film covering the back of the tile off by lifting one edge and pulling the film. This easily-removed film is placed on the back of the tile so that the tiles can be stacked without adhering to each other.

Photographs courtesy of United States Rubber Co.

How To Install Flagstone Asphalt Tile

Flagstone asphalt tile is the first basically new design in asphalt tile flooring since the industry's inception. Previously, the term "tile" in the trade was synonymous with the conventional square or rectangular tiles. The "flagstones" are irregularly shaped—just like real flagstones. Perhaps best described as jig-saw like in shape, the simulated flagstone tiles are precision cut to fit tightly into different size openings in an 18″ x 18″ frame or "grid." Grids are cut out of plain gray asphalt tile

3. Set the tiles in place on the clean floor, following the same technique as you would when laying tiles with adhesive. For a tight, professional-looking joint, butt one end of the tile against the tile already in place and then press it into place. Maintain slight pressure against the installed tile while pressing the new one into position.

and resemble mortar used to hold flagstones in place. Since there are no straight lines in the finished floor, the flagstone design is completely authentic.

GENERAL INSTRUCTIONS

1. Flagstone asphalt tile can be installed over any floor that is firm, level, and dry. For a satisfactory installation, floors must be completely free of wax, paint, enamel, grease, and dirt before the tile is installed.

2. Tile should be kept in a

warm room for at least twenty-four hours prior to installation. During installation the room must be at least 70° for easy handling of the tile and adhesive. Caution: Don't install in interiors, such as summer cottages, where there is no heat during the winter.

3. Before starting the installation, take all furniture and removable fixtures from the room. Pry up quarter-round at the baseboard so the tile can be slid underneath during installation.

4. Remove old floor coverings, wax, grease, dirt, and paint with paint remover or a scraper or with a sanding machine when necessary.

5. Fill cracks and holes in concrete with crack filler. Prime basement and grade level slabs with asphalt primer if concrete surface is new, dusty or porous.

6. Plug holes and cracks in wood floors with small pieces of wood, Plastic Wood, or cover them with smoothly nailed pieces of tin. Plane off high spots and renail loose

boards. Apply a coat of floor size over new or freshly sanded wood to help prevent warping.

7. Cover wood floors with a layer of lining felt laid across the boards and paste in place. First cut the felt to fit with seams butted but not overlapped, then move the strips back and spread paste over half the floor. Lay the felt in the paste and smooth it in place. Lap back the strips the other way and repeat this procedure.

HOW TO LAY OUT THE ROOM

1. Measure the room and determine the number of grid units required to cover the floor in both directions. (Use this simple table of 18″ Unit Equivalents.)

Photograph courtesy of Armstrong Cork Co.

1. Before the felt and tile may be laid, plane off high spots as shown above and renail loose boards. Plug or cover holes and cracks. Apply a coat of size over new or freshly sanded wood to help prevent warping.

TABLE OF 18″ EQUIVALENTS

LENGTH OR WIDTH	BORDERLESS NO. UNITS
3′ or less	2
4′ 6″ ″ ″	3
6′ ″ ″	4
7′ 6″ ″ ″	5
9′ ″ ″	6
10′ 6″ ″ ″	7
12′ ″ ″	8
13′ 6″ ″ ″	9
15′ ″ ″	10
16′ 6″ ″ ″	11
18′ ″ ″	12
19′ 6″ ″ ″	13
21′ ″ ″	14
22′ 6″ ″ ″	15

2. If the number of units required along the short wall is *even*, (8, 10, 12, 14, etc.) strike a chalk line connecting the center at the two short walls. If the number of units required is *uneven*, (7, 9, 11, 13, etc.) the starting line should be moved 9″ to either the left or right of the center.

3. Locate the center of this line, and using a framing square draw a perpendicular.

4. Along this perpendicular, strike a chalk line connecting the two side walls. Repeat above procedure for determining if an even or uneven number of grids is required along the long wall. If the number of units required is *uneven*, the perpendicular line should be moved 9″ to either the left or right.

2. After smoothing the boards, a layer of lining felt should be laid across the boards and pasted in place with linoleum paste. Cut the felt to fit with seams butted but not overlapped, then move the strips back and spread paste over half the floor. Proceed as directed in text.

3. Lift out two or three grid pieces. The grids match each other side-for-side and top-to-bottom.

4. Put several shaped tile pieces in place within the grids. Notice that each tile will fit only one space in each of the grids. Tiles along all edges of the grid interlock with adjoining grids. The pattern has an 18" repeat.

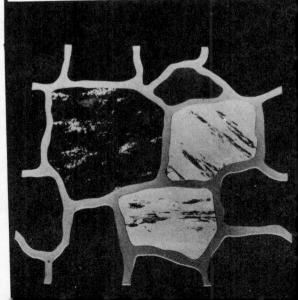

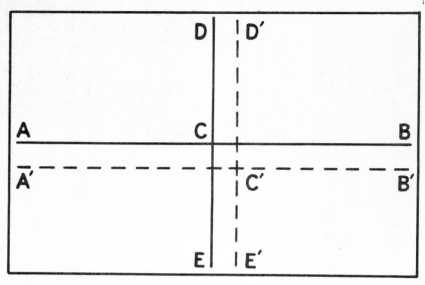

5. Find the center point of each of the short end walls and connect these points by snapping a chalk line down the middle of the room—line AB. Locate the center point C of line AB and erect a perpendicular. Strike a chalk line DE connecting the two side walls. Lay a row of uncemented grids from the center of the room to the side wall and another row to the end wall. If the space between the last whole grid and the side wall is less than 9", installation will be easier if the line down the center of the room is moved 9" (half the width of a grid) to either left or right—line A'B'. Likewise, if the space between the end wall and the last whole grid is less than 9", the perpendicular cross line should be moved 9" to either the left or right—line D'E'. (After you have found the proper starting lines by this test placement of uncemented grids, remove the loose grids used in the test and you are ready to start the actual installation.

6. Using a notched trowel, spread adhesive over one-half of the room as shown. Be sure to leave the chalk guide lines exposed.

7. Lay the first grid at the intersection of the guide lines. It's important that each of the "fingers" of the grid are lined up accurately with both lines.

8. Lay a second grid unit against the first and line up with the longer guide line. Lay a "key" interlocking piece (shaped like a boot) between the two grids. Repeat procedure until first row is complete except for "border" unit. Do not lay any grids or tiles requiring cutting and fitting until all field units are installed.

Photographs courtesy of Armstrong Cork Co.

9. Install all remaining interlocking pieces and "filler" pieces in first row. Do not install interlocking pieces for second row until next grids are in position.

10. Lay two or three grids in second row, installing interlocking "keystone piece" (shown above) as each grid is installed. Again be sure "fingers" are lined up with perpendicular guide line. Then install key interlocking "boot pieces" between grids in second row.

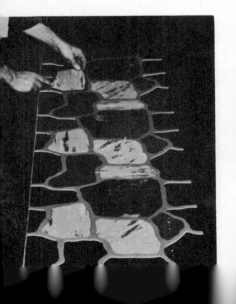

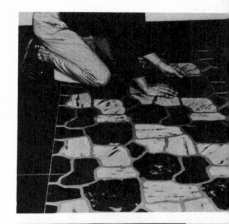

11. Continue laying grids, "interlocking" pieces and "filler" pieces. Don't install interlocking pieces which extend into border areas until all but the "border" area of one half of the floor is installed. Repeat the entire procedure for all but border area for the other half of the floor.

12. If regular asphalt tile border material is not used in the border areas, grids and tiles must be cut to fit. Place a grid exactly over the last grid already cemented in place nearest the wall. Next put all pieces requiring cutting in place in this loose grid. Then, using an 18" template of some stiff material, mark the grid and the pieces at the same time, as shown. However, the grid and pieces should be removed and cut separately.

13. The cut grids and pieces should fit exactly into the adjacent border area. Repeat this procedure until all border grids are installed and fitted with tile.

Floors—Wood

Photograph courtesy of E. L. Bruce Co.

Wood floors can be secured directly over the joists in a house or even over concrete. A subfloor, however, is used for added strength.

Today, most subfloors are made of plywood which is nailed across the joists. The finished flooring is attached over the subfloor. Normally, tongue-and-groove boards are nailed to the subfloor. It is necessary to press the boards close together so that gaps between boards are at a minimum. Flooring nails, driven at a diagonal through the tongue, are concealed when the next board is set into place.

These tongue-and-groove boards come prefinished as well as unfinished. If you have a perfectly smooth subfloor, you should encounter no difficulty in laying a wood floor. However, covering of uneven subfloors should be left to the professional.

Although moderately expensive, prefinished wood squares can be used as the finished flooring. These blocks are held in place by an adhesive. Note instructions later in this section.

Tongue-and-groove boards are secured by blind nailing. A flooring nail is driven diagonally through the tongue of the board into the subfloor. When the next piece of flooring is added, the groove conceals the nail head.

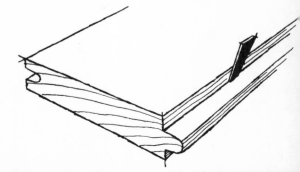

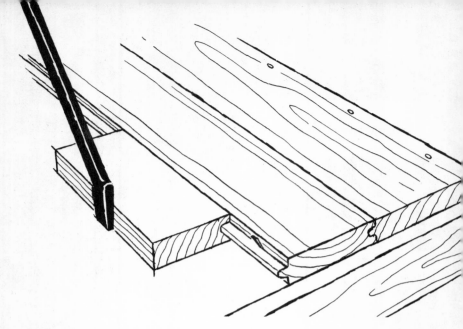

To keep the boards together tightly when nailing, it is best to use a pinch bar and a wedge (piece of flooring with one edge square).

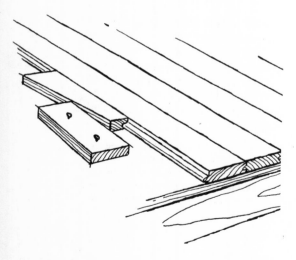

Another method to keep the boards together when nailing is to fasten a block to the subfloor and use a wooden wedge to press against the flooring boards.

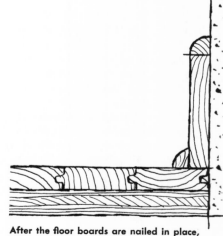

After the floor boards are nailed in place, the joint between the floor and wall are covered with a molding, a baseboard. See **Baseboard.**

Nailing prefinished ranch type flooring in place. Note that a waterproof paper has been laid over the subfloor.

Photograph courtesy of E. L. Bruce Co.

How To Install Laminated Oak Blocks

SUBFLOORS

Laminated blocks can be installed over subfloors of concrete, dressed and matched wood, or plywood. Under certain conditions, old surface floors of wood or asphalt tile are equally suitable. Depending on type, subfloors should answer the following specifications:

Concrete—Subfloors should be sound, level, dry, smooth, and clean. Remove grease or oil stains with a

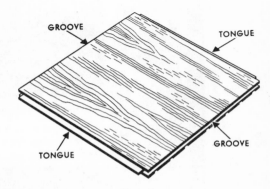

Fig. I

Laying Prefinished Wood Squares

1. The wood block is set in place over the center line after the mastic is applied over the floor.

2. Additional blocks are set in place with tongues and grooves interlocking.

3. Lay all the full squares to fill the area. Make certain that the blocks are properly spaced.

4. Fill in the remaining areas by cutting blocks to the required size and setting them in place.

Photographs courtesy of E. L. Bruce Co.

solution of industrial lye, using about one pound of lye to each three gallons of water. Level high spots with a terrazzo grinder, Carborundum stone, or hammer and chisel. Fill low areas to general subfloor level with a good-quality concrete patching mix, according to directions on the container.

Wood or Plywood—Newly-constructed wood subfloors should be of dressed and matched boards not over 6″ wide. New plywood subfloors should be well-nailed at all edges and through tthe center. Rough edges should be sanded smooth. Either type subfloor must be sound, level, and well-nailed.

Renail old wood subfloors or old surface flooring where neces-

sary, and level any raised edges by rough-sanding. Roughsand old surface floors to remove varnish, paint, shellac, or wax.

Asphalt Tile—Laminated blocks may be laid directly over old asphalt tile if the tile is not crumbled, loose, or otherwise in poor condition. Make sure that tiles are firmly bonded; if not, remove all tile down to subfloor level, and sand or scrape the subfloor to remove all traces of old tile cement.

If tiles are well bonded, roughsand the surface to remove wax. This may also be done satisfactorily by cleaning with water and a good-quality household scouring powder. Allow ample drying time afterward.

Remove base shoe molding and

doorway thresholds before beginning installation of blocks over old surface floors of any type.

DAMPPROOFING THE SUBFLOOR

Laminated blocks are unusually stable under adverse moisture conditions. They do not expand unduly except when subjected to "flooding" or actual immersion in water.

No dampproofing between subfloor and surface floor is necessary where blocks are to be laid over wood or plywood subfloors or over a concrete slab subfloor suspended above ground level. Do not use a paper underlayment of any kind over subfloors of these types.

However, a full two-ply, damp-proofing membrane should be installed over concrete subfloors at ground level or in direct contact with the ground where capillary moisture (seepage of water upward through the concrete) is suspected. Check for capillary moisture as follows:

Put 5 to 6 tablespoonfuls of powdered calcium chloride on the concrete; build a "well" of putty about 1″ high around the chemical, then cover with a piece of glass 8″ or 10″ square. Seal edges with putty to keep out air.

If, within 24 hours, water droplets appear on the glass or the chemical shows signs of caking, capillary moisture is present. A competent waterproofing contractor should then be employed to install a damp-proofing membrane, as follows, before laying any floor:

(1) Sweep the surface and prime with asphalt primer.

(2) Coat the subfloor with hot asphalt or with Bruce Everbond "X".

(3) While asphalt or mastic is

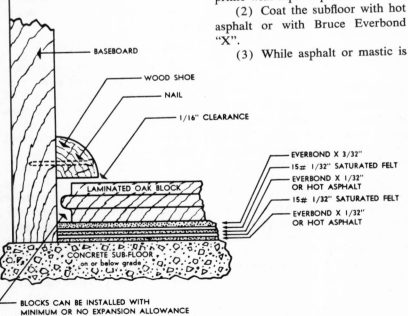

WALL LINE

BASEBOARD

WOOD SHOE

NAIL

1/16″ CLEARANCE

LAMINATED OAK BLOCK

EVERBOND X 3/32″
15# 1/32″ SATURATED FELT
EVERBOND X 1/32″ OR HOT ASPHALT
15# 1/32″ SATURATED FELT
EVERBOND X 1/32″ OR HOT ASPHALT

CONCRETE SUB-FLOOR on or below grade

BLOCKS CAN BE INSTALLED WITH MINIMUM OR NO EXPANSION ALLOWANCE

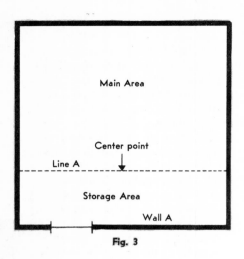

Main Area

Center point

Line A

Storage Area

Wall A

Fig. 3

hot, embed a layer of 15-pound asphalt-saturated felt, starting with a half-sheet at one wall and butting all seams. Mop firmly to press out wrinkles and blisters.

(4) Cover felt with another coating of hot asphalt or mastic and embed second layer of felt. Start with a full sheet instead of a half sheet so that seams of the first layer are covered.

Priming the Subfloor

Concrete subfloors that have not been waterproofed should be primed with asphalt primer before spreading mastic to settle dust and provide the best possible bonding surface.

Priming is unnecessary on subfloors other than concrete. Do not, under any circumstances, prime asphalt tile. Remove dust on asphalt tile by mopping with warm water, then allowing to dry completely. Remove dust on wood or plywood

subfloors by thorough sweeping.

Laying Out Working Lines

The following instructions deal with the installation of blocks in a square pattern without regard to balanced borders at walls. Installation should begin nearest the wall containing the main entranceway.

1. (Figure 3): From Wall A, measure off at two points an equal distance sufficient to provide a convenient initial working space and storage area for materials. This measurement should be carefully calculated to allow a full or nearly full block in the doorway. After determining the distance desired, check by laying a row of blocks loosely on the subfloor from the point established through the doorway; the final block should reach past the center of the door jamb.

2. Snap a chalk line, Line A in Figure 3, from wall to wall across these two points. This line should be parallel to Wall A.

APPLYING THE MASTIC

Everbond "X" Mastic requires heating, and is applied to the subfloor while hot. Note: Do not attempt to lay blocks in mastic when room temperature is less than 45°F. A temperature of about 70° is preferable.

1. Heat Everbond "X" to a liquid consistency over a coke or charcoal burner or over an outside fire, first removing the cover. Stir while heating. Do not allow mastic to boil, and guard against accidental contact with water to avoid uncontrollable frothing. If using pails of mastic, keep one pail over heat while

Fig. 4

a second is in use; if using drums, dip hot mastic from drum to pail for ease in handling.

2. Begin applying mastic to subfloor at the wall opposite the entranceway. Pour from pail and spread evenly with a notched trowel with ¼" teeth on ⅜" centers to gain the desired depth of ³⁄₃₂". Hold trowel in a nearly vertical position while in use, (Figure 4).

3. Let mastic dry and "set" until a glaze appears on the surface.

LAYING THE BLOCKS

After mastic has set, begin laying blocks as directed below. When laying blocks see that edges of blocks coincide with the line rather than tongues or grooves, to secure true alignment.

When placing blocks in position, insert groove over tongue or tongue into groove and drop block lightly into place. Tap on the exposed sides to complete positioning. Do not attempt to slide blocks into place; mastic will pile up on the leading edge, impeding the fit. Use mineral spirits to remove any mastic adhering to the surface of blocks by accident.

1. Locate the approximate center point of Line A.

2. (Figure 5): Lay Block No. 1 on Line A at this point. Place this initial block with a grooved side along the working line. This is the key block; make sure it is positioned correctly to make exact alignment of additional blocks easier.

3. (Figure 6): Next lay Blocks 2 and 3 on either side of Block 1, fitting tongues and grooves as required. Align these blocks carefully with Line A and with each other.

4. (Figure 6): Place Block 4 directly over Block 1, establishing a "pyramid" pattern extending from Line A into the main area of the room.

5. (Figure 7): Lay Blocks 5, 6, 7, 8, and 9 around the pyramid pattern established in Step 4. Make sure that Blocks 5 and 9 are positioned exactly on Line A, and that Block 7 is perfectly aligned with Block 4.

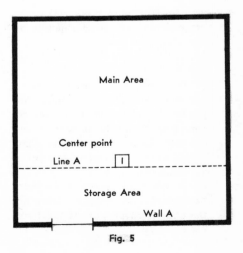

Fig. 5

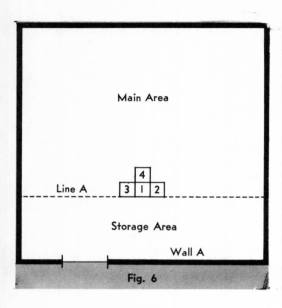

Main Area

Line A

Storage Area

Wall A

Fig. 6

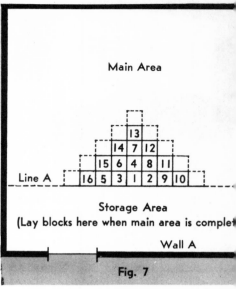

Main Area

Line A

Storage Area
(Lay blocks here when main area is complete)

Wall A

Fig. 7

6. (Figure 7): Continue laying Blocks 10 through 16 around the pyramid in the manner described in step 5. Follow with additional blocks in this fashion until walls are reached. Trim part blocks to fit at wall lines, around pipes and other projections, and around jambs at doorways. Let border blocks extend as far as possible into door openings.

No expansion allowance is necessary at walls or around projecting obstacles since the laminated blocks are relatively stable even under poor moisture conditions; lay blocks as snugly as possible against all vertical surfaces.

7. When the main area has been partly laid, move all materials onto the completed portion of the floor and spread mastic over storage area between Line A and Wall A (Figure 7). Then continue filling in main area as instructed in step 6. When main area is completed and freshly-spread mastic has "set," lay blocks along Line A until storage area is covered. Follow the same procedure as before. Cut part blocks, if necessary, to fit along Wall A.

8. When floor is completed, install new factory-finished base shoe mold of proper size, or re-install old molding.

If there is any appreciable difference in elevation between the new floor of laminated blocks and old floors in adjoining rooms, overcome by using a special $\frac{7}{16}'' \times 1\frac{1}{2}''$ factory-finished oak nosing strip obtainable through any lumber dealer.